FRANK

THE LIFE AND POLITICS OF
FRANK McKENNA

Election night, 1991.

FRANK

THE LIFE AND POLITICS OF
FRANK McKENNA

PHILIP LEE

GOOSE LANE

The Publisher gratefully acknowledges the financial contributions of several Canadian businesses, without whose support this book would not have been possible.

Edited by Laurel Boone.
Book design by Ryan Astle.
Printed in Canada by Friesens.
10 9 8 7 6 5 4 3 2 1

Canadian Cataloguing in Publication Data

Lee, Philip J., 1963 -
Frank : the life and politics of Frank McKenna
Issued also in French under title: Frank: la vie et la politique de Frank McKenna

Includes bibliographical references and index.
ISBN 0-86492-303-1

1. McKenna, Frank J. 2. Prime ministers — New Brunswick —
Biography. 3. New Brunswick — Politics and government — 1987-
I. Title

FC2477.1.M34L44 2001   971.5'104'092   C2002-901728-6
F1043.M32L44 2001

Published with the financial support of the Canada Council for the Arts, the Government of Canada through the Book Publishing Industry Development Program, and the New Brunswick Culture and Sports Secretariat.

Goose Lane Editions
469 King Street
Fredericton, New Brunswick
CANADA E3B 1E5

For Fernand Landry

CONTENTS

ACKNOWLEDGEMENTS

I am grateful to the many people who generously contributed to this project, in particular the staff at the Provincial Archives for endlessly hauling boxes and retrieving files, Francis McGuire for sharing his time and personal records, Donald Savoie for offering his wisdom, research and early manuscript of his Frank McKenna project, Aldéa Landry for her graciousness during a difficult time, Scott Anderson for his friendship and support, Peter Dale and Elizabeth Dingman for offering me a home in Toronto, Jackie Webster for giving me the use of her screened porch at Youghall Beach, my mother Roberta Lee for reading and editing the manuscript, and Ruth McCrea, who was marvellous and indispensable in every way. For assistance in assembling photographs, I am grateful to Harry Mullin; to Howie Trainor, of the New Brunswick *Telegraph-Journal*; to Bill Witcomb and Tracy Carr, of the Fredericton *Daily Gleaner*; and to Anne-Marie Beaton, of Canadian Press. Susanne Alexander of Goose Lane Editions patiently shepherded this project from conception to completion.

I am indebted to the patience, good humour and candid co-operation of Frank and Julie McKenna, their children and other members of the McKenna clan. Frank and Julie McKenna sat for many hours of interviews and contributed their personal papers and photographs to this project. The story could not have been told without the work of two researchers. Emelie Hubert spent hours in archives and libraries, doggedly compiling essential files, in particular tracing the genealogy of the McKennas. Deborah Nobes, a fine journalist and writer, conducted essential interviews, collected documents and critiqued the manuscript; every page reflects her indomitable spirit and enthusiasm. Finally, the book belongs to the three people who lived it with me, Danielle, Gabrielle and Aaron, children of my heart.

Public life is regarded as the crown of a career, and to young men it is the worthiest ambition. Politics is still the greatest and the most honourable adventure.

— *John Buchan, Lord Tweedsmuir*

Your name is Francis. There was never a St. Frank. That's a name for gangsters and politicians.

— *Frank McCourt*

Frank McKenna in Wilmot Park, Fredericton, 1993.

1

BAY STREET BLUES

If you move, you're a target. But I won't stand still.
— *Frank McKenna, diary entry, September 16, 1996*

He opens his front door and steps out into the awakening city. He pauses to button his navy trench coat and stretch the morning stiffness out of his legs, then crosses the street and cuts through the park. A gentle spring rain splashes on the pathway in front of him. Other early risers carry umbrellas and walk their dogs across wet grass that is beginning to turn green as winter releases Toronto from its embrace. The subway station that serves the moneyed neighbourhood of Rosedale is just ahead, but he prefers a forty-minute walk to a ten-minute ride, even in the rain. He turns right on Yonge Street, picking up his pace as the pulse of the city quickens with each passing block. If Francis Joseph McKenna moved any faster, he'd break into a jog. His best days begin when he's up early and out walking.

Early morning walks have been one of McKenna's rituals for years. When he was Premier of New Brunswick, he left his white clapboard home in Fredericton at six-thirty on weekday mornings and walked beside the St. John River to his office near the province's legislative building complex. Navigating the bustling sidewalks of Toronto, Frank McKenna carries himself in much the same manner as he did on the sleepy streets of Fredericton. His brown eyes are bright and alert; his body bristles with energy. He doesn't need coffee in the morning to clear his head.

He has notes to himself stuffed in his pockets — "eat right," "exercise," "be optimistic," "be decisive," "call home" — the scribbled reminders of a man who must be disciplined in all things. His to-do lists are a bulwark against the pace of his life. He is sucked easily into the vortex of work until he is whirling so fast that he loses sight of the kind of man he aspires to be. And so he reminds himself — "listen more than you speak," "take time out to think," "don't forget your family." When he loses control and forgets about his lists, he feels a measure of failure as he walks back home at the end of the day.

He diets constantly to keep the pounds off his stocky five-foot-eight-inch frame, notes his weight in his diary each day, and periodically subjects himself to three-day fasts to cleanse his system. He plays golf now instead of hockey, but he still carries hard muscle on his shoulders, arms and thick hands, his body forever defined by the hayfields he worked as a boy on his family's farm in Apohaqui, New Brunswick.

He is still consumed by the incessant drive that propelled a boy with big dreams out of a life of poverty and rural isolation. When a man moves so quickly from there to here, parts of the character he has fashioned on the journey are only sketched in. Therefore Frank McKenna remains elusive. When you think you have him standing in front of you, he slips away again. He has always been the fastest man on the street.

He rarely follows the same route downtown, leaving Yonge Street to avoid waiting at traffic lights, pausing to pour a fistful of change into the hands of every panhandler he meets. Back home, New Brunswickers watch Frank McKenna's every move. Here in Toronto he is anonymous, just another man in a hurry, on his way to make his fortune on Bay Street. At the corner of Bay and King Street East, he stops and looks up at the three imposing Toronto Dominion Bank office towers. "Welcome to the heart of capitalist greed," he says with a smile. Then, still speaking with the proprietorship of a premier, he notes, "If I had just one of these buildings in New Brunswick, I'd have zero unemployment." He turns abruptly and pushes through a revolving door into the sprawling lobby of First Canadian Place.

He takes the express elevator to the sixty-sixth floor and enters the offices of Osler, Hoskin and Harcourt. This international legal powerhouse, specializing in mergers and acquisitions, administered eight billion dollars worth of deals in 1999 through its offices in Toronto, Ottawa, Calgary, and New York. Shortly after eight a.m. the office is humming. No one throws McKenna a second glance as he makes his way to his small office, which is outfitted with a desk, a computer, a round glass meeting table and three chairs. McKenna is one of more than two hundred and fifty lawyers who work here in the firm's Bay Street office. He is a consulting counsel for Osler, Hoskin and Harcourt, on the payroll to stir up business rather than practise law.

Soon after leaving the premier's office, McKenna established his business home base in New Brunswick at the rapidly expanding law firm, McInnes Cooper & Robertson, in Moncton, where he is counsel and a partner. He sold his residence in Fredericton and built an elegant beach-front home in Cap-Pelé on New Brunswick's east coast, beside the warm waters of the Northumberland Strait. But McKenna is on the road more often than he is home, and for four months every winter he and Julie, his wife, live in Toronto in a rented three-storey home, modest by Rosedale standards. Julie McKenna looks forward to her time in the city because she enjoys the theatres, art galleries, stores and restaurants that she can't find back home. Frank is more of a sports fan than a patron of the arts and prefers a hockey rink or a baseball stadium anytime to an art gallery, although he enjoys attending the theatre with Julie. She, in turn, attends sporting events with him — to watch the people, not the game. As he and Julie entered the Skydome for the second Blue Jays home game of the 2000 season, he remarked, "This is kind of like eating early lobster." He's a fine companion in a baseball park, munching on peanuts, sipping beer, leading the wave in his section, singing "Take Me Out to the Ball Game" louder, more out of tune and with a bigger grin than anyone around him. He knows how to surrender himself to the moment.

Whereas Frank and Julie always look forward to the simpler pleasures of life in their home beside the ocean, he is not unlike scores of Maritimers who for generations have been drawn to Toronto by the magnet of opportunity. Bay Street is the most influential twenty blocks of real estate in Canada, the corporate power centre of the country, housing a work force that rivals the population of the city of Fredericton. Bay Street "is Canada's version of Hollywood, a mythical domain where dreams may be dashed, but still a place where dreamers test themselves against their destinies," writes Peter C. Newman, the foremost observer of the Canadian establishment.

On Bay Street, McKenna tests himself against his destiny after politics. He lives a simple, unpretentious life, although he is becoming wealthy: he earns more money in one year here than he did in ten years in the premier's office. McKenna has never cared much for money, but on Bay Street a person's income is a way of keeping score. He works for his law firms and holds a dozen corporate directorships, including the Bank of Montreal,

Noranda Inc., United Parcel Service, CanWest Communications Corp. and General Motors of Canada. He is also a regular on the national public speaking circuit.

Two-thirds of Canada's major law firms have offices on Bay Street. In his life before politics, McKenna was an impressive courtroom lawyer, but he found his way to Bay Street because he has access to power, which in Newman's terms "means getting through on the telephone to anyone at command level." With his vast and growing network of business friends and his position close to the heart of the Canadian political establishment, McKenna is a rainmaker.

He is a confidant of Prime Minister Jean Chrétien, who has often urged him to enter federal politics, solidify a strategic beachhead of Liberal support in Atlantic Canada and position himself as a future party leader and Prime Minister. On January 5, 1996, McKenna noted in his diary that he had met with Chrétien to discuss his future. The Prime Minister suggested that McKenna had three choices: he could make a lot of money, he could be the best premier in the history of Canada, or he could position himself to become prime minister. "He said I would have an excellent chance of being PM," McKenna noted. "He said if I have any aspirations I should follow them. I would always regret it if I didn't. Therefore, I should run federally this time. I told him it was highly unlikely, but I was flattered. I would be deeply honoured to run with him and to serve with him, but I was connected to New Brunswick."

On this April morning in 2000, a potential investor is on the line. McKenna is acting on behalf of the owner of a restaurant chain who is planning to expand into hotels. "What's your normal appetite for risk?" he asks, adopting the language of his new environment. "Would you be in the ten-million to twenty-million range?" Pause. "Ten million. Okay. What you're saying is that you've got a big appetite for risk, but only ten million." He smiles and listens. "I'll tell him this, tell him what your maximums are, that you are interested in talking with other people if he's interested in talking with you." He nods, then quickly brings the conversation to a close. "If he wants to pursue this, he'll put a business plan in front of you, and if not, that's fine, too, neither of us has wasted anything on it. More importantly, now that I know more about you I'll try to place other people in front of you." McKenna gathers the pieces of the business puzzle and puts them on the table, leaving the creation of the picture to others.

He still takes a special interest in Atlantic Canadian business opportunities, still obsessed with job creation, an issue that dominated the public agenda during his decade as Premier. However, since the Progressive Conservatives came to power in New Brunswick in the spring of 1999, he has been relegated to the sidelines of the job hunting game. He is frustrated by the Tory government's lack of interest in aggressively courting new businesses. Still, whenever he sees an opportunity, McKenna tries to make business deals happen in New Brunswick and at the same time channel more work into his Moncton law firm. "I just operate under the theory that what goes around comes around," McKenna says. "It always does."

While the move to Bay Street seemed natural for McKenna, he is the first Atlantic Canadian premier to be so warmly embraced by the Canadian establishment. Donald Savoie, a distinguished public policy professor at the Université de Moncton, is the author of *Pulling Against Gravity: Economic Development in New Brunswick During the McKenna Years*. No one was surprised, he writes, when corporate Canada came calling on the leader of an administration that was so friendly to business, although his Bay Street career is unprecedented among Atlantic Canadian premiers. Savoie notes that it would be hard to imagine former premiers Joey Smallwood, Alex Campbell, Louis J. Robichaud or John Buchanan being greeted so warmly by the business establishment.

It didn't hurt McKenna's post-political career that he often visited Bay Street when he was Premier, setting up shop in a suite at the Royal York Hotel (which he jokingly referred to as his second home) and hustling jobs with his chief salesman and deal-closer Charlie Harling. "It didn't matter if it took thirty meetings and five different trips to Toronto, if he landed one or one hundred jobs, the deal was worth it," recalls Maurice Robichaud, McKenna's former director of communications. "It was what drove him. He loved going to Toronto to get deals and jobs."

Before he left politics, McKenna enjoyed widespread and largely positive exposure in the national media, appearing on the covers of *Canadian Business*, the *Canadian Business Review*, *Maclean's*, and the *Globe and Mail's Report on Business* magazine. His name appeared in the headline or first paragraph of more than three hundred stories in the *Globe and Mail* during his time as Premier.

McKenna's critics argued that his entry into the business world came too soon after he left politics. They found it unseemly that he accepted a position as a director of Bruncor Inc., the holding company of NB Tel, which had benefited greatly from his campaign as Premier to recruit call centres. They also pointed out that he had joined the board of UPS, the courier company that had been recruited to New Brunswick with, among other incentives, a pocketful of taxpayer's money. They contended that there should have been a cooling off period before private citizen McKenna began working for the very companies which had been so close to his political agenda.

However, McKenna never broke any rules because there weren't any conflict of interest guidelines for retiring politicians in New Brunswick. And even his staunchest political rivals had a hard time genuinely arguing that he recruited UPS to the province so he could later sit on the company's board of directors. After a brief dust-up in the New Brunswick media, McKenna quietly went about his business. Most New Brunswickers seemed to feel that they shouldn't begrudge a man who had worked so hard in public life the opportunity to make some money after he left office.

Moreover, McKenna's acceptance on Bay Street wasn't simply the result of positive press and business contacts. Corporate Canada had welcomed Premier McKenna's vision for a self-sufficient New Brunswick. When he spoke to national business audiences, he insisted he was asking for investments, not handouts from central Canada. "This was a major transition in Maritime politics," says former Ontario premier David Peterson. "Maritime politics was patronage-ridden, paternalistic, a bunch of boys from the old school who thought you'd win by pumping money into things. The new wave of leadership in the Maritimes really started with Frank and signalled a new kind of idealism. 'Roll up your sleeves and get the job done. Let's look ahead. Let's use all our resources. Let's get the goddam job done and not sit here and whine, and then *we'll* start contributing to equalization and *you* can whine about being a have-not.'" Peterson says that when McKenna brought his vision for a self-sufficient New Brunswick to Bay Street audiences, their reaction was uniformly, "God bless him."

"It was entrepreneurial politics," Peterson says. "It's so much easier, if you have a problem, to blame central Canada, blame the federation. This creates regional cleavages and divisions. McKenna understood instinctively the new world, the new information-based world. He wanted his place in that. He was ahead of his time."

McKenna, the farm-boy-turned-premier, projected self-reliance and dignity, which were attractive to the members of the Ontario business community. There are few images more satisfactory to a business person than that of a self-made man. Furthermore, as Donald Savoie points out, the economically comfortable regions of Canada want to believe they became that way on their own merit, without the help of governments, which of course is not the case. "The message not only lets them off the hook, it also confirms their belief that market forces and their own abilities explain their economic success," Savoie writes. McKenna's Toronto audiences welcomed the optimism and ambition of this young New Brunswick lawyer, partly because he made them feel good about themselves.

On April 2, 1997, six months before McKenna stepped down as Premier, Gerry Schwartz, the president and chief executive officer of the multi-billion-dollar Onex Corporation, and Heather Reisman, then chief executive of Indigo Books and Music Inc., and now the president and chief executive officer of Chapters Inc., held a dinner in honour of their favourite Maritime son at their Rosedale mansion. Schwartz is the former chief bagman of the federal Liberal Party; Reisman was co-chair of Finance Minister Paul Martin's first leadership bid. Schwartz and Reisman, Bay Street's foremost power couple, represent the innermost circle of the Toronto Liberal establishment. Whenever the Prime Minister visits Toronto, "the Schwartz parlour is a compulsory stop," Newman notes.

Frank McKenna Night in Rosedale was an intimate evening with a short list of influential guests and their partners: Paul Godfrey, publisher of the *Toronto Sun*; Peter Godsoe, the chairman and chief executive officer of the Bank of Nova Scotia; Brian Levitt, president and CEO of Imasco Ltd; Rob Prichard, president of the University of Toronto; and Dick Currie, president of Loblaws Companies Limited. The evening featured a round of tributes to McKenna. In a note to Schwartz and Reisman after the dinner, McKenna expressed thanks, humility and respect for his new friends. "I found our conversations to be stimulating and proactive," he wrote. "There is nothing more useful to a person in my position than the unscreened advice of people I respect. I do not pretend to be the person you described, but you have set a standard and an expectation that I will be relentless in pursuing. There is no way of adequately expressing my thanks to you, other than continuing to do everything in my power to ensure that my province and country prosper and remain whole." The dinner was about establishing friendships and connections that would outlive a political career. As Godsoe had told Newman, "I believe deeply in networks. Networks are information — people doing business with people, or working out political solutions." McKenna had joined the Canadian power network.

When in Toronto, the McKennas socialize with other expatriate Maritimers who cling together in the big city, never fully belonging to Toronto, just people doing what they have to do and enjoying a taste of the good life along the way. Among Frank and Julie McKenna's closest friends are Wallace and Margaret McCain. The McCains moved to Toronto in 1995 after a nasty family feud resulted in Wallace McCain being ousted by his brother Harrison from the international frozen food empire they had run as a team out of Florenceville, New Brunswick. When Wallace left New Brunswick, Margaret McCain continued serving as the province's Lieutenant-Governor for a time before resigning her post and joining her husband in Toronto.

"Business people in this city know Frank McKenna and respect him very much," says Wallace McCain, the chairman of Maple Leaf Foods, who works out of a small office tower several blocks north of Bay Street. "I've never heard anyone in this city say anything negative about Frank McKenna. Zero. They thought he was fiscally responsible. They felt that he was generally trying to better the province of New Brunswick. And he's aggressive. People don't mind that around here."

Wallace McCain tells his business friends in Toronto that sooner or later his New Brunswick friend will be Prime Minister of Canada. "And people say, 'Do you think so?' I say, 'Yeah.' They say, 'Well, gee, that's a good idea,'" McCain continues, speaking in his staccato St. John River valley rhythm. "Toronto votes Conservative, but there are a lot of Liberals here, and most of them don't want to admit they vote Liberal. They look at Frank as running under a Liberal banner but being conservative. Politics gets in your blood. I don't think he's lying in bed scheming about how he's going to be prime minister. He's politically astute. If he saw the right time in Ottawa, and the right circumstances, would he give it a go? Yes, he would. Would he get elected? In my opinion, yes, he would."

Down the street from First Canadian Place in the Bank of Nova Scotia Tower, David Peterson relaxes in his office at the law firm of Cassels Brock and Blackwell and reflects on life after politics. Embracing the casual style of the moment on Bay Street, Peterson wears jeans and a cotton dress shirt as he leans back in his chair, sipping a morning latte and smoking a cigarette.

"He's a tough little rascal, you know," Peterson says with a smile. He recalls that McKenna used to tell former Ontario premier Bob Rae, the man who bounced Peterson's Liberal government from office, that his New Democratic government was the best job creation program New

Brunswick ever had. "He used to make Bob Rae mad as hell. There's a protocol that you give a car and driver to a visiting premier. Frank would be here every goddam week, and he'd take the car and go and steal jobs. It used to drive Bob nuts. Frank would approach business people and say, 'You better come to New Brunswick because these socialists are screwing up Ontario.' It was a bit of a game."

Peterson also makes a good living as an inhabitant of Bay Street, attracting business to his blue-chip law firm and sitting on corporate boards. When McKenna asked Peterson for career advice as he prepared to leave politics, Peterson suggested that he maintain a New Brunswick base and become the Peter Lougheed of Atlantic Canada — in reference to the former Tory premier of Alberta, who has enjoyed a lucrative business career after politics. However, there are no free rides on Bay Street, and many former politicians, especially retired premiers, don't adjust well to life in the private sector. Peterson notes that McKenna isn't merely a regional figurehead for these corporations and law firms. "Your reputation doesn't last very long if you're a screw-up," he says. "Frank puts the same enormous energy into all the things he does. He's a hustler. He doesn't sit there and wait for opportunity to come to him."

McKenna works long days and travels constantly. His April, 2000, schedule, sent to him by e-mail from his Moncton office by his long-time scheduling assistant Ruth McCrea, is mind-boggling. After a few days working in Toronto, he travels to New York City on the weekend, then back to Toronto for meetings at the law firm and a speech. Then he flies to Montreal for board meetings, then on to Australia and New Zealand, and back to London, England. Without taking a day off, he goes home to Fredericton and Moncton and then comes back to Toronto. It's a whirlwind that never stops.

The schedule leaves McKenna little chance for spontaneity in his life, although he now spends more time with Julie and his three children, Toby, Christine and Jamie, than he did when he was Premier. He has also shed the often overwhelming anxiety that consumed him when he was in public life. "I would wake up in the middle of the night and not get back to sleep," McKenna recalls. "I would just lie there with my mind racing, my body almost pulsing, thinking nothing productive, just having obsessive thoughts."

However, what's missing from his Bay Street life is a sense that his long days have a purpose larger than the particular events that fill his schedule. He is no longer part of a common journey. At times he expresses deep ambivalence about his life. Even attracting jobs to Atlantic Canada doesn't generate the same thrill that it used to. "That's a small piece of what I do," he says in between telephone calls at his Toronto office. "I do other things. I can't tell you what I do because even I don't always know. It gets so busy here at times. And I really can't tell you that I do anything useful. I do a lot of things that have value to somebody."

The tasks that fill his days rarely move him. He has a hole in his life and can't replace the sense of satisfaction he had when he was premier. Then he felt he was doing something important, that he was enhancing people's lives. He wonders whether he should either learn to live with the fact that his life has changed irrevocably or consider doing something more focused — start a new business or take on a new cause.

When he was premier, nothing could deter him from his plan to transform and modernize New Brunswick. Winning three huge majority governments and occupying the premier's office never satisfied his drive. He wanted to be the best premier in history in the same way that he wanted to be the best at everything he did — playing centre for his high school hockey team, running for office as a student politician, practicing law.

"Perfectionism has always been part of my character, and it's not something that I've been fond of at all," he says. "I've always had to perform to the best of my ability and to overcome whatever deficiencies I've had through hard work and through extra effort. It's hard to live with. I don't know what the hell you'd call it, almost a compulsive thing. I won't take things on unless I feel I can do a good job. I'm a long way from perfection in any of the things that I do, but I'm driven in that way. It's not a lot of fun."

When he entered politics as a Member of the Legislative Assembly representing the Miramichi River town of Chatham, he was motivated by raw ambition, to see how high on the ladder he could go. His motivation changed when he became premier. "Whether it was a rationalization or a justification, I came to believe that I could make New Brunswick a better place, that I could make people feel better, that I could bring more prosperity to this province," he says. "It may be a case of believing my own rhetoric, I don't know. I can't honestly tell you that when I started I was as purely motivated as that. I hated controversy, hated hurting anybody's feelings, hated acrimony. But I became comfortable with making difficult decisions and, if necessary, offending people. I did it all because the force of the ideas was so powerful that I had to be prepared to endure any indignity or to undertake any rigorous decision to get there. That sustained me. That drove me night and day. I still feel it intensely now. I feel deeply wounded when I see New Brunswick slide back into the valley of self-doubt, becoming a supplicant again."

Julie McKenna thinks her husband needed to slow down and spend time with their children. "Frank's kind of become like the favourite uncle," she says. "He takes them places, he gives them things. He never had the time to do this. He's enjoying that time. And our relationship has changed. We see each other a lot, and I've really enjoyed that. I've enjoyed him. But he's not challenged."

Few experiences match the excitement and adrenalin rush of being first minister. "You live on the tightrope all the time, always action-packed, always with hundreds of decisions to make," Peterson says. "In our system, the first minister has an enormous amount of authority. I think Frank misses that."

Despite the perpetual motion of the corporate fast lane, Frank McKenna feels as if he is standing still for the first time in his life.

The dinner at Fredericton's Sheraton Hotel the day after the June 7, 1999, election was supposed to celebrate the continuation of Liberal rule in New Brunswick. The Dr. Everett Chalmers Hospital Foundation in Fredericton was holding a high-profile fundraiser, "An Evening of Appreciation for Frank and Julie McKenna." All the Liberal heavyweights in the province were on the guest list. Frank McKenna would be the keynote speaker, making his first public appearance in Fredericton since his resignation. However, it was risky to bank on the outcome of an election, especially in New Brunswick, and especially when a party has been in power long enough to project an aura of invincibility. The omnipotent Liberals were demolished at the polls by Bernard Lord, a baby-faced thirty-three-year-old Tory lawyer who led his party back from the brink of oblivion.

When Maurice Robichaud arrived at the Sheraton, he grumbled that he felt as if he had been tied down in a schoolyard and pummelled by small children. "The function room, crowded with Liberal walking wounded, resembled something between a trauma centre and an intensive care unit," Dalton Camp observed.

Liberal leader Camille Thériault's team had run a disastrous campaign, complete with a condescending slogan, "Making It Happen," and an annoying faux-rap song that blared from speakers at the leader's public appearances. Thériault, the son of Norbert Thériault, a retired senator who had run unsuccessfully for the party leadership in 1971, had tried to portray himself as an agent of change, a softer, left-of-centre Liberal, while embracing Frank McKenna's fiscally conservative legacy. Thériault claimed he was a man of the people yet acceded to the demands of big business, granting Irving Oil an exemption from an environmental impact assessment for a major refinery expansion and agreeing to allow large companies to buy natural gas directly from Sable Island suppliers instead of going through the distributor that was building the gas network for consumers. He cancelled an income tax cut McKenna had scheduled for 1999 in favour of putting more money into the health care system. His ambition for power was clear; his vision for the province was murky.

Thériault and his colleagues had fallen victim to the insidious complacency of a political party settled too comfortably into power. Whatever Liberals thought was good was by extension good for New Brunswickers. "A party securely in power carries with it a musk of well-being and reeks with the essence of its affluence and comfort," Dalton Camp writes. "Men quickly learn to shift their gaze from that which they do not want to see, or to view with indifference things to which they have become strangely accustomed."

McKenna's single-minded determination had kept complacency at bay. His three election campaigns were meticulously planned, his platforms and communications strategies tested by extensive polling. Thériault wanted the job badly, but he didn't apply himself to the details. He turned away from the gifted McKenna campaign team and put his brother, Mario Thériault, in charge of strategy. The younger Thériault is erudite, charming and talented, but he was a political neophyte facing the most challenging of electoral mindsets, an electorate that had decided to vote for change. Camp had asked Thériault six months before the election was called what would happen if the central theme of the campaign became a call for change. "If the issue is change, we can't win, and there's nothing I can do about it," he replied matter-of-factly. In Camp's view it was "a no-fault election with a no-one-to-blame result."

Watching from the wings, Frank McKenna's political instincts told him that his plan to create a Liberal dynasty in New Brunswick had gone terribly awry. McKenna had promised Julie, who hated life as a political wife, that he would resign after ten years in the premier's office. Shortly after he was elected Premier, Julie McKenna told *Chatelaine* magazine that she intended to hold him to his promise. "Frank will leave while he's still a star," she said. He announced that he was quitting politics two years into his third mandate, ten years to the day after his election victory in 1987. He kept the timing of his departure a closely guarded secret, but privately he had been counting down the days for more than a year.

He carefully scripted his final moves to give a new leader time to put his own stamp on government before going to the polls. While he was tempted to extend his time in office by another few months, in the end he decided there would never be an easy time to walk away. He had pushed the patience of his family and friends to the limit. He left behind a Liberal Party holding a strong hand: forty-nine of fifty-six seats in the Legislature, a hundred thousand card-carrying members, more than a million dollars in the bank and one of the best-organized political machines in Canada. As a final gesture, McKenna anointed as interim premier Ray Frenette, his loyal Acadian lieutenant and rival for the leadership in 1985. "I thought, if there was ever good succession planning, I've achieved it," he says. "I thought we had a rich field of candidates. I thought I had in Ray Frenette a perfect transition, someone who could take the ball and run with it in the interim. The plan was brilliant, it just didn't work."

After winning the leadership in the spring of 1998, Camille Thériault could have governed into 2000, but instead he chose to call an early election the following spring. "I knew it was all unwinding," McKenna says. "I just watched the way things were going. The election timing was terrible. I knew the campaign and platform weren't the quality that we needed. I'm probably one of the only people in New Brunswick who sensed that we were going down. It was a classic front runner's campaign where you go turtle and just get through the campaign as best you can."

Meanwhile, Bernard Lord emerged as a solid choice for voters. Lord speaks both English and French fluently. His Acadian wife, Diane, has similar language skills and shares her husband's quiet charisma. He showed himself to be the kind of leader who would make a good impression for New Brunswick on the national stage. During a CBC television debate, NDP leader Elizabeth Weir said she saw Bernard Lord's lips moving but heard Frank McKenna's voice. Unintentionally, she may have thrown a compliment Lord's way. On June 7, 1999, the Progressive Conservatives surpassed even their most optimistic projections, winning forty-four of fifty-five seats.

The evening after the election, Frank and Julie McKenna rest in their room at the Sheraton Hotel, preparing to make their appearance at the hospital fundraiser. News reporters pace in the lobby, hoping McKenna will comment on the outcome of the election. Maurice Robichaud finds himself back in the familiar role of arranging for a media scrum, something he has orchestrated hundreds of times before. After receiving a telephone call from Robichaud in the lobby, McKenna steps off the elevator and calmly walks into the glare of television lights. He speaks in a subdued voice about his legacy and says he shares the responsibility for the crushing defeat of his party. When asked what advice he has for Bernard Lord, McKenna lifts his head and stares directly into the bank of cameras.

"He's now receiving one of the most precious things I've ever had in my life, which was the stewardship of the Province of New Brunswick," he says. "It consumed me. It was everything to me. He's going to have to go in there with a lot of heart and a lot of passion and believe so strongly, so fervently in making things happen that, by sheer force of personality, he can move the people around him. Otherwise, he'll be just another politician."

McKenna is describing himself, not the young premier-elect. Robichaud, who has positioned himself behind McKenna's right shoulder, steps in and stops the questions, but McKenna seems reluctant to leave the lights. As he walks away, he turns back to the reporters, smiles and says, "I've missed you guys."

Later that evening, McKenna steps up to the podium and tells the crowd that he believes the timing of the event is perfect. The best time to show appreciation for politicians, he says, is after an election campaign, regardless of the outcome. Then he addresses his Liberal colleagues: "To the people who have tasted defeat, there is nothing, no matter how you gloss it over, as heart-wrenching and as hurtful as losing a political battle."

He raises his voice, his words flowing more quickly. "We have to stand aside momentarily and not be able to carry the torch that we believe in. They keep saying to themselves, 'Don't these people know what it is I was going to do for them? Don't they know how much I love them and care for them and want to serve them?'" His voice falls and he pauses. "That's what hurts the most. The moment of birth, the moment when you're the most excited and the most fulfilled, is the first moment of your death. It's the first moment when you start down that path which inevitably will lead to either your defeat or your resignation.

"You start with all this political capital in the bank. And you spend that bit by bit as you go through your political career. And if you don't spend that political capital, you may not be defeated, but you are a failure, because you have not honoured those people who put their trust in you to lead courageously and not to be afraid to spend your popularity to do what was right and good and just and would stand the test of time."

McKenna knows he has spent his political capital and a good part of his party's. The Sheraton ballroom is hushed as he pauses, preparing for his closing. While he admits that he has made mistakes, that he has sometimes pushed too hard, made changes too quickly and left casualties in his wake, he makes no apology for the driving idealism behind his reforms.

"I know that people look at our province with different eyes," he says. "Some people look at it as a province that's disadvantaged and poor and needs help and needs support. I look out at a province that's just brimming over with opportunity, a province of people who, for over a hundred years, pioneered their way and made life what it is for them today. I look out and I see a province that is on the move, that is modernizing, that is activist, that is interventionist, that is looking to the future with more confidence, and more hope and more pride, and more opportunity and more potential."

Then he expresses his own paradox: not a day goes by that he doesn't miss being premier; however, not a day goes by that he regrets leaving. He still has the passion for the job, but he recognizes that he pushed his agenda as hard and as far as he could.

"There's nothing I've ever done in my life that was as fulfilling," he says. "There's nothing that I've ever done in my life that compares to the satisfaction that I felt every single day on the job of being the premier of your province. I can't get it out of my blood. It's like a song in my head that just beats in my heart all of the time, this province of ours. I just can't leave it. I just can't get rid of this sense of destiny that we have."

———

Four days after McKenna's remarkable performance at the Sheraton, on a perfect blue Saturday, a light breeze pushes waves into the horseshoe cove that shelters the sands of Friel Beach. About noon, guests begin to arrive at Frank and Julie McKenna's new home, which is built into a bluff above the beach in the tiny francophone community of Cap-Pelé that Julie visited with her family when she was a child. When McKenna announced on October 7, 1997, that he was stepping down as Premier and leaving politics, he held a press conference, then went back to work. Four days later, he cleaned out his office, said goodbye to his staff and walked home alone. In the months that followed, his staff and advisors disbanded, most of them landing jobs in the private sector. It had taken twenty months for all of these "eminent knights of the McKenna round table," as Dalton Camp likes to call them, to reassemble in the same place.

From the moment McKenna announced that he intended to be leader of the New Brunswick Liberal Party, he began to recruit a loyal political team. By the time he was established as Premier, he was surrounded by a tightly knit group of professionals, most of whom remained at his side for ten years. These are the guests who are arriving that afternoon with their partners and families.

Fernand and Aldéa Landry arrive on their twenty-four-foot sailboat, *L'erre d'aller,* which they anchor in the cove. Fernand Landry, a Harvard-educated lawyer born in the tiny community of Evangeline on the Acadian Peninsula, co-chaired all three election campaigns and was McKenna's first deputy minister in the premier's office. Aldéa Landry, the former president of the Liberal Party in New Brunswick, was his first deputy premier and the minister of intergovernmental affairs during the constitutional crisis of the late eighties. The three have been friends since their University of New Brunswick Law School days.

Raymond Frenette, loyal soldier and political fixer, drives up the driveway dressed for the golf course, his clubs in the trunk of his car. Francis McGuire, McKenna's deputy minister of economic development, brings his trademark never-ending conversation and laughter to the beach. For ten years, McKenna depended on McGuire's agile mind and mastery of political strategy.

McGuire is followed by Maurice Robichaud, the gregarious communications wizard who controlled the media agenda in New Brunswick and helped to make his boss a star in the national press. At Robichaud's side is Steven MacKinnon, a bilingual political junkie from Prince Edward Island who personifies the kind of youthful passion and loyalty McKenna admires.

The guest list is rounded out by Georgio Gaudet, a resourceful career civil servant who was the deputy minister in the premier's office during McKenna's final years; Charlie Harling, consummate corporate deal maker; Ruth McCrea, the scheduler who continues to construct all the details of her boss's life; Nat Richard, a neighbour and former executive assistant; speech writer Nicole Picot; and secretaries Pierrette Battah and Zona Bovingdon.

McKenna leads an expedition to the golf course. Others go sailing with the Landrys, and the less adventurous relax on the deck, basking in the sea breeze on this unusually hot June day. When the golfers and sailors return, they feast on lobster and steak, then wander down to the beach, where they talk around a bonfire until the early hours of Sunday morning. The couples who stay overnight in the guest wing share a subdued brunch with the McKennas on Sunday and depart about noon.

Political gossip in New Brunswick spreads like wildfire, and the gathering of McKenna loyalists in Cap-Pelé that Saturday in June became the subject of much speculation. What's Frank McKenna up to now? A week later, the reunion was the subject of a front page column by Roy MacGregor in the *National Post*. "This is how these things get started," MacGregor wrote. "Last weekend — with the prime minister, Jean Chrétien, musing once again about his own possible or probable retirement — word leaked out of New Brunswick that a private gathering was under way at McKenna's home at which his former advisors and assistants were musing openly about the possibilities of a Frank McKenna leadership run. A new name had, not officially, joined the unofficial race to replace Mr. Chrétien."

When MacGregor tracked down McKenna, he insisted that the gathering was social, not political — a golf game, a few beers, nothing more. He issued as firm a denial as possible about his federal leadership aspirations. "I'm not seeking it and I'm not looking for it and I'm not offering for it," he said. "I was able to walk away from the premier's office with a very strong mandate and at the height of my popularity, so I can look this ambition in the face and walk away from it." To which MacGregor added: "For the time being at least."

The consensus in political circles was that Robichaud had leaked the news of the gathering to float McKenna's name across the country and gauge public reaction. Robichaud knows the value of a strategically leaked news story; however, he insists that on this one his conscience is clear. As it turned out, McKenna's description of the Saturday afternoon gathering was accurate. In the months that followed, no leadership bid emerged. However, MacGregor was correct in reporting that there had been talk of politics on the beach and a consensus that the old team would love to recreate the magic.

"I would walk through a concrete wall for any of the people in that office, and everybody there would have done the same thing for me,"

Robichaud says. For years, Aldéa Landry has been urging McKenna to position himself to occupy 24 Sussex Drive. "This was not a post mortem about the election or a rally for Frank running federally, but I don't think these people would ever get in the same room with him without telling him, 'If you ever go, we're there, and if the opportunity arises, please go,'" she says. "I don't think he has got politics out of his blood at all. If he runs, it will be because he thinks he can win, and I think he can win. It's obvious from talking to him that he misses politics big time."

There is no doubt that Frank McKenna misses politics, but the crisis that swept over his family in the months following the Cap-Pelé reunion convinced him without a doubt that leaving when he did was the right thing to do. In fact, the timing of his resignation may have saved his wife's life. When they moved to Cap-Pelé, Julie McKenna changed doctors, and her new doctor recommended a physical, including a routine mammogram despite the fact that she wasn't scheduled for a breast screening for at least another year. She had a mammogram in August 1999. On Thanksgiving weekend she received a call that the test had revealed a small mass in her left breast. Her doctor performed a biopsy and diagnosed her with breast cancer. Julie McKenna was numb, paralyzed with fear. "I couldn't believe it. I thought, this is not happening. How could it be? My mother didn't have breast cancer, none of my aunts, my sisters. And I'm fine. I feel fine. This isn't possible."

She had a small tumour and lymph nodes removed and then took a course of radiation treatment. Because the disease was detected early, which wouldn't have been the case if she had remained in Fredericton, she has a good prognosis. But Julie knows she isn't out of the woods yet. Their world doesn't look the same as it did before her illness. "I think Frank and I have both come to appreciate nature, just to watch the sunset, to do gardening and be outside," she says. "Breast cancer can always return, so there's constant fear that it's going to come back. If it returns, the chances of survival are not as great. We spend a lot more time together now. I think he sees his family as a much higher priority than some of the speeches he's asked to give or some of the places he's asked to go."

While Julie says she wouldn't stand in the way of her husband if he decides to re-enter politics, he has put politics on hold indefinitely. "For me to do more politics is a very selfish gesture until we have a lot better appreciation of where we stand health-wise," McKenna says. "Right now we're much more focused on getting through all this."

So Frank McKenna stands at a crossroads in his life, watching his political legacy being dismantled by the Tory administration and dissected by pundits. Soon after the Tories came to power, Lord accused the Liberals of cooking the province's books. He toned down McKenna's economic development program and gutted a multi-million dollar tourism campaign that Francis McGuire had been building for years. A string of extravagant campaign promises, including reversing McKenna's decision to charge tolls on a new stretch of Trans-Canada Highway, packed almost a billion dollars onto the province's debt.

In *Pulling Against Gravity*, Donald Savoie concludes that, while McKenna made a difference and New Brunswick outperformed other provinces of similar size during his time in office, he was fighting against entrenched federal policies that kept his province in a disadvantaged state, still miles from economic self-sufficiency. "McKenna pushed and pulled all the economic levers he could, as far as and probably better than anyone else could have done in promoting economic development in the province," writes Savoie, who admires McKenna. "His effort did have an impact. But one can only imagine the kind of impact there would have been had the federal government also pushed and pulled in the same direction."

For a man obsessed with perfection, the political and academic assessments of his legacy have been painful. McKenna has had to learn the hard lesson that political legacies are fleeting at best. However, history moves through the particulars of many stories into broad, sweeping themes. David Peterson unabashedly calls him "the best political leader of my generation," not only because McKenna shared Peterson's vision of a new Liberalism and worked hard to transform the economy of a have-not province, but also because he fundamentally changed the attitudes and spirit of his people.

Frank McKenna understood that his province was in much the same position as he found himself as a boy. Poor and isolated from the corridors of power, he began his journey with no natural advantages other than a determination to work harder than anyone around him to fulfill a destiny he believed in absolutely. "He gave New Brunswick confidence," Peterson says. "He made the average guy feel good about being a New Brunswicker. The toughest thing in the world in politics is to change attitudes. That is what great politicians do." However, for both Frank McKenna and his province, nothing came easy.

*Frank McKenna and Louis Robichaud after the New Brunswick
Liberal leadership convention, May, 1985.*

2

ACROSS THE GREAT DIVIDE

Sometimes it feels like a lonely battle — the whole world
stacked against us.
— *Frank McKenna, diary entry, February 10, 1987*

By the time Frank McKenna became Liberal leader in New Brunswick in
the spring of 1985, the Liberals had spent fifteen frustrating years on the
Opposition benches. McKenna and his campaign co-chairmen, Fernand
Landry and John Bryden, were determined not to let a victory over
Premier Richard Hatfield slip from their grasp. This time, they were
going to do it right.

Late in the summer of 1985, they hired Francis McGuire, a brash
young communications specialist from Nova Scotia, who had gained a
reputation as a shrewd operator in Ottawa. McGuire suggested that
McKenna and his team commission a thorough baseline poll that would
become the foundation for their strategy. At McGuire's suggestion,
McKenna enlisted the services of one of his former professors, George
Perlin of Queen's University, an eminent political scientist and pollster.
Perlin had been researching attitudes of Atlantic Canadians since 1970,
when Flora MacDonald, the former head of the political science department at Queen's, asked him to conduct polling for Richard Hatfield's first
campaign. Since then, Perlin had continued to study Atlantic Canadian
politics, in particular conducting in-depth research about language
attitudes for the Pepin-Robarts Commission on national unity in the late
1970s. Perlin agreed to work with the McKenna team on the condition
that he could use the data from the polls in his academic research without
restriction. And so an unusual collaboration between an innovative academic
researcher and an active political campaign began, creating a polling
laboratory in New Brunswick unlike any other in Canadian history.

Political campaigns generally commission either tracking polls, which take snapshots of public opinion to measure voting intentions and determine what people think about issues at a particular moment, or more thorough research to test public opinion about a specific issue to guide campaign strategy. Perlin and McGuire had more ambitious plans. They prepared to conduct baseline polling that would become the foundation for a search to understand the soul of a people — not only their political views, but also what caused them to think about their lives in the way they did, their hopes and dreams, their prejudices and fears.

In the fall of 1985, McKenna's campaign team dispatched a small army of pollsters to gather enough data to paint a scientific portrait of the people of New Brunswick. "We were going to create hypotheses, test them, make choices and then stick with them," McGuire says. "We were going to understand the attitudes of the public." Perlin would prepare an analysis of the data and make broad recommendations; McGuire would take Perlin's conclusions and direct political strategy on the ground.

In March, 1986, Perlin produced a lengthy confidential report for the McKenna campaign team developed from the data gathered in the first round of polling. On the surface, the numbers were good news for McKenna. The Liberals held a two-to-one lead among decided voters, although Perlin warned that more than half of those surveyed remained undecided about how they would vote in the next election. Richard Hatfield, unable to shake off a pall of scandal over accusations of drug use and recklessness in his personal life, was heading for a massive defeat at the polls. However, beyond his political preamble, Perlin's portrait of New Brunswick society was deeply disturbing.

"The polling was showing incredible discord between English and French communities," McGuire recalls. "It was about as goddam black as you could picture it. We were saying, 'Oh my God, we could have people shooting each other here.' It was that intense." Anti-French sentiment in English New Brunswick was rising. Less than fifty per cent of the province's anglophones believed Acadians "contribute to what is good about New Brunswick." More than half said they felt closer to English-speaking Canadians in other provinces than to their French-speaking neighbours, who comprised one-third of the 710,000 people in the province. Less than half of the people surveyed supported official bilingualism. One in two anglophones believed that official bilingualism had gone too far: Acadians were being treated better than the English. More than seventy per cent of anglophone New Brunswickers said they would agree to reductions in the government's French language services. Almost half of English New Brunswick believed that the French had no reason to feel that they had been discriminated against in the past, a belief that illustrated either remarkable ignorance of or callous disregard for history.

It was not surprising then that Perlin could find little sense of common purpose or community in the province. Only half of the people surveyed could articulate why they found living at home more attractive than moving to Ontario. Those who did attempt to describe a New Brunswick identity spoke of the relaxed pace of living in smaller communities and the natural beauty of the province. This was a weak foundation for a community of common interest. A majority of New Brunswickers felt dependent on governments and were overwhelmed by economic insecurity.

Perlin suggested that McKenna needed to change the attitudes of his people, to convince them to feel pride in their homeland by creating an image of New Brunswick as "the most Canadian province" because of its bilingual, bicultural character. Perlin concluded that the only issue that could bridge the linguistic and social cleavages would be a united campaign to create jobs. McKenna should try to convince "New Brunswickers, wherever they live, and whatever their language, to join in a common and concerted campaign to deal with the problem of unemployment," he wrote. Perlin's message in that first report defined McKenna's political mission. "The goal was to get both communities to share the same vision, the same dream," McGuire says.

At that moment, McKenna immersed himself in the divisive currents of his province's history. Richard Hatfield, who never trusted polls and instead relied on his remarkable political instincts to guide him, understood better than most the enormous challenge of striving to heal the wounds of history. By the end of his political career, Hatfield had reached the conclusion that the soul of his province was best expressed as a collage. On August 1, 1990, three years after he was crushed at the polls by Frank McKenna and less than a year before he died, Hatfield wrote an essay about his province that was published in the *Telegraph-Journal* to celebrate New Brunswick Day. He began by touring the province's landscapes, arranging the pictures on his imaginary canvas. He visited a summer house party on Miscou Island, the landfall at the extreme northeast corner of the province. He picked baskets of fiddleheads as he travelled in the valleys of the province's great rivers: the Restigouche, slicing through northern forests before spilling into the waters of the Bay of Chaleur beneath the hills of Gaspésie; the Miramichi and its vast network of tributaries, embracing the wilderness hinterland of the province; the St. John, rising in the Maine wilderness in the north and running south through a grand valley the length of the province. In his imagination, Hatfield unearthed new potatoes in farming communities throughout the St. John River valley. He visited the fishing villages that cling to the coastline of the Acadian Peninsula on the northeast shore of the province. He watched fishermen tend herring weirs in the Bay of Fundy off the south coast. He lounged in the living room of poet Alden Nowlan's bungalow, and then he returned to his home beside the river late at night, walking in silence along Fredericton's peaceful, elm-lined streets.

In Hatfield's vision, all these images were united in a people he had come to love and admire. "Premium is the word for the people," he wrote. "The Malicites who observed Champlain's arrival on the Isle de St. Croix. And the Micmac and les Acadiens and the Planters who came for land. The Loyalists who escaped persecution and the Irish who remained despite it. The farm makers in New Denmark, the Brayons in the Republic of Madawaska. . . . It doesn't matter where you come from if you call New Brunswick MY PLACE/MON FOYER. We have more in common with each other than any other peoples in the world."

Hatfield had created a splendid collage; a man so generous in spirit was able to unite these images in his own mind. Perhaps Hatfield can be forgiven this moment of wishful thinking. As premier, he had applied his considerable political talents to the task of trying to bridge his province's greatest divide by drawing New Brunswick's French and English communities together into the embrace of his Conservative party. But did the people of his province really have that much in common?

For a century, an invisible political boundary had split the province on an east-to-west diagonal line from Moncton to Grand Falls. North of the line was French New Brunswick — largely Roman Catholic, rural, and disconnected from the economic and political establishment. Voters in the north elected Liberals. South of the line was English New Brunswick — predominantly Protestant, urban, the seat of economic and political power in the province. Voters in the south elected Tories. For generations, chasms of prejudice, envy and suspicion had separated northern and southern communities, rural and urban families.

Throughout the 1970s, Hatfield acted as a political missionary, making casual appearances at Acadian festivals, arriving unannounced at meetings of the Société des Acadiens du Nouveau-Brunswick to share coffee and conversation as best he could in his rudimentary French. "He was highly respected and well liked in francophone communities, which goes to show you really don't have to speak the language in order to communicate with people," says Fernand Landry, who came to admire Hatfield during these years. Hatfield legitimized Acadian aspirations in his public policy, splitting the Department of Education into French and English divisions and relentlessly promoting bilingualism, but in his first decade in power he could elect no more than four Acadians, all of whom he appointed to his cabinet. When Jean-Pierre Ouellet turned down a cabinet post because he wasn't bilingual, Hatfield replied curtly, "Neither am I." In 1981, Hatfield passed the landmark Bill 88, an Act Recognizing the Equality of the Two Official Linguistic Communities. Before the 1982 election, Hatfield dispatched his French lieutenant, Jean-Maurice Simard, to deliver seats in the north. Simard, brazenly seeking help from Parti Québécois strategists in Quebec, turned the Acadian nationalist vote toward the Conservatives.

On October 12, 1982, Hatfield marched triumphantly across the divide, electing Tory members in traditional Acadian Liberal ridings in the north, winning thirty-nine of fifty-eight seats, his largest majority. However, Hatfield's bridges, resting solely on his own credibility, were weak. Five years later, when he withdrew from public life in political and personal disgrace, his bridges collapsed behind him. It would take more than the political will of Richard Hatfield to change the course of history. New Brunswick society, a melting pot of natives and European and American settlers, carried with it a history of wars and prejudices fostered for centuries in far-away lands as well as at home. The battles raged on uninterrupted; only the weapons and the character of the battlefield changed.

The French explorers who arrived in New Brunswick early in the seventeenth century encountered about three thousand members of the Algonquin nation: the Maliseet, who patrolled the St. John River valley, and the Micmacs, who fished and hunted on the eastern shore. Samuel de Champlain sailed up the mouth of the St. John River on June 24, 1604, the Feast of St. John the Baptist, and in the years that followed established French settlements in the land he called Acadia. When England and France went to war in 1689, the fighting spread into French and English settlements in Acadia. The French, with little support from Europe, valiantly defended strongholds in the St. John River valley before France ceded Acadia to Britain under the Treaty of Utrecht in 1713. However, the boundaries of Acadia were unclear, and the French continued to lay claim to the land, establishing Fort Beauséjour on a ridge overlooking the Isthmus of Chignecto, the key communications passage for the region. In 1755, the British attacked Beauséjour, and the fort fell with little resistance.

The fall of Beauséjour thrust Acadia into its darkest hour. The British army, in a systematic campaign of ethnic cleansing, burned French settlements, drove their inhabitants off the land, and transported thousands from Nova Scotia to Louisiana, Massachusetts, Virginia and even back to France. Acadians retreated into the northern wilderness of New Brunswick, pursued by British forces. Colonel Robert Monckton sailed up the St. John River and destroyed French settlements at Grimross and St. Anne's. A French "commander of a forlorn hope" named Boishébert made camps for the refugees on the east coast and beside the Miramichi River, only to see them destroyed by troops dispatched by General Wolfe. "The last stroke fell in 1760, when Boishébert, with his Canadian irregulars, Acadian partisans, and Indian allies, sullenly looked on as Commodore Byron destroyed, in the estuary of the Restigouche, the last fleets sent by France to the St. Lawrence," writes the dean of New Brunswick historians, W.S. MacNutt. During the Expulsion, Acadians who escaped deportation retreated into Quebec and the wildest fringes of New Brunswick and Nova Scotia.

After the peace of 1763, New England settlers called Planters moved north into the new British territory, pushing up the St. John River valley in search of farmland. Acadians also began to return home, leaving behind their scourged settlements in the south, moving quietly into the north and the interior of New Brunswick to create new communities protected from their oppressors by a wilderness wall. In the northwest corner of New Brunswick, Acadian and French Canadian settlers converged in the fertile Madawaska region, forming a society of people who would call themselves *les brayons*.

At the end of the American Revolutionary War, a new wave of immigrants arrived who would forever change the character of the colony. More than thirteen thousand members of Loyalist regiments and their families trekked north to start over again in British territory. The arrival of the Loyalists prompted Britain to detach the region from Nova Scotia and create a new colony, New Brunswick, dominated by these Protestant settlers.

The Revolutionary War also launched the Maritime timber trade that supplied masts and lumber to the British fleet. The forests fell and the economy prospered in the restricted trading system of the Empire. Immigration from the British Isles increased as empty timber ships offered cheap passage for settlers. By the middle of the nineteenth century, more than seventy per cent of the immigrants landing in New Brunswick ports were poor Irish Catholics, who found themselves relegated to the bottom of the colony's social and economic order.

The New Brunswick appendage of the Loyal Orange Order, which had spread throughout the British Empire, became the public voice of the Protestant rejection of these Irish Papists, suspect because they maintained a loyalty to Rome, not Mother England. Periodic clashes between Orangemen and Irish Catholics escalated into full-scale riots in Woodstock and Fredericton. The violence peaked in 1849 in the Irish Catholic ghetto of York Point in Saint John when the Orangemen planned to march through York Point to celebrate July 12, the day Catholic King James II was defeated at the Battle of the Boyne by the Prince of Orange, King William III. The Irish Catholics erected an arch of pine boughs to force the Protestant marchers to lower their flags and banners in a symbolic act of submission. When six hundred Orangemen reached York Point, the Irish showered them with rocks before they reached the arch. The marchers opened fire, and the street exploded in a pitched battle.

The official estimates after this confrontation indicated that twelve people were killed, including one Irish Catholic woman, and more than one hundred were injured. However, there were likely many more casualties because the proud Irish had quietly held their funerals before investigators from Fredericton arrived the following day. The horror of the York Point riot served only to solidify the cleavage between British and Irish, Protestant and Roman Catholic communities in New Brunswick.

The British Colonial Office granted responsible government to New Brunswick in 1848; however, the Loyalists continued their rule without interruption. For a century after the Expulsion, Acadians played no role in political life and had little contact with English communities. They survived by farming and fishing, isolated from the booming southern economy that was supported by the timber trade. The Loyalist governments preferred to consider the Acadians a foreign race who could manage their own affairs. While the Irish were an enemy that needed to be engaged, the Acadians remained outcasts who could be ignored.

The years before Confederation were a golden era for the economy of the Maritimes, which included, in addition to the timber trade, a strong manufacturing base, a wealthy merchant shipping fleet and financial institutions that would become the foundations of the Royal Bank and the Bank of Nova Scotia. Donald Savoie notes that the Maritime region was at that time "an economic powerhouse" and, of course, it wanted to stay that way. At the dawn of Confederation, the Maritimes were no charity case. Leonard Tilley, New Brunswick's leading politician of the day, began to explore the possibility of a political union of the three Maritime governments to enhance their already strong economic position. In 1864, with the support of Charles Tupper, a rising star in Nova Scotia politics, Tilley arranged for a meeting in Charlottetown to discuss Maritime Union. However, by the end of the conference, a Canadian delegation had convinced Tilley and Tupper to embrace the vision of a wider Confederation.

Tilley returned to New Brunswick to sell the idea of a Canadian union, but he and his supporters were crushed at the polls in 1865. Two years later, with Irish Fenian outlaws threatening invasion at the American border and New Brunswickers feeling increasingly isolated and insecure, the province reluctantly entered the new Canadian union. It was Tilley who suggested the name Dominion of Canada after reading a passage from the Psalms one Sunday morning: "And his Dominion shall stretch from sea to sea and from the river to the ends of the earth."

The great promise of Confederation, the trade routes that the Intercolonial Railway would open, never materialized for the Maritimes. To make matters worse, the shipping world was converting from wood to steel. Lumber markets were collapsing, bringing shipyards and mills down with them. Tens of thousands of New Brunswickers migrated out of the province in the decade following Confederation. The province's most promising political leaders set their sights on Ottawa. The artificial east-west trade routes of the new nation had isolated the Maritimes, and the new railway system reduced New Brunswick to a supplier of raw materials and a market for central Canadian manufactured goods. New Brunswick became "a stagnant economic backwater on the periphery of a booming continent — a forgotten society," writes Arthur Doyle. "Once, it was a successful offspring of the British Empire; now it was a poor cousin in a new nation."

As its economy declined, the province found itself dependent on the Canadian government; New Brunswick had become a supplicant. The spirit of self-determination and the seeds of unity that had been sown as the economy boomed in the decades before Confederation were lost.

"The fierce, unyielding spirit of local independence and self-sufficiency, brought to the country by the Americans in the eighteenth century and by inhabitants of the British Isles in the nineteenth, was channelled off in a dozen directions," writes MacNutt. "If the spectacular and the grand were possible in New Brunswick, it was the violent spirit of sectionalism, so clearly apparent in all political, social and economic activity, that denied them free expression. A community of interest based upon a single economic impulse was denied to New Brunswick because there were so many ways to the outside world. Mercantile capitalism as well as government had failed to impart a spirit of unity."

Political initiatives designed to bring a measure of unity to the new province only stoked the fires of prejudice and division. In 1870, George E. King, a thirty-year-old lawyer and son of a Saint John shipbuilder, was elected Premier. The next year, King's Conservative coalition government tabled the Common Schools Act, progressive legislation that provided public non-religious schools for all children. Irish and Acadian Catholics, who for decades had been locked in a bitter struggle for control of their church, joined forces to fight the act. When Acadian Catholics rioted in Caraquet, the government dispatched a constabulary division from the Miramichi. Shots were exchanged, and two men were killed. The *Freeman*, Saint John's Irish Catholic newspaper, urged citizens to withhold taxes. Bishop Sweeney of Saint John had his books, horses and carriages seized by tax collectors. Timothy Anglin, the strident editor of the *Freeman*, took his church's case to John A. Macdonald to no avail. King stood his ground and won a huge majority in 1874, riding a wave of Protestant, anti-Catholic sentiment under the slogan, "Vote for the Queen and against the Pope."

Eventually, the government compromised, allowing religious education, allowing members of religious orders to work as teachers, and agreeing to rent school buildings from the Catholic Church. Now it was the Protestants who expressed their outrage at the weakening of King's position. At the age of thirty-eight, King resigned; after trying unsuccessfully to enter federal politics, he was appointed to the Supreme Court of New Brunswick and later the Supreme Court of Canada.

In 1879, the six-member Liberal opposition in the Legislature chose thirty-five-year-old Fredericton lawyer Andrew Blair as their leader to challenge the Conservative government, which was led by Daniel Hanington, a devout Anglican who had taken the unusual stance for a Protestant of opposing the Common Schools Act. A tall, handsome man with prematurely grey hair and beard, a Presbyterian and a ruthless political operator, Blair built the base for the modern Liberal Party in New Brunswick. He reduced the government's majority to four in the next election, a precarious majority indeed when a politician's vote often went to the highest bidder. Blair secretly lined up the necessary defectors and engineered a vote of non-confidence in the government. In 1883, Blair became Premier and, by judiciously controlling a system of patronage for steadfast Liberals, created a system of party loyalty. He also began drawing the support of Acadians who identified with the French Catholic leadership of Wilfrid Laurier in Ottawa.

In Blair's political world an election was never lost, even after the votes were counted. In the 1890 election, Blair lost his majority, forfeiting four crucial seats in Northumberland County because his government had increased stumpage rates on Crown land. Refusing to concede defeat, the ruthless Blair immediately travelled to Chatham, met with the four new Tory members in a hotel room, negotiated new stumpage rates and offered them whatever other favours they required to cross the floor. His government held. In 1896, he resigned to join the Laurier cabinet, leaving a profound impression not only on his friends but also on his enemies. At a Tory rally in Gloucester County in 1907, a man stepped up to the podium to announce that Andrew Blair had died. After a moment of stunned silence, the crowd spontaneously erupted into cheers.

In the first decades of the twentieth century, New Brunswick remained a rural province. Less than twenty per cent of the population lived in the cities of Saint John, Fredericton and Moncton. Small towns that had enjoyed healthy economies during the shipbuilding and lumber boom had lost their self-sufficiency and retreated further into self-imposed isolation. The distant government in Fredericton was unable to unite a province fragmented by persistent regional, religious and cultural conflicts.

Five years after Blair's death, James Kidd Flemming, an orator without equal in the province, led the Tories to a landslide victory, leaving the Liberals with only two seats, both in francophone Madawaska County. The Liberals hired Acadian journalist Peter J. Veniot, along with journalist E.S. Carter of Saint John and Frank Carvell, the Member of Parliament for Woodstock, to lead them out of the political wilderness. The Conservative Press referred to the three as the "Dark Lantern Brigade," after the Confederate spies who operated behind union lines during the American Civil War. Veniot, dapper, charismatic and bilingual, travelled through the Acadian villages, preaching Liberalism and raking muck. Eventually, he, Carter and Carvell unearthed evidence that Flemming had been taking kickbacks from lumbermen and railway contractors. A royal commission found Flemming guilty on one count and not guilty on another. He resigned, and the Tory government fell to Liberal Walter Foster in 1917.

Peter Veniot became Minister of Public Works in the Foster government and took control of the highways program and the patronage system. For the first time, he included Acadian communities in the allotment of graft and largesse. Foster's government took steps to modernize New Brunswick, creating the Electric Power Commission and Canada's first Department of Health. Foster led the Liberals to victory again in 1920; then he resigned and Veniot became premier. But the province was not yet ready to be led by an Acadian, and when Veniot went to the polls, the Tories returned to power. The vote split strictly along religious and ethnic lines, with English Protestants voting solidly for the Tories.

On the eve of the 1930 election, fearing another Protestant backlash, the Liberals ousted interim leader Allison Dysart, a lawyer from Loyalist stock who had all the makings of a premier except that he was Roman Catholic. William Jones, a Protestant from the St. John River valley, was routed at the polls. The Liberals turned back to Dysart for the Depression election of 1935. Even though the Ku Klux Klan, standing in for the Orangemen, published a circular during the campaign denouncing Dysart as a dangerous Papist, he won a majority government, becoming the first Roman Catholic elected premier in New Brunswick.

When Dysart resigned and was appointed to the bench in 1940, John Babbit McNair became Premier and created a Liberal dynasty. A Rhodes scholar and war veteran, McNair remained the star of the political stage for more than a decade. He pushed electricity into rural communities and solidified the capital in Fredericton by expanding the civil service. A fine speaker and strategist, he brought modern election tactics to New Brunswick, hiring a Montreal advertising firm to run his election campaigns.

When McNair went to the polls in 1952, Tory leader Hugh John Flemming, who as a child had watched his father leave the premier's office in disgrace, hired a young, disaffected Liberal to run his advertising campaign. Dalton Camp moved into the Lord Beaverbrook Hotel and set up a war room to engineer the downfall of McNair. "To do battle with McNair, I believed, you must enter his lair, and the struggle must be renewed each day," Camp recalled. In Camp's view, the Liberalism he had once supported had become not a faith but a command. "The society of

New Brunswick remained an egalitarian one; the only aristocracy was power," Camp later wrote. "What had ennobled Liberalism was its charity and compassion; what now corrupted it was its expedience and the haunted insecurity that led it to accompany humanitarianism with the menace of fear. This became the gist of Liberalism — everyone was better off being Liberal, everyone would be worse off being anything else."

Camp decided to exploit the anemic provincial press and purchased space for his own editorials in all of the daily newspapers. He encouraged public debate, supplied ammunition for Tories in the field, and gave the public something lively to read. Each day he ridiculed the McNair government, signing his editorials, "Yours truly, L.C. House," a not-so-subtle reference to the Tory slogan "Let's Clean House." In one of the great upsets in the province's political history, McNair was defeated.

Unwittingly, Camp had contributed to a renewal within the Liberal Party that would change the course of history. Since Confederation, the premier's office had been dominated by English Protestant lawyers from the south. It took the energy and courage of Louis Joseph Robichaud, a young Acadian lawyer, to drag New Brunswick into the twentieth century. Robichaud's ancestors were driven from southern New Brunswick during the Expulsion and had settled in Quebec before returning to establish a new home on the province's north-eastern shore. Although proud of their Acadian heritage, Robichaud's parents didn't allow linguistic or religious conflicts to dominate political discussions at their home in Saint-Antoine. "Few families in Saint-Antoine had time to dwell on events far in the past," writes Della Stanley, Robichaud's biographer. "Immediate family needs required their full attention. For that reason, Louis did not grow up identifying his political attitudes with a grudge against English Protestants. Rather, he was brought up to take pride in family, church and country."

Robichaud was educated at the birthplace of Quebec's quiet revolution, Laval University's École des sciences sociales. There, he came to believe that progressive governments could move society toward equality and social justice. He returned to New Brunswick to practice law. When he was elected to the Legislature in 1952, he could speak little English; six years later, at the age of thirty-four, he was elected Liberal leader and travelled to festivals, county fairs, graduations, main streets and meeting halls in every corner of the province. In the north, he drove a shiny new Chrysler, reflecting the ambitions of a people who wanted a symbol of Acadian political success; in the south, he drove a Ford, reflecting the frugal Protestant work ethic. The diminutive orator, known affectionately as Little Louis, stunned Flemming by winning thirty-one of fifty-two seats in the 1960 election. The Acadians had a champion and at that moment became a political force that could never again be ignored.

When Robichaud came to power, government services, including health care and education, were dispensed by municipalities, which also collected taxes. Robichaud asked Edward Byrne, a lawyer from Bathurst, to conduct a study into municipal taxation. His report, presented in March, 1965, under the innocuous title White Paper on Government Responsibilities, revolutionized the province. Byrne found an antiquated host of taxing agencies and government service providers. His report stated that children in poor regions of the province, especially rural Acadian communities in the north, attended dilapidated schools run by poorly trained teachers, and that families outside the economic centres of the province were living with inadequate health care services and welfare programs.

In response to the Byrne report, Robichaud introduced his Equal Opportunity reforms to create a uniform taxation system, remove control of health care and education from municipalities and eliminate local tax collectors. He centralized political power in Fredericton and called his cabinet in from the regions.

Once again, reforms that were intended to create unity exposed the depth of the province's divisions. The opposition to Equal Opportunity teemed with anti-French rhetoric. Robichaud received death threats, and for a time RCMP officers escorted his children to school. At the centre of the storm was the most powerful economic force in the province, industrialist K.C. Irving, who was angry about losing the sweet deals he had negotiated with local tax collectors. When Irving appeared before the Law Amendments Committee to speak against Robichaud's reforms, the Fredericton *Daily Gleaner* suggested the industrialist was pleading "for the very life of his industries."

In 1966, with encouragement and financial support from Irving, former Restigouche-Madawaska Member of Parliament Charlie Van Horne returned to New Brunswick from his adopted home in Texas and defeated Richard Hatfield for the leadership of the Conservative Party. The Tories believed that Van Horne, a flamboyant, bilingual political street fighter, was the man to take out Robichaud.

Brigadier Michael Wardell, publisher of the *Daily Gleaner*, who had come from Fleet Street to Fredericton, considered his vitriolic opposition to Equal Opportunity the last great journalistic campaign of his career. Wardell told his readers that Robichaud "seems to have forgotten what he owes Mr. Irving." Two days before Christmas in 1965, he editorialized: "This is no time for Christmas revelry, as an interlude in a friendly bout of charades. This is war *à l'outrance* — to the death." Wardell supported Van Horne over Hatfield, saying that Tories needed "not a mama's boy but someone who knew how to fight."

If Wardell believed his grandstanding would intimidate Little Louis, he was mistaken. "We have had enough of the old palliatives and panaceas that did more to ease the public conscience than to correct the basic faults which have existed," Robichaud thundered in a speech in Saint John. "And if, in due time, my government and I are defeated on the head of this, then we will have the satisfaction of having been defeated for doing something, rather than doing nothing."

"I see as my duty the complete and absolute suppression of the Robichaud dictatorship," Van Horne retorted during the 1967 election campaign as he handed out his signature white cowboy hats. Wardell praised Van Horne's "magical qualities" and "tremendous personality," calling him a "giant on the New Brunswick political scene." The Conservatives described Equal Opportunity as "robbing Peter to pay Pierre." Van Horne, referring to Robichaud's drinking habits, said, "These half-breeds shouldn't drink liquor. Louis can't drink, he has too much Indian in him." Robichaud countered, "We must unmask the hypocrites and make the thinking people aware of the perils inherent in letting loose the forces of bigotry and prejudice." Little Louis held his party's thirty-two seats in the election to win his third majority government.

Van Horne lost his own seat, but he returned to the Legislature in a by-election and again challenged Richard Hatfield for the Tory leadership. In 1969 the Tories chose Hatfield; Wardell's "mama's boy" would prove to be the political giant.

Hatfield seemed destined for politics from the day his mother named him Richard Bennett after the family friend and former Conservative Prime Minister from New Brunswick R.B. Bennett. His father, Heber Hatfield, owned a potato chip plant in their hometown of Hartland in the St. John River valley potato country; Heber Hatfield was the area's Member of Parliament and largest employer. His son was a gifted student but applied himself only when absolutely necessary. When he was thirteen, his parents sent him to Rothesay Collegiate School, where he was teased relentlessly, his frail, fine features and blond hair earning him the nickname "Mary." He returned to Hartland's public school system the next year, studied at Acadia University, and then went on to graduate from Dalhousie Law School, earning his degree for its value as an admission ticket into the world of politics rather than for any passion he had for the law.

His biographers, Michel Cormier and Achille Michaud, explain that Hatfield's first and only court case sealed his decision to leave law. "He had been assigned to defend a boy charged with stealing a heart-shaped box of chocolates from a Truro candy store. The boy said he wanted to give the chocolates to his mother on Valentine's Day but could not afford them. Hatfield believed the boy's mother had instigated the theft. Despite his plea for clemency and the extenuating circumstances of the case, Hatfield did not sway the judge. The boy was sent to an institution." At that moment, Hatfield decided law was not for him.

Politics, and the social networks the profession offered him, became his passion. "My preoccupation was about wanting to help people," he said. "Individuals, not necessarily societies or communities or provinces or the nation, but people." New Brunswickers were intrigued by this Kennedy-like figure who was wealthy, educated and eccentric. He told *Maclean's* magazine that his favourite pastimes were walking alone in the country and listening to music.

Meanwhile, Robichaud was exhausted when he went to the polls in 1970. For a decade, he had been challenging political tradition, the intolerance and parochialism of his people, and generations of social and economic disparity. He was looking for a way out of public life and his party was in shambles. Hatfield won a majority with a campaign that needed to say little more than "We need a change." Robichaud's Acadian and Irish Catholic coalition had collapsed. He lost important seats in Moncton, the setting of a Université de Moncton student uprising to protest the anti-bilingualism policies of Moncton Mayor Leonard Jones. The anti French forces carried the city for Hatfield in a campaign that "was silent and superbly efficient," recalls Robert Pichette, Robichaud's executive assistant.

Even Robichaud described his loss in the context of New Brunswick's great divide. "I'd been there for ten years. A change was inevitable. I'd done too much for the Acadians, and the English wanted a break," he told Della Stanley. However, Robichaud left his people with a road map to Equal Opportunity. The Acadians had discovered a new nationalism. He had created the Université de Moncton and, during his final year in office, introduced an Official Languages Act. The Société des Acadiens wanted to keep their agenda moving forward. The more militant Parti Acadien, formed in 1971, wanted to decentralize government services and eventually form a new Acadian province.

The anti-French forces in New Brunswick, hoping for a champion in Richard Hatfield, were sorely disappointed. Hatfield would later say his proudest political achievement was implementing Robichaud's reforms. Furthermore, Hatfield was determined to create a New Brunswick identity based on harmony between French and English. "Although Hatfield never explained clearly what he meant by a New Brunswick identity, he did say it depended on enabling everyone in the province to share the same symbols," write Cormier and Michaud. "This was the pact he made with the Conservative Party: he would make it a truly provincial party by opening it up to francophones."

In the fall of 1972, Hatfield made his first trip abroad. In Paris, he attended the premiere of Antonine Maillet's play *La Sagouine*, which told the story of the survival of the Acadian people. The play received rave reviews in *Le Monde*. Maillet became famous and Hatfield a larger-than-life political force.

Hatfield drove a black Mercury Cougar, collected art and fine crafts, listened to rock music, socialized at Truman Capote's parties in New York City and, at home, held court in his suite at the Lord Beaverbrook Hotel. He drank and danced at Fredericton's disco, Club Cosmopolitan, stumbling to his office late in the morning, guzzling endless cups of black coffee to clear his head. He was routinely late for appointments and rarely attended cabinet meetings. He bought ties in Montreal and ordered custom-made suits in New York City when he took the government airplane south to party at Studio 54.

Two years into his first mandate, Hatfield fired Charlie Van Horne, his Minister of Tourism. Never a man to concede the spotlight, Van Horne had encouraged tourism employees to wear white cowboy hats while he engineered plans to build casinos, liberalize liquor laws and make New Brunswick the Las Vegas of the Maritimes. Van Horne had overspent his budget; Hatfield ordered an audit of the department's accounts and then passed the report to the RCMP. After an investigation, Van Horne was charged with accepting a bribe from a developer. At his trial in 1974, Van Horne alleged that the Hatfield government was financed by an elaborate scheme that would "make Watergate look like any Sunday bingo game."

His remark, largely ignored by the press, captured the attention of RCMP investigators.

Meanwhile, Hatfield was riding high. He cut a deal with thirty-five-year-old Arizona promoter Malcolm Bricklin to build a sleek acrylic sports car with gull-wing doors in New Brunswick. Bricklin would invest two million dollars, the province three and a half million, taking a majority position in the company. "The project represented everything he wanted for the province," write Cormier and Michaud. "Innovative, ambitious and idealistic, the venture would give New Brunswick a forward-looking image, an international trademark." Bricklin and Hatfield unveiled the car at the Four Seasons Hotel in New York City in June, 1974; the Bricklin was featured in *Playboy* magazine, and Hatfield appeared on the *Tonight Show* with Johnny Carson. If nothing else, Hatfield was allowing the people of New Brunswick to dream.

In the fall of 1974, Hatfield went to the polls, driving proudly across the province in an orange Bricklin. The Liberals fielded a candidate of great promise, Robert Higgins, a handsome Irish Catholic lawyer from Saint John. But Higgins, for all his natural abilities as a leader, proved to be undisciplined and ran a haphazard campaign. And Hatfield had kept an ace in the hole: before the election, he had created fifty-eight single-member ridings, ending the traditional multi-member riding system, a reform he manipulated to Tory advantage. As a result, Hatfield won an eight-seat majority.

In the final days of the campaign, the *Financial Post* published a story about an RCMP investigation into political fundraising in New Brunswick. The story was too late to change the result of the election, but the scandal to come would destroy one political career and leave Hatfield fighting for his own survival.

On February 10, 1977, RCMP investigators searched the law office of Francis Atkinson, the Tory Party's chief bagman in Fredericton. They hit pay dirt. Atkinson, whose father was also a Tory bagman, was an obsessive note-taker. His files revealed the finance committee's efficient system of tollgating. Businesses that won government contracts made contributions to the party, often at established percentage rates. The finance committee kept a list of companies doing business with the government and the level of their political contributions. Companies who refused to pay the party were placed on a negative list for government business.

Atkinson's files also suggested that the party had planted a mole inside the Department of Supply and Services to pass on information about government contracts to the finance committee. For fourteen months in the early seventies, Allan "Chowder" Woodworth received $616 a month in civil service pay and $384 a month from the Conservative Party. As far as Atkinson and the members of the finance committee were concerned, they were simply continuing the practices of their predecessors, including Robichaud's Liberals. On November 1, 1971, shortly before Woodworth began his job as a government "buyer trainee," Atkinson wrote a letter to Richard Hatfield marked "Personal and Confidential," in which he noted that the "recommendation of your Finance Committee on the appointment of a Co-ordinator in Purchasing has been finally carried out, and this should solve a lot of our problems." Hatfield would later deny he had ever received the letter.

Rumours swirled through Fredericton, and information about the search of Atkinson's office and the investigation leaked into the Opposition offices. On March 3, 1977, Robert Higgins rose in the Legislature, supposedly to reply to the Speech from the Throne but actually to accuse the Hatfield government of interfering in the police investigation into party fundraising. "I am informed and believe that, in 1972, the Premier of this province met with a committee of the Progressive Conservative Party," he began. "Some cabinet ministers were also in attendance at this meeting. I am informed that, at this meeting, discussion took place relative to the system used in the collection of monies for the Progressive Conservative Party." Higgins demanded a Royal Commission of inquiry, and he told reporters that if his accusations were proven wrong, he would quit.

Hatfield countered by asking Chief Justice Charles Hughes to conduct an inquiry into the relatively narrow question of whether there had been political interference in the investigation. He would leave the question of Tory fundraising tactics to the RCMP. The day after Higgins made his public accusations, Hatfield summoned Gordon Gregory, the deputy minister of justice, to his office. For two years, Gregory had been receiving regular briefings from the RCMP on the status of the investigation.

"Do you know what that's all about?" Hatfield asked, referring to the allegations of political interference in the investigation.

"Yes," Gregory replied.

"Is there anything wrong?"

"No."

"Okay, thank you," Hatfield said and dismissed him.

Gregory recalls that he could "smell the fear in the room."

Later, Hatfield asked Gregory to draft the terms of reference of an inquiry which would examine the accusations of political interference only. Gregory sent the terms of reference to Hatfield, and Hatfield passed them on to Hughes, who redrafted them in consultation with Hatfield and Gregory.

A year later, Hughes cleared the government of political interference, and Higgins resigned. Using his own nasty scandal as a weapon, Hatfield had managed to eliminate a Liberal rival who appeared to be on the verge of becoming premier. Hatfield advisor Dalton Camp, writing in the *Toronto Star*, expressed the completeness of the political victory: "What has been most astonishing about all this has been the reaction of the local media, which responded to these events as though Higgins had just rescued a boy scout troop from the freezing waters of the Bay of Fundy and afterwards soon perished from his exertions. If indeed, as one keening editorial primly intoned, Higgins quit with his head held high, it could only have been because he was feeling his neck."

The police investigation continued. Woodworth was charged with being a corrupt agent inside government, paid by the Tories to pass information to the finance committee. The Progressive Conservative party chose a young legal prodigy to defend him, a lawyer named Frank McKenna, who practiced in the town of Chatham beside the Miramichi River. McKenna asked for a retainer of $2,500 from the Conservative Party and was eventually paid $10,000 for his services. The essence of McKenna's defence was that Woodworth did not make any decisions about contracts or purchases while in government, that he passed on no information that was not already public, and that his payment from the Tories did not directly relate to his work within government.

"I spent months right in the middle of the worst of politics in New Brunswick," McKenna recalls. He was asked to join Francis Atkinson's defence team, but Judge Paul Barry, a Liberal Irish Catholic from Saint John, ruled that he was in conflict and asked him to step aside. "I think maybe he was trying to get me out of it for the good of my political health," McKenna says. "The Liberals were really quite incensed that I was representing these guys because it took me right into the heart of the Tory establishment." One day when he was in Fredericton working on the Woodworth case, McKenna walked to the Legislative Library to do some research. He remembers meeting Liberal staffer Don Hoyt and future Liberal leader Douglas Young in the hallway. Young, who was an acquaintance from the University of New Brunswick Law School, turned to McKenna and said, "You've fucked yourself in the Liberal Party in New Brunswick."

In the end, Atkinson was convicted of influence-peddling. Judge Barry paused before sentencing to offer the Crown a chance to cut a deal with Atkinson for his testimony at future trials. The Crown refused the offer. Barry handed Atkinson an absolute discharge anyway. Charges against fundraiser Lawrence Machum were dropped at a preliminary hearing. Charges against Woodworth were dropped because Atkinson refused to incriminate him. Atkinson took the fall; Hatfield had his scapegoat.

In 1978, Hatfield's government introduced the Political Process Financing Act, which placed limits on contributions and election spending and provided public funding for political parties. "It was, at the time, among the most advanced election-financing legislation in Canada, and it made the methods of the Conservative finance committee irrelevant," writes Jeffrey Simpson in his study of patronage in Canadian politics. "But the Atkinson affair served a long-term political purpose by exposing the corruption in New Brunswick politics — similar to that found in some other Canadian provinces."

The storm seemed to have passed, and Hatfield called an election after announcing early in 1978 the collapse of his Bricklin venture, along with the news that the boondoggle had gobbled twenty million dollars in public funds.

The Liberals felt certain they would return to power under the leadership of Joseph Daigle, a former judge the party hoped would become their new Acadian star. But where Robichaud had exuded passion and energy, Daigle appeared methodical and wooden. Daigle's Acadian heritage was once again stirring up the anti-French forces, but it was the Liberal leader's attack on Hatfield that defined the campaign. When Hatfield referred to Daigle as a "second-hand rose" in reference to his policy platform, Daigle responded with a witticism coined in private by Don Hoyt. "Better a second-hand rose than a faded pansy," Daigle said at a campaign rally, much to Hoyt's dismay. Voters made it clear that they had personal affection for Hatfield, despite his eccentricities. Hatfield clung to his majority government by two seats and bought himself some breathing room by convincing a Liberal to occupy the speaker's chair.

When Daigle was forced out of the party's leadership by a caucus revolt, Douglas Young, an ambitious bilingual lawyer, was chosen to duel with Hatfield. At the close of the leadership convention, Robichaud appealed for party unity: "Let's get together and make sure we crush the Tories in the next election." But the party never united behind Young, who was perceived to have masterminded the revolt against Daigle.

When Hatfield went to the people in 1982, he had become the champion of Acadia. Young found himself under attack, even though his riding of Tracadie was in the heart of Acadia. The Société des Acadiens suggested that August 15, the *fête nationale des Acadiens,* be made a holiday, whereas Young suggested that it be merged with New Brunswick Day on August 1. The Parti Acadien attacked Young in the Acadian daily newspaper *L'Évangéline,* linking Young's ancestors to the death of Louis Mailloux, a local hero during the Caraquet school riots of 1875. Hatfield won his largest majority and achieved his ambition of breaking down the French-English political divide in New Brunswick.

The Liberals were demoralized. When the party managed to win only one seat in the 1984 federal election, commentators began to write off the Liberals as a political force in New Brunswick. "People started saying the Liberal Party in New Brunswick was gone," Fern Landry recalls. "Traditional political parties are more difficult to kill than that."

On May 4, 1985, six thousand Liberals braved a fierce spring snow-storm to gather at the Moncton Coliseum to elect a new leader. In the three years since his astonishing political breakthrough, Richard Hatfield had dug himself into the deepest political hole of his career. Late in 1984, he had been charged with drug possession after an envelope of marijuana had been found in his suitcase in a routine RCMP search during Queen Elizabeth's tour of New Brunswick. Hatfield was acquitted early in 1985; however, news stories after the trial alleged that he had shared drugs, including cocaine, with male university students and in fact had flown two young men in the government plane to Montreal for a party. Hatfield claimed he was the victim of a conspiracy, but the political damage appeared irreparable.

Fresh off a by-election victory, the Liberals who had gathered in Moncton believed they were on the verge of a return to power, although they still feared Hatfield's magic. "After he won the 1982 election, it seemed as if Hatfield almost had the divine right to govern," says Julian Walker, a former staffer in the opposition office. "The guy knew how to win elections. No one underestimated Hatfield. He had this talent for letting things fester, allowing people to tear each other's hearts out, and finally at the last minute he would walk in and fix it. He was the hero. He did that time and time again."

The two candidates in the race were a study in contrasts. Ray Frenette, a fifty-year-old grandfather, was the choice of the party establishment. An Acadian businessman who had launched his public career in Moncton city politics, he had been recruited by Robert Higgins to run provincially. Frenette had represented the Moncton East riding for nine years, had run twice for the party leadership and had become interim leader after Young resigned. Frenette was an Acadian Higgins, a voice of experience, a man who commanded respect; on the other hand, he was a constant reminder of Liberal lost opportunities.

During the two-month leadership campaign, a new political force was emerging. Frank McKenna, the freshman member from the riding of Chatham, a thirty-seven-year-old father of three young children, was travelling the province in a blue Ford station wagon, promising "to open the doors and the windows" of the party. He told Liberals that times were changing, and that they needed to change with the times. When McKenna burst into the convention hall wearing his navy suit jacket unbuttoned, his campaign's rainbow banner jammed into his breast pocket, delegates noted that he appeared to be an English Louis Robichaud.

A week before the convention, the CBC had commissioned a poll predicting a McKenna romp. Frenette had said publicly that he might pull out of the race, a statement Liberal columnist Don Hoyt called "one of the worst political mistakes any politician has made in New Brunswick in the last twenty years." Although Frenette decided to continue his campaign, there was speculation in the convention hall that he might concede to McKenna and make the choice unanimous in his speech.

McKenna spoke first. He stood at the podium, nervously clearing his throat, his left hand shoved awkwardly into his pocket. Opening his speech in halting French, he told the audience that "more than anything, this campaign has been filled with hope." Raising his voice just short of a shout, the single volume of his early public speaking days, McKenna poured his passion into the cavernous hockey arena, projecting the anger of New Brunswickers about the chaos in Fredericton. He spoke of bringing together the two linguistic communities. He ridiculed Hatfield's legendary expense accounts. He promised to improve the quality of education, to allow businesses to flourish, to promote pay equity, to battle poverty and unemployment. He enumerated the concerns of every interest group in the province. He presented no clear vision of how he would govern the province, yet everyone who listened to the speech felt the force of his personality.

"I cannot accept the morality of this government any longer," he said. "We have had enough of the politics of despair, the politics of cynicism. The time has come for our province when hope is an acceptable four letter word. Where is the self-esteem, where is the pride? Dignity includes the right to work and have a meaningful job. What this province needs and so richly deserves is a change in government."

Ray Frenette arrived at the podium with a speech in his breast pocket that he did not want to deliver. The text, prepared by a Toronto speech writer, harshly attacked his young opponent. Frenette had been convinced by his handlers, including his fiercely competitive campaign manager, lumber baron Bev O'Keefe, that he was obliged morally and financially to pull out all the stops to try to stop McKenna.

Frenette told the crowd he had two speeches, one he had started writing more than a month ago, a speech full of ideas and vision. He admitted that his campaign had fallen into crisis, and his team was forced to step back and ask why they were in the race. Frenette said he could live with the embarrassment of losing but not with letting the party down. "I saw a vision of myself with my new young leader, still in Opposition, with an arrogant Hatfield still in power, and me with a speech in my pocket that could have changed all that. I am not prepared to suffer through another four years of Richard Hatfield. If I withdraw from this race, we will not only assure Frank McKenna the leadership of this party, but we will be giving the Tories another five years in office."

The Coliseum erupted, cheers from the Frenette camp and boos from McKenna supporters. McKenna rose to his feet and gestured for his people to listen in silence.

Frenette then presented his version of the recent Liberal failures. In 1978 and 1982, the Liberals had watched young lawyers be defeated by Hatfield. "And now, in 1985, I do not believe you will once again jeopardize our chances of victory by sending another young lawyer to the polls against Richard Hatfield," he said. "How often do we as a party need to be given a message by the electorate?" The problem with Frenette's revisionist history was that New Brunswick voters were attracted to young lawyers, electing one in the 1960s for the Liberals and another in 1970 for the Tories.

McKenna leaned back in his seat with his arms folded across his chest, struggling to maintain his composure. Julie McKenna was livid. "I couldn't believe some of the things he was saying," she recalls. "I was beside Frank, and of course our supporters were booing. That's how I was going to handle it, too, but Frank said, 'Just look up.'" He turned to the people around him and said, "Leave it, let it go."

"It's a choice between now and someday," Frenette shouted. "It's a choice between chasing the elusive pot of gold at the end of the rainbow or forming the next government. I think we have been chasing rainbows long enough. We are so close to finally getting our opportunity to change this province. We cannot let Hatfield off the hook this time." Frank McKenna was on his feet again, silencing his crowd. "I have waited eleven years for this moment. My time is now. Our time is now."

Minutes later, the CBC placed a headset on McKenna, who proceeded to answer questions calmly, displaying remarkable discipline in such a heated moment. "Ray Frenette's a fighter," he told the CBC's Mark Pedersen. "Ray just showed he was going to fight to the end. I don't take it personally. It's up to me to convince the voters I can win an election. Politics is a rough game, and if you're going to play, it's going to get rough at times. I have a tremendous amount of respect for Ray, and my respect hasn't changed one iota."

McKenna received 1,901 votes, Frenette 847. A beaming Louis Robichaud met the new leader on the stage and raised his hand in victory. Frenette urged his supporters to "follow me behind Frank McKenna." McKenna told the crowd that he would spread the word to New Brunswickers: finally somebody had faith in them. And he noted that, outside, the nasty spring storm had finally passed. "The sun is shining, the sky is blue, and there might even be a rainbow out there."

Ray Frenette soon learned the Liberals hadn't chosen just another young lawyer as their leader. McKenna poured his seemingly limitless energy into preparing the party to return to power. His first order of business was to assemble his election team and commission the baseline poll that would bring substance and vision to his campaign.

The first George Perlin poll, which revealed the profound cultural divisions within the province, also alerted the campaign team to a problem that had to be addressed immediately. New Brunswickers were deeply disillusioned with politics and politicians, and while they may have made up their mind about Richard Hatfield, they knew little about the province's new Liberal leader. When the polling results arrived, Francis McGuire realized that even the people who were working closely with the new leader didn't know his story. Who was Frank McKenna? How did he get here? Where would he take them? How far would he go? McGuire remembers telling his new boss, "Okay, Frank, it's time, we need to know."

*Mary Ita McKenna and Francis McKenna,
about 1963.*

*Joseph McKenna
with his son Francis,
1948.*

*The McKenna house
in Apohaqui, New
Brunswick, 1963.*

*Francis McKenna
and Susan McKenna,
June, 1966.*

3

THE CHOSEN ONE

Goals: Confidence, toughness, effective use of time, peace of mind. I must do better tomorrow.
— *Frank McKenna, diary entry, January 1, 1987*

Had Horatio Alger Jr. known Frank McKenna, he would have written his story. The early life of Frank McKenna mirrors the rags-to-riches formulas of the prolific nineteenth-century Massachusetts-born author. Alger's hero is a teen-age boy, "well-knit and vigorous, with a frank, manly expression and a prepossessing face." Often, this boy is the sole support of a widow. They live together on a farm mortgaged to the story's villain, who usually has a bully for a son. By the end of the book, the hero, who courageously stands his moral ground, is climbing onto the first rung of the ladder of success, the villain is in financial ruin, and the bullying son is exposed for the lout that he is.

In rural New Brunswick in the 1950s, boys were still devouring Alger's works. McKenna learned to read before he started school and soon consumed every Alger book he could lay his hands on, titles such as *Do and Dare, Fame and Fortune, Frank and Fearless, Strive and Succeed, Sink or Swim*. While modern critics have chastised Alger for his shameless promotion of the American Dream and the blessings of capitalism, boys like McKenna found inspiration in his stories.

New Brunswick poet Alden Nowlan, a Horatio Alger boy himself who emerged from a childhood of unbearable poverty to become a Canadian literary legend, believed that the author profoundly influenced his young readers. However, in Nowlan's view, Alger's youths were inspired by the promise of power, not money. "It has been said that Alger heroes were without distinct personalities," Nowlan wrote. "Ah, but the reason should be obvious. The hero's face was left blank so that it would always reflect the face of the reader, not as he was but as he would have liked to have been. The money in the Alger books isn't real money. It's another name for King Arthur's sword." Alger boys believed in the power of the individual to shape his own destiny if he found within himself the will and strength to pull the sword from the stone.

In the spring of 1986, Frank McKenna was asked by his campaign strategists to dictate his life story into a tape recorder; he began in the fashion of an Alger tale. "I was born in Apohaqui, Kings County, New Brunswick, January 19, 1948," he said. "I was born on a farm."

That was the beginning of the creation of Frank McKenna, the image. "Frank was a poor farming boy," Francis McGuire says. "Suddenly I had a feeling for where this guy is coming from. He believes in hard work. He believes in opportunity. We said, 'This is the guy we've got, these are the polling numbers. Let's take the guy we've got and, no sense faking anything, let's emphasize things.'" McGuire selected the facts he needed to create the image he had in mind, jettisoned material that didn't fit and then destroyed the tapes.

The portrait of Frank McKenna as a hard-working, clean-living farm lad was repeated time and again in media profiles. A *Toronto Star* reporter gushed that Frank McKenna's childhood "was a Norman Rockwell scene, white clapboard farmhouse in a village called Apohaqui. He'd practise his slapshot in the barn so noisily the cows objected and stopped giving milk." On the campaign trail, McKenna kept his story simple: he was just an average New Brunswick boy who had a few breaks along the way. "I lucked out on some good cases, and then the seat came open and I ran," he'd say. "Then, when I got there, the leadership was open and nobody else wanted it, so I ran for that, and here I am. Now nobody wants to be premier, so I'm running for that. I've just been at the right place at the right time so far. There's nothing I've got that isn't typical New Brunswick. I'm a typical New Brunswick boy, a little bit country and a little bit rock and roll." This official biography was a mask, and he wore it well. In fact, there was nothing average about McKenna's life at all.

McKenna grew up on a farm but was never a farmer in spirit. From an early age, he understood that he was living a life he was destined to leave behind. "I am part of all I have met," he says. "I am a product of my background. It's inescapable. I have never felt better than other people and oftentimes have felt inferior. I'm comfortable in corner stores and farmyards, but I am different from them.

"I left the farm, and I don't subscribe to all the same things those people subscribe to. I'm not as anxious to support unworkable enterprises.

I understand where people are coming from and I understand the pain, but at some point life has to go on. I would like to say things like 'You're a fisherman, and you should always be entitled to fish,' but sometimes I look at a coal miner and say, 'No, God doesn't give you the right to mine forever.' This has created a lot of dissonance in my life. The kind of communities I came from, sometimes they are doomed."

The true story of McKenna's youth, the real-life Horatio Alger version, begins on the outskirts of a village too small to accommodate an ambitious boy's dreams in an achingly beautiful river valley that would continue to define his character long after he moved away. Apohaqui, a community of 325 people situated at the confluence of the Kennebecasis and Millstream rivers, adopted its name from the Maliseet word for "the merging of swift waters" by which the Maliseets identified their own village and burial ground.

The shell of the McKenna homestead still stands four kilometres south of the bridge at Apohaqui. Larry and Kevin McKenna, the youngest of Frank McKenna's seven siblings, still own more than three hundred acres in Apohaqui, and their farm extends from the gentle, hardwood-covered hills above the Kennebecasis down to rich lowlands fertilized by spring freshets. The McKenna brothers, well-educated professional farmers, have built new riverfront homes across the road from their parents' two-storey gabled white-and-green saltbox, the downstairs of which has been converted into a storage shed for farm equipment. "It's probably in better shape now than when we were kids," says Kevin McKenna as he passes a critical eye over the old house.

Upstairs, a sun-faded portrait of Apohaqui's most famous son hangs in one of the three bedrooms. In another bedroom, Kevin McKenna's children discovered stamps and ink pads that belonged to their uncle when he was a student politician. They have decorated the room with his campaign slogans – "McKenna for President" and "Student Union: McKenna-Dolan."

Gnarled apple trees and ancient lilacs compete for space in the front yard. Behind the house, a patched tin barn stands near the foundation of what was once a large, hip-roofed cattle barn. Further back in the woods, the brothers raise pigs in a pristine modern barn. They operate one of only a handful of working farms that remain in a valley that has become a suburb of two cities, connected by a four-lane highway to Saint John in the south and Moncton in the northeast. The railway station, which gave birth to the village, has closed.

The first European to join the Maliseets at the mouth of the Millstream was Major Gilford Studholme, an Irishman, professional soldier and Loyalist who helped defend Fort Cumberland in 1770. He retreated to Saint John, where he built and manned Fort Howe, welcoming the Loyalists who landed in Saint John in 1783. Retiring from the army, he moved into the backwoods with plans to establish a farm and country estate on a 5,000-acre land grant he received for his service to the Crown. He built his house on a hill overlooking the Millstream, damming the waterway to create a saw and grist mill. But Studholme was soon defeated by the wilderness. In 1788, he stood on his front porch watching help-lessly as a spring flood washed away his dams and hemp fields and drove him into financial ruin. When he died, all of his lands and possessions, right down to his woollen underwear, were seized by creditors.

More Loyalist families followed Studholme into the river valley, experiencing similar hardships as they built rough log homes and cleared land, planting their first crops of potatoes around the stumps in "the chopping." Most of them lived desperately from season to season, focused on survival rather than progress. Many abandoned their farms, but early in the nineteenth century, waves of new immigrants from the British Isles began to push north to the Kennebecasis valley. The majority of these immigrants were Irish, both Protestants and Catholics, driven by poverty and famine from their homes into a land of promise they called New Ireland. Starving families began flooding out of Ireland in 1845 after the repeated failure of the potato crop. Saint John became an important port of entry in North America, and by 1871, the Irish made up 100,000 of New Brunswick's population of 285,000. Historian Peter Toner points out that the Irish farmers "had the largest, least valuable, least profitable, most populous, and most independent farms of all."

Frank McKenna's great-great-grandparents arrived in New Brunswick in the years before the Great Famine. Their son, Hugh Osmond McKenna, was born in New Brunswick in 1841. While the family often speaks of Hugh McKenna as an Irish immigrant, he consistently reported in census records that he was a New Brunswick native, born of Irish immigrant parents. The names of his parents and the date of their arrival have been lost. However, it is likely they arrived in New Brunswick as immigrants from County Monahan, Ulster, which was ruled by powerful chieftans of the McKenna clan for more than eight hundred years.

In the spring of 1997, Frank and Julie McKenna and their children

Jamie and Christine travelled to County Monahan, where they walked through graveyards full of tombstones engraved with the name McKenna. While a lack of written records has stymied Frank McKenna's attempts to make a direct genealogical link to County Monahan, he and his family were all made honorary members of the clan, and this pilgrimage firmly established his spiritual connection to the land of his ancestors.

Hugh Osmond McKenna farmed land east of the town of Sussex, the hub of the farming communities in the Kennebecasis valley. In the fall of 1872, Hugh McKenna married Ellen Elizabeth McManus, the daughter of Luke McManus, an Irish Catholic, and Julia Ann Montgomery, an English Protestant. According to family tradition, Julia was the daughter of Lord and Lady Montgomery, British Protestants, who disowned her when she married an Irish Catholic. Ellen Elizabeth was a midwife and a musician of some renown, and their home overflowed with guests when she played the accordion and fiddle. They raised ten children, including Durward James McKenna, Frank McKenna's grandfather, who was born in 1884, the sixth child of Hugh and Ellen McKenna.

Durward McKenna bought a farm near Sussex, where, soon after the turn of the twentieth century, he met the love of his life, a stylish, strong-willed Newfoundlander named Mary Ita Corbett. She was born in St. John's in 1883 but spent part of her childhood in the seaport of Brigus, the home of her most famous relative, Captain Bob Bartlett, the renowned Arctic explorer. Throughout her life she told tales of Bartlett's heroism and daring rescues on the ice as leader of expeditions to the North Pole. Her father, Joseph Corbett, a constable and notary public, saw to it that his daughter received a complete Catholic education at St. Bonaventure's College in St. John's. In 1901, Mary Ita travelled to New Brunswick with her sister Margaret, who was engaged to marry a man in Sussex. The marriage plans fell through, but the sisters stayed on in Sussex, and Mary Ita met Durward McKenna. The sisters travelled to Boston to find work, and Durward followed them. Mary Ita and Durward returned to Sussex, married in 1905, and later moved downriver to Apohaqui to establish a permanent homestead.

A city girl who loved fashion and books and pined for Newfoundland, Mary Ita reluctantly settled into her new life as a rural farm wife. Her husband taught her to cook, and she sewed clothes for the family. She maintained her independence as much as possible, keeping a trotting horse and sled, which she used to travel to Sussex in the winter. Durward played the fiddle, Mary Ita played the grand piano that she had brought back from Boston, and they hosted musical gatherings of young people from up and down the valley.

Durward and Mary Ita were devoted parents who raised seven children and encouraged them to educate themselves and seek opportunities beyond life in Apohaqui. However, throughout her life, Mary Ita never stopped grieving for the children she had lost. James Harold Paul, born on October 30, 1908, lived just thirteen months; his twin brother, Joseph Durward, survived. John Duncan, born four years later, lived only six months. For years afterwards, Mary Ita would descend into deep bouts of depression, and she turned to her religion for comfort. Every Sunday morning without fail, dressed in her finest clothes and draped in a fur stole, heavily perfumed and wearing a feathered hat, she would lead her flock into the Catholic church in Sussex.

Mary Ita and Durward's daughters became nurses and moved to Boston and Toronto. Their youngest son, Jack, attended St. Francis Xavier University in Antigonish, Nova Scotia; he joined the army and served overseas in the Second World War, returning home as a Lieutenant Colonel. Joseph Durward McKenna, the surviving twin, a quiet young man who shared none of the ambitions of his siblings, stayed home during the war to help his father on the farm. In 1942, Joseph married twenty-one-year-old Olive Moody, a native of Sheffield, England, who had arrived in Quebec City at the age of seven with her English father, Robert Moody, and Scottish mother, Margaret Helena Cairns. The Moodys settled near St. Stephen in southern New Brunswick. Robert Moody was a natural leader, deeply involved in community life, a man to whom everyone turned for advice. Like him, his daughter, who never lost her Yorkshire accent, was eminently sensible, not openly bossy but always in control. Olive Moody McKenna began working side by side with her husband on Durward and Mary Ita McKenna's farm in Apohaqui.

Their first child, Theresa Anne, was born in September, 1943. Two more girls followed, Loretta Mary and Cynthia Margaret. During a fierce snowstorm on the evening of January 19, 1948, Olive went into labour with her fourth child. Joseph McKenna was away working at a woods camp. His brother Jack was at home on leave from the army, and Olive asked her brother-in-law, a bachelor, to drive her to a midwife's home in Apohaqui. Jack, who had never helped a woman in labour before, drove his car into a snowbank, where it stuck fast. Panicking, convinced that Olive was going to give birth in the car, he ran to a nearby home and recruited a group of men to help him dig and push the car out of the bank. Throughout all of this, Olive remained calm. She knew her labours tended to be long, and she figured they had time. With the car safely back on the road, Jack drove white-knuckled to Apohaqui, parked in front of the midwife's home, and took Olive by the arm to the front door. Later that night, Francis Joseph was born.

Before Francis arrived, Mary Ita had once again fallen into dark depression, but the moment she laid eyes on her grandson, she found a reason to live again: the baby bore an uncanny resemblance to the twin boy she had lost. This bright-eyed boy with dark curls, she believed, was destined for great things, and she made it her mission see to it that he would fulfill his dreams and hers. By the time Francis was five years old, Joseph and Olive McKenna had saved enough money to buy their own farm down the road. However, when the family moved, Francis stayed behind with his grandparents. He never again lived with his sisters and brothers, although he moved into a room off the kitchen in his parents' home when Mary Ita visited her children in Toronto and Boston in the winter. All his childhood memories are of living with "Grammie," who became the greatest influence in his young life.

"What my grandmother did that separated me from my siblings, who are wonderful and smart and have every attribute that I would ever have, is that she established very high expectations for me," McKenna says. "I believed I was destined to do something great just because she always put it in my mind."

Mary Ita had a house full of books and taught Francis to read before he started school. He spent hours exploring her eclectic library and listening to her stories. In the evenings, Mary Ita would sit at the kitchen table and ask Francis to read to her. When he finished reading, he and his grandparents would kneel and say the rosary together. Then his grandfather would light his pipe and tune the radio to *The Irish Hour;* before the show ended Papa McKenna would be sleeping in his chair.

When Papa McKenna became seriously ill, his daughter, Mary Alexander, who was a nursing assistant, moved to Saint John so she could help look after him. Mary was a devout Catholic, and her daughter Elaine entered the Sisters of Charity Convent in Saint John to become a nun. Mary hoped her nephew Francis would follow in his cousin's footsteps and devote his life to the Church.

Papa McKenna died in the spring of 1960, and Francis became the sole focus of Mary Ita's life. She encouraged him to excel in school, telling him that he was destined for one of two callings — the priesthood or politics, the only two professions worthy of his talents. She was almost as devoted to Liberalism as she was to Catholicism. "We'd listen to it, watch it and talk about it," McKenna says. "She created my political ambitions. I can't remember her saying, You're going to be the prime minister or the premier, but she made it such a value-charged subject that it was obvious to me that politics was a high calling."

Joseph and Olive McKenna's politics amounted to little more than greeting the local candidates when they visited to deliver their obligatory chocolate bars and nylon stockings before voting day. But Mary Ita sat her grandson in front of the television to watch Paul Martin Sr. and Lester Pearson battle for the federal Liberal leadership. They followed American politics and idolized John F. Kennedy, their Irish Catholic hero. She hated "Godless communists" and saw one hiding behind every tree. "With my grandmother, there were only extremes," McKenna says. "My parents were tolerant and moderate in their beliefs. As Catholics, they practiced their faith modestly. They would never have pushed me to become a priest. But my grandmother, definitely. A priest, a prime minister, but nothing in between."

While Francis wouldn't openly defy his grandmother, he didn't blindly follow her fanaticism. "Because she was so didactic and firm, it became very easy to accept those opinions," McKenna recalls. "I spent years of my life resisting that, discovering that there were no universal truths at all, that I had to find these things for myself. I recall trying to defend her position on the Papacy or communism and finding out there were some very strong arguments to the contrary. It became a useful exercise for me to realize that nobody has a monopoly on knowledge."

His grandmother provided more than intellectual stimulation; Francis also lived more comfortably than his brothers and sisters. Mary Ita's home had indoor plumbing, while Joseph and Olive and their other children continued to use an outhouse. When Mary Ita travelled to Toronto and Boston to visit her daughters, she stole clothes from her grandchildren and brought them home to Francis. At school, he usually had money in his pocket to buy candy at the general store, and he shared it with his brothers and sisters who had candy only at Christmas and Easter. He often had a fancy lunch of sandwiches and goodies packed neatly in a chocolate box. "I can remember when we'd go up to Grammie's farm, and she'd be sneaking little treats to him in the background, and of course he'd laugh about it and give everybody something," recalls Anne, his oldest sister.

At Joseph and Olive McKenna's farm, the children ate well from the gardens and wore decent hand-me-down clothes, but there was never any money. "We were dirt poor, but we didn't know it until later," recalls McKenna's younger sister Doris. In the winter, the children would line up by the stove to receive a hot brick to take to bed, a nightly ritual in the wood-stove-heated farmhouse, which was cold and drafty upstairs. Invariably the brick would crash out of one of the beds in the middle of the night, waking up the household. Despite their poverty, the McKennas never cried hard times. When Olive's sister was going through a divorce and needed a place for her two children to stay, Joseph and Olive immediately offered to take them in and treated them as their own.

Joseph McKenna rarely left the farm except for trips to woods camps during the winters. He did not rush any job, working steadily from dawn until dusk. As a young man, he was a fine athlete and promising hockey player, but the long days in the cold, damp barn took their toll on his body. He suffered from debilitating arthritis but refused to see a doctor. He poured gasoline in his rubber boots in the mornings to dull the pain. Frank McKenna remembers his father returning from the woods after a day of cutting firewood with his hand badly mangled from a chainsaw accident. He had cut his hand early in the morning but finished his work before treating his injury at home. When he was in his sixties, he suffered a stroke while working in the barn. "The whole side of his face was crippled and twisted, and he could hardly talk," McKenna recalls. "He had to talk out of the corner of his mouth for the last ten years of his life. He never ended up seeing anybody about it. He was so arthritic and crippled that he could hardly walk from being out there morning, noon and night in the wet and cold and everything else."

When Larry and Kevin attended agricultural college and learned the science of farming, their father drove them to distraction with his primitive methods of working the land and breeding livestock. Olive kept breeding records, but their style of farming included no other form of organization. He was always the last farmer in the valley to have his cattle out to pasture in the spring and the last to make hay in the summer.

His children remember him as a gentle man who didn't have a mean bone in his body. Frank McKenna recalls the day his father had to clean a new litter of kittens out of the barn. As was the rural custom, he filled a feed sack with rocks, placed the kittens inside and walked through the woods to the creek to drown them. The children followed him, wailing about the fate of the kittens. Grim-faced, Joseph McKenna descended the bank of the stream and then came up again, the sack empty and the kittens trailing behind him all the way back to the farm. Every Christmas, the children bought their father a case of beer. He opened one bottle at Christmas dinner and poured each child an inch in the bottom of a glass. He would nurse his beer slowly over the next few weeks, sometimes sipping only half a bottle before replacing the cap and returning it to the fridge for another night.

"I enjoyed my father because he loved to watch the hockey games," Anne recalls. "I'd sit up with him and watch hockey and wrestling and all those things. When he got in at night, that's what he enjoyed, the television. He was just a steady person, and Mom was the one who did all the planning and looked after the money and made sure we were all fed and clothed. He just let her go ahead and do everything."

Olive worked with Joseph in the barn every morning and evening. Once when she was pregnant and went into labour, she finished washing the milking machines before she went to the hospital. Even on Christmas morning, Joseph and Olive would work in the barn, and the children would have to wait for them to return before opening their presents.

Joseph and Olive weren't strict disciplinarians. The children understood the rules and were expected to follow them. They avoided confrontations and encouraged their children to be self-reliant. The children understood that they would never ask their parents for money because there wasn't any. If they needed to buy something, such as a new pair of skates, they would go out and find work to earn the money they needed. Francis earned the money for his first bike by picking raspberries. In the spring, he and his friend Joe Monahan ran a trapline along the banks of the Kennebecasis, drying muskrat pelts on boards and selling them in Sussex. Joe would bike down from his home in the village, and the boys would walk their trapline and watch the early morning mists lift off the river.

As the older children left home to go to work, they started sending money home. Anne remembers a day after she had landed her first nursing job, when her father was dropping her off at the train station. She was feeling proud of her new situation, bundled up in a stylish new winter coat. Before she boarded the train, her father cleared his throat and hesitantly asked her if it would be possible for her to send a little more money home. "I just felt so guilty for buying these new clothes and things," Anne says. "Dad never said much, but that one time it really bothered me that he needed the help and I didn't realize it." As soon as she saved enough money, Anne financed the installation of indoor plumbing in the family home.

Joseph and Olive's farm was operated jointly with Mary Ita's property up the road. Francis would rise early in the morning at his grandmother's home and meet his father outside to milk the cows in the field. Mary Ita was a later riser, so after helping his father with the farm chores, Francis would make his own breakfast, wash up and head for school. He and his father built a relationship around the chores they did together, but as Francis grew older, he found more outside interests.

"I think Dad sometimes found Frank a little frustrating because Frank spent so much time away from the farm, but the rest of us kids picked up the slack," says his younger sister Rosemary. "Dad was quite proud of all of Frank's accomplishments, although he wasn't involved in sports because he was too busy looking after the family. But when Frank came home from hockey, he always wanted to know what the score was and who scored.

"My father had a great love for sports, watching sports on TV. So they enjoyed that together. Francis always liked the Montreal Canadiens, and Dad would always take the Boston Bruins. Dad would take great delight if the Bruins did well and the Canadiens didn't."

While Mary Ita was grooming Francis for the priesthood, he and his friends had other ideas for their future. "We wanted to be hockey players and baseball players," says Joe Monahan. The Apohaqui school consisted of two rooms — grades one through four in one and five through eight in the other — separated by a common corridor where the children stored boots, coats and hats. The building was heated by a wood furnace in the basement. When the windows were open, the students could hear the saws ripping through timbers at the Jones Brothers sawmill beside the Millstream. In the spring and fall, the school children took part in an endless softball game in the mornings, at recess and at lunchtime. The field ran downhill toward the school's two outhouses and then into a hayfield. When a player hit the ball beyond the outhouses into the tall grass, they called it "a shithouse bunt." The boys in the village formed a softball team and travelled to play other boys in the nearby towns of Norton, Penobsquis and Sussex Corner. Jones Brothers, which owned the mill and general store in Apohaqui, provided an old feed truck for a team bus, and the players piled in the back for road trips. When Joe and Francis played by themselves, Joe was the catcher and Francis was the pitcher, pretending to be Sandy Koufax perfecting his curve.

In the winter, the boys played hockey on the frozen river or on the town's outdoor rink, which had a change hut beside it that was heated by a woodstove made from an old oil drum. Francis was a sure skater, but he was small for a centreman and had to make up for his lack of size through sheer hustle and strength. Francis and Joe laid a sheet of plywood on the floor of the McKenna barn and shot pucks against the wall – wristers like Gordie Howe and slappers like Bernie "Boom Boom" Geoffrion. They strapped hay to the legs of Francis's younger sister Rosemary and made her stand in as the goalie.

"I remember times we'd come home from hockey games in Moncton or Fredericton close to midnight, and we'd pass a rink with the lights on, and we'd all jump out of the car and go play hockey for another hour or two," McKenna recalls. His grandmother worried constantly about his passion for sports. She believed that overworking the heart could kill a person. Bundled in a black sealskin coat, she would watch Francis play hockey, yelling throughout the game, "They're going to kill you. Get off the ice, Francis."

When Mary Ita told Francis that she didn't want him to play hockey in the village, he would climb down over the riverbank and skate to town, play hockey for a few hours and then quietly return the same way he came. When his teams made the sports page in the *Kings County Record*, he would hide the newspaper from his grandmother.

A dozen students graduated with Francis and Joe from the Apohaqui school and travelled to the large three-storey red brick high school in Sussex. The boys and girls entered the building each morning at opposite ends beneath high white stone archways. One day while he was waiting for the bus near the girls' entrance, Francis met the girl who would become his best friend throughout high school. Susan McKenna shared his last name but was not related to the McKennas of Apohaqui; she came from a well-to-do Sussex family. Her father, J. Louis McKenna, was the owner and publisher of the *Kings County Record*. She was born the day before Francis, and their mothers used to joke that the same snowstorm brought them into the world.

Susan was Francis's first girlfriend; he was her first boyfriend. They went to school dances together. When he played hockey on Friday nights, she would watch the game and he would walk her home afterwards. Margaret McKenna, Susan's mother, laid down the law: "I want you home ten minutes after the game ends. If there's a wind at your backs, I want you home in five minutes."

They both loved sports, and Susan was as fine an athlete as Francis. They travelled to track and field meets and badminton tournaments, playing mixed doubles together. Francis became a regular visitor to her home, where he would talk politics and business with her father; J. Louis McKenna had been trained as a newspaperman on Fleet Street, and his father, James McKenna, was a friend of Lord Beaverbrook, the New Brunswick-born newspaper magnate and philanthropist.

Francis earned enough money doing odd jobs to buy himself an old Mercury Zephyr, and he and Susan would take long drives together and talk for hours. A confident young woman herself, Susan was never in awe of Francis's accomplishments and considered herself his equal in every way. She says he never boasted, just quietly continued to push himself. A disciplined and responsible teenager, he was careful not to do anything that would upset his grandmother. "Frank didn't spend any nights out carousing and drinking," Rosemary says. "Grammie certainly wouldn't have approved. He did a lot to get her approval. He might not have agreed with all her opinions, but he certainly wouldn't have disagreed with her openly, just because of his affection for her."

In February, 1965, when Francis was in grade eleven, Mary Ita travelled to Toronto to visit one of her daughters. She had been shopping and was showing her daughter the shirts and pants she had purchased for her Francis when she suffered a stroke. She died three days later in hospital; she was seventy-seven years old. When Francis arrived at the funeral parlour in Sussex, the room which had been filled with chatter fell silent. He walked up to her casket and crossed himself, tears streaming down his face. "I was her life," he says. "They knew how traumatic this was for me. She had a big heart, and she filled it with me to the point where it was unfair to my brothers and sisters. I replaced something in her life, and it was my good fortune to be there."

Francis returned to live with his parents during his final year of high school, and while he no longer had his grandmother pushing him, she had already completed her mission. Francis was filled with quiet confidence. Susan McKenna believes he understood from a young age that he had gifts of energy and intellect that would allow him to become a leader. "He never asked for anything," Margaret McKenna recalls. "He never searched for any poor-boy sympathy. He never acted poor. As far as he was concerned, he was on top of the world. He was in competition with himself, nobody else."

At Sussex High School, Francis emerged as a leader, excelling at everything he did. He was president of the Key Club, a junior affiliate of the

Kiwanis, and he became Lieutenant Governor for all the Key Clubs in New Brunswick. He became school president in his final year of high school, winning the election with the slogan, "If you want more dances vote for Francis" — his first foray into political opportunism. That year, Margaret McKenna remembers giving Francis five dollars to take with him on a train trip to Toronto to attend a Key Club convention. He needed the money to rent a pillow from the porter and buy food. Despite her objections, he wrote her a cheque for five dollars. "Francis, I'm not going to cash this," she told him. "I'm going to use it as an entry to your office when you are Prime Minister of Canada."

When Francis graduated from Sussex High School, he considered attending the Université de Moncton to play hockey and learn French, but the pull to St. Francis Xavier in Antigonish, Nova Scotia, was too strong. His uncle Jack had attended St. FX and played hockey, and his grandmother had always assumed that he, too, he would study at the small-town Roman Catholic university. In the end he decided to follow the course she had set out for him. Through his Aunt Mary, he received a scholarship from the Diocese of Saint John, and so in the fall of 1966, he arrived in Antigonish as a candidate for the priesthood, although he wasn't focusing entirely on theology when he enrolled in a political science and economics program.

The three thousand undergraduates who lived on the campus in the western corner of the town were under strict church control. A priest lived in every residence, drinking was forbidden, and girls and boys were not allowed in each other's dorms. All students attended Mass in the chapel, and the girls at Mount St. Bernard College lived under curfew. Antigonish wasn't a town where a student could get into serious trouble. It offered one bar, where local talent such as John Allan Cameron and Anne Murray sometimes performed, and one pizza joint called the Wheel. For the students, life revolved around the campus, and McKenna soon placed himself at the centre of the action.

As he unpacked his bags at St. FX, he began launching his career in student politics. He became known as "Frank"; "Francis" had been left behind in Apohaqui. The first step on the political ladder was freshman class president. He developed a base of support among the girls at Mount St. Bernard College, and they helped to design campaign posters that were based on the *Peanuts* comic strip, with slogans such as "Lucy says Vote for Frank McKenna." He won the class presidency and a new nickname — "Charlie Brown."

John Friel, an economics student from Moncton, lived in residence with McKenna. He recalls that while McKenna was personable, charming and well liked on the campus, he always seemed to live outside the orbit of the group. "He was a real hick, a goody two-shoes," Friel says. "He didn't get drunk with us. He'd be part of the group, but he didn't seem to pick up the bad habits that we seemed to pick up. We used to laugh at him because we'd be wanting to go out and party, and he'd say, 'I can't go, I have to study, I've got this meeting or that meeting.' He was involved in everything."

He was also developing political skills. McKenna made a point of trying to remember people's names and details about their lives. If he had conversations with people on campus, he would recall the specifics of what they said weeks later. McKenna soon realized that his future was not in the church; while he appreciated the financial support from the Diocese of Saint John, he would look elsewhere for scholarships in the future.

McKenna's home base at St. FX was the Student Union Building, which had been converted from an old chapel into offices, a dry lounge and a games room with pinball machines. Beginning in his second year, McKenna had an office there, where his friends would find him talking on the phone or writing letters. He took his roles in student government seriously, at least in part because these jobs carried with them honorariums; it wasn't long before he began sending money home to his family in Apohaqui. He bought books and newspapers but rarely spent money on himself. When his friends were heading out to eat, he would stay on campus because he had already paid for the food they were serving in the cafeteria.

His summer holidays became a frantic race to earn as much money as possible before classes resumed in the fall. In the summer of 1967, he travelled to Toronto to search for work. He marched into the offices of the Toronto *Telegram* and told an editor that, if he helped him find a job, he would remember him and someday grant him an exclusive interview because he was going to do something great. The editor, as amused as he was impressed by the ambitious young Maritimer, helped McKenna secure a job with the York University security force. In his spare time, Frank would buy used cars at discount prices on lots in Toronto. Then, on his days off, he would drive them back to New Brunswick (a sixteen-hour trip), sell them for a profit, hitch a ride back to Toronto, and return to work.

In early September, 1967, he found himself working security at the Conservative leadership convention at Maple Leaf Gardens, the convention at which Robert Stanfield was elected on the fifth ballot and John Diefenbaker made his dramatic last stand. McKenna found himself guarding a trailer where veteran organizer Norm Atkins, a native of Lower Millstream, New Brunswick, was working. When McKenna met Atkins and the two realized they were from the same small part of the country, members of the group started calling the trailer "Operation Apohaqui." McKenna worked for the Tories during the convention, carrying the speeches Dalton Camp wrote in one hotel to Stanfield in another hotel. Whereas this convention marked an ideological coming of age for a new generation of young Conservatives such as Joe Clark and Brian Mulroney, for McKenna the thrill was just being in the midst of high-stakes politics for the first time.

"It whetted my appetite for party politics," he recalls. "I loved the convention and the buzz and all the Machiavellian plots and twists, listening to Diefenbaker flailing out at his enemies. It was high drama." The drama wasn't enough to turn him to the Tory Party, however. The next summer McKenna was back in Toronto working and, on his days off, campaigning for Pierre Trudeau, working for Liberal candidates in city ridings.

After his second summer in Toronto, McKenna returned to St. FX with the first real luxury of his life, a red Austin Healey Sprite two-seater sports car. Whenever he drove back and forth between Apohaqui and St. FX, he always had two New Brunswickers in tow, one in the front seat and the other jammed in the luggage area behind it. "He was a poor farm boy, but he worked hard," John Friel says. "He was one of the few who had a car. He was doing paying jobs everywhere. It was only later that I realized he was smarter than everybody else. He didn't show it. He always tried to keep at the level of whoever he was with and not intimidate anyone. I've seen him doing it. I know now he was a lot smarter than the rest of us, but he didn't show it."

One winter evening, McKenna dropped John Friel off in Moncton during a fierce winter storm. John's mother insisted that McKenna stay the night with them and drive the last leg of his trip when the roads were clear. That night, McKenna met John's sister Julie, who was in grade twelve and planning to attend St. FX the next year. A couple of months later, she arrived in Antigonish to attend Winter Carnival. The boy who was to be her date had gotten drunk and put his fist through a window;

he was in the hospital and didn't meet her at the train station. Without a place to stay, she reluctantly sought out her big brother at his dorm, found him playing bridge with his friends and knocked on the window.

John knew exactly who could help his sister. While Julie waited outside the door of the men's residence, he went upstairs to find his friend Frank. "I said, 'Frank, you know all the girls at the Mount. Take care of my little sister.' And he did," Friel recalls. He thinks the romance between his sister and McKenna started at that moment. "How could she help but like him? This was the guy who really helped her out when she was in a jam. She was in such a jam that she was going to spend the night sleeping in the room with the brother she hated. That's how desperate she was."

Julie's recollection of her first encounter with Frank McKenna is somewhat different. "I thought he was a total nerd," she says. "He studied and played bridge all the time. He and his friends did weird things, like crossword puzzles and word games. It was a Friday night when I met him, and he was studying."

When she arrived at St. FX the next year to begin studying secretarial arts, a woman's version of a business degree in those days, she started to find the young student leader more appealing. "A lot of women found him very attractive," she says. "He had power, but he was easygoing. He knew everybody. He made a point of being friendly to everyone, both students and professors."

When he and Julie began dating regularly, McKenna felt he needed to see Susan McKenna to tell her what was happening in his life. They had drifted apart soon after he went to St. FX and she moved to Fredericton to attend the University of New Brunswick. In Susan's mind, the relationship was over. She was dating other men and had no illusions about a future with Francis McKenna. During the Christmas holidays in 1970, Susan was at home recovering from pneumonia when McKenna arrived unannounced. "He told me he had met someone he quite liked and that he would be spending a lot of time with her," she recalls. "I remember being surprised, but I didn't know why I should be surprised." She never expected them to spend their lives together, but in her mind, Francis McKenna had been frozen in time, a dependable friend who would always be there when she needed him. The high school sweethearts closed a door on their childhoods that Christmas, but they went their separate ways with their friendship intact.

McKenna continued to turn heads at St. FX, winning awards first as the outstanding sophomore and the next year as the top junior in his class. He shunned the student Liberal association, focusing on Student Union work, which he and his friends considered to be real politics. He began attending conferences organized by Students for a Democratic Society, absorbing the radical views of society orators. "He actually started espousing socialist ideals," Friel recalls. "We were all socialists then. We hated the establishment and all the things which he later became."

McKenna was struggling to reconcile his new leftist views with the conservative values of his grandmother and the rural village of his youth. "All of the political philosophy I was reading and the movement I was part of tended to radicalize me," he says. "But there was always the other side: my own instinct, based on my own life experiences of hard work and self-sufficiency. Sometimes, when the pendulum was swinging too far, I'd have a lot of what I'd call cognitive dissonance, where what I was reading and studying differed from what I instinctively believe about life. Every one of my friends was telling me that socialism was the philosophy we should be embracing, but this just didn't ring true with what I knew about the world. How do I square this circle? I had to find my way through it."

In his final year at St. FX, when McKenna was elected president of the Student Union and president of the Nova Scotia Union of Students, he found himself thrust into the middle of the greatest turmoil in the university's history. The students were demanding that the university relax its social rules, a deadly serious fight at that time. The boys wanted girls to be allowed to visit them in their dorms, and the girls wanted an end to their curfews, to which boys were not subjected.

"We called it the battle for democracy and relevancy, but it came right down to having girls in our rooms," McKenna recalls. "We won it, over time, but I ended up taking the university to the point of a strike."

During this period, McKenna became overwhelmed with anxiety. All his life, he had avoided confrontations. He was accustomed to rigid discipline from his family, his domineering grandmother and the church. When he arrived at St. FX, he easily accepted the discipline of the church and university. But he had been elected to represent students who were becoming increasingly militant, occupying buildings, demonstrating and threatening violence. He found himself leading a movement against a religious system he had been taught was infallible. Frank listened to his fellow students, but he resisted their pressure to escalate the protests and attempt to shut down the university.

"It was the most traumatic situation I had ever faced in my life," he recalls. "I was caught between the students, who were more radical than I was, and the administration, which was traditionally Roman Catholic, and the professors, who tended to be more liberal but who were still Roman Catholic. It was extraordinarily stressful." At one point during the dispute, he became physically ill, collapsed and had to be taken to the infirmary by his friends. His political accomplishment that year was to keep the peace and stabilize a potentially explosive situation. McKenna helped to organize a meeting between students and the Board of Governors. Both sides made some concessions, the dorm rules were relaxed, and the university went back to normal for a time. The next year, under new student leadership, the campus erupted. A firebomb was thrown, a building burned, and the university temporarily closed.

In the spring of 1970, McKenna submitted his honours thesis in political science: "Changing Canada's Federal Constitution: The Background." The thesis, thoroughly researched with the cautious analysis of an undergraduate, received top marks. "Almost without exception, the basis of constitutional disputes has centred around the division of powers between the Dominion and the several provinces," he wrote, naïvely foreshadowing the very question that would haunt him throughout his political career.

McKenna attended his convocation at St. FX and then drove all night to Kingston, Ontario, so he could begin his Masters program in political science the next day. By the time John Friel arrived at Queen's in the fall, McKenna had arranged lodging for them in a small boarding house. The elderly woman who owned the home had fallen for her new young tenant and was allowing him to use her car and her summer cottage; she was also feeding him three meals a day, which wasn't part of the deal.

During his first year at Queen's, as he became more sure that politics was his calling, he began to question whether his academic studies were taking him in the right direction. During a class that examined John Porter's seminal work, *The Vertical Mosaic*, which explores power structures in Canada, McKenna realized that if he wanted to be a politician, he was in the wrong field. He had a choice to make. He had the opportunity to attend the University of Melbourne in Australia on scholarship to begin his doctoral studies, or he could change gears entirely, abandon his masters studies before they were complete, and go to law school, which Porter's research showed was the surest route to political power. Friel recalls McKenna marching into his room and handing him an application for a Beaverbrook Scholarship at the University of New Brunswick. "We're wasting our time here," McKenna told him. "I'm interested in politics, but the politicians are all lawyers."

"That was when it first hit me that he wanted to run in politics in New Brunswick," Friel recalls. "Anybody who looked at things objectively, even back in 1966, should have known he had political ambitions, but that's not the way we thought of Frank. He was such a humble guy."

McKenna discussed his options with the only lawyer he knew. John and Julie's father, Moncton lawyer Donal Friel, was a long-time Liberal backroom activist. Friel recommended that he attend the University of New Brunswick Law School, despite the fact that Dalhousie Law School in Halifax was considered to be a better school, because the most important thing for him was to get to know the people who would be his peers in his home province. Frank and John filled out the forms for Beaverbrook Scholarships and were interviewed and selected by the committee. John was less than enthusiastic. "I was perfectly content to waste my life where I was as opposed to wasting my life being a lawyer. But they gave me this scholarship, so I came down."

In the summer of 1971, McKenna worked in Ottawa as a special assistant to Liberal MP Allan MacEachen, the president of the Privy Council and an alumnus of St. FX. He became deeply immersed in Liberal Party politics for the first time. In the fall of 1971, when he began his studies at the University of New Brunswick Law School, his career path was now clarified — first the law, then politics.

Julie and Frank had maintained their relationship when he was in Kingston and she was completing her studies at St. FX, and they spent time together in Ontario in the summers. In February of 1972, Julie became pregnant, and soon after that she and Frank decided to get married. "There were times I wanted to get married and he didn't, and times he wanted to get married and I didn't," Julie says. Her pregnancy helped them make the decision. They were married on April 29, 1972, in Moncton, and Julie graduated from St. FX that spring. Their honeymoon was a trip to Ottawa to work and make enough money so they could continue their education. On October 15, 1972, Tobias John McKenna was born. Both Frank and Julie shared the duties of caring for their young son. In January, 1973, when Julie took a teaching job in the nearby town of Minto, Toby became a fixture at law-student hangouts in Fredericton. That fall, Julie decided to return to academics and earn her Bachelor of Education at the University of New Brunswick.

Frank McKenna, 1970.   *Julie Friel McKenna, 1972.*

McKenna excelled at law school, was elected president of the student law society and graduated in the spring of 1974, second in his class behind Ernest Drapeau, who would eventually be named Chief Justice of the New Brunswick Court of Appeal. Julie also graduated that spring and prepared to begin a career in the classroom. They carefully weighed their options. McKenna was astute enough to know that his choice of where to practice law would be a critical first step toward a career in politics down the road. While any large city law firm would have welcomed the promising young graduate, McKenna had met Paul Lordon, who was looking for a young lawyer to join his small firm in Chatham, a blue-collar Irish Catholic town situated at the mouth of the Miramichi River. Lordon had been accepted to study at the London School of Economics and needed someone to help his brother Denis at their firm. While this seemed a strange career move for an ambitious young man, McKenna decided Chatham and the Lordons would put him right where he wanted to be. McKenna the country boy wanted to live in a small community; Paul Lordon assured him that he would become a major player at the firm right away; and the Lordons were Liberal movers and shakers who would open political doors for him when he was ready. Paul and Denis Lordon's father had served in Louis Robichaud's government, and no Liberal made a political move on the Miramichi without checking with the Lordons first.

"I liked the look and the feel of it," McKenna says. "I had looked at New Brunswick in terms of keeping my political options open. I needed to be in an area that would at least have some hope for a Liberal, because I realized by that time that that was where I was and there was no changing it. Where was there a possibility for me to run and win? I excluded all the Acadian parts of New Brunswick, which were the most Liberal parts, because I didn't speak French well enough. It came down to looking at some of the Irish Catholic parts of New Brunswick. The only one that was a consistent supporter of the Liberal Party was the Miramichi. I looked at the political map and said, 'If there is ever a future for me in politics, this is at least a place where I start with a chance.'"

During the wave of pre-famine immigration, a large community of Irish Catholics had settled at the mouth of the Miramichi River, and Chatham had become the strongest Irish Catholic community in New Brunswick. Julie, too, was attracted to Chatham; she had been offered a teaching job there, and it was the home of the Creaghans, her relatives on her mother's side, who ran a chain of department stores.

"I don't think Frank's political ambitions at that particular time were any secret," says Denis Lordon. "To do it right, you have to put yourself in an area, you have to get established, you have to become known and trusted, and you have to get the local people on side. This is not a short-term thing at all. If we were going to develop him as a viable potential candidate, we knew it was going to take time. But first and foremost in our minds was to hire somebody who would be a competent legal professional. We had an expanding law practice, and we needed someone we could groom and depend on."

Frank McKenna laid eyes on Chatham for the first time on the late spring day in 1974 when he arrived in town to start work. As he drove slowly through the smoke spewing from the paper mills that fuelled the local economy, the sister towns of Newcastle on one side of the Miramichi River and Chatham on the other were shaking off the effects of a long, cold winter. He parked his car at the side of a street lined with mud and slush and walked up to the Lordons' cubbyhole of an office on Henderson Street next to the post office in downtown Chatham. He paused in the doorway and looked up the hill at the grey stone spire of St. Joseph's Cathedral, the one dominant and elegant structure in the rugged river town.

Author David Adams Richards, a native of Newcastle, recalls hearing of the arrival of McKenna, the new lawyer who had come to the Miramichi from the Sussex area. "I heard that there was something of the salesman about him, along with a slight naïveté that is somehow forgivable and even, at times, charming," Richards later wrote. "Not unlike Willie Loman; or more to the point, an old time southern politician from the thirties. Huey Long briefly comes to mind. That is, if his naïveté is somehow, at times, forgivable and charming, you can bet he plays it that way. You can bet it is also encased in a will of iron."

The people of the Miramichi would encounter the paradoxes of Frank McKenna's character. At times, he was genuinely humble. At other times, he had to remind himself to express humility. He had always been quietly confident that he had gifts of leadership, yet he often found himself overcome with the feeling that he was an impostor, that he would wake up one day and be exposed as just an ordinary farm boy from Apohaqui. While he was writing notes to himself to project humility, he was struggling to keep his feelings of self-doubt at bay.

A Horatio Alger novel would end with McKenna opening the door to his new law office, a young man destined for a better life than he had known as a child. However, McKenna knew his story wouldn't end there. Although he still nurtured his political ambitions, he was patient. For now he would apply himself to the law, and soon his name would be known from one end of the province to the other.

Frank McKenna, Theresa Durelle, Yvon Durelle,
and Denis Lordon, September, 1977.

THE FIGHTER

It was him or me. I will live longer.
— *Yvon Durelle, statement to police*

The Saturday morning radio newscast had just reported the death of a man in Baie-Sainte-Anne when Frank McKenna's home telephone rang. He casually reached for the receiver, expecting a call from one of his clients, a victim of Miramichi River spring fever arrested after a Friday-night drinking binge. When the caller identified herself as Theresa Durelle, McKenna snapped to attention. She told him her husband Yvon, the Fighting Fisherman from Baie-Sainte-Anne, had shot a man, and they needed his help. McKenna hung up the phone, grabbed a jacket and tie and raced out the door.

Earlier that Saturday morning, May 21, 1977, Chatham Police Chief Daniel Allen had arrived at the town lockup, where he found Yvon Durelle in tears. "I'm no murderer," he mumbled. He turned to his long-time friend and said, "Chief, I can't take it. I'm better off dead. I'm better off dead."

Allen knew the RCMP had taken Durelle into custody after a man was shot to death in the parking lot of the Fisherman's Club, the bar and restaurant Yvon and Theresa operated next door to their home in Baie-Sainte-Anne. He could see that his friend was in no shape to make coherent decisions. Durelle at forty-eight was punch-drunk, suffering from the silent affliction of retired boxers. Too many blows to the head during more than two hundred amateur and professional fights had left Durelle living with irreparable neurological damage. Durelle had been talking to RCMP investigators all night without a lawyer. That may have been exactly the way the Mounties wanted it. Regardless of which side of the law he was on, Allen figured it was time to make this a fair fight.

He told Theresa and Yvon that they needed a lawyer and suggested they call Frank McKenna. During the three years McKenna had been practicing law in Chatham, he had made a name for himself in the Miramichi criminal courts as a prodigious worker who would stop at nothing to defend his clients. While Allen and the twenty-nine-year-old McKenna often found themselves locking horns in the courtroom, the police chief could appreciate a promising young lawyer when he saw one.

When McKenna arrived at the police lockup, he found Durelle, his eyes red from crying, sitting in an interview room with Theresa at his side. Both of them were pale and exhausted. McKenna closed the door and perched on the edge of the desk, one foot resting on the floor. "Yvon, I'm Frank McKenna," he said calmly. "I'm your lawyer. I'm going to represent you, and I want you to listen carefully to everything I'm going to say. Don't talk to anybody, especially the police. If they ask you something, you tell them you can't talk. Don't trust anyone except me."

By silencing Durelle, McKenna was trying to take control of a situation that, from a defence lawyer's point of view, was already a disaster. When RCMP Constable Owen Arthur had arrived in the parking lot of the Fisherman's Club shortly before midnight on Friday, he found Durelle standing beside a green 1958 Pontiac that had crashed into the rear of another car parked beside the front door of the club. Thirty-two-year-old Albain Poirier was slumped across the front bench seat on his right side, an empty wine bottle wrapped in a paper bag pinned under his arm. He had been shot in the face, left arm and chest. His jeans, denim shirt and tan suede jacket were soaked with blood. An animated Durelle, waiting for the RCMP to arrive, waved Arthur over to the car.

"I plugged him," he told the constable. "I plugged him."

Arthur calmly coaxed Durelle away from the car. "Yvon, okay, would you please come over to the police car with me."

As they walked toward the cruiser, Durelle handed Arthur a loaded .38 Smith & Wesson revolver. Arthur decided then and there to take a statement from the co-operative Durelle, and he read him the police warning. Durelle replied, "Yes, I know all that, I know, I understand." He then blurted out the short version of his story.

"Poirier came around and came into the bar, and I told him that he had to go. He said that he wouldn't. He said, Who was going to make me go? I said I would take him out, and I did. I had taken the gun from the till, and when we got outside, I put him into the car. I had a hard time. He backed up and down, trying to get in front to run me over. He came up beside me, and I stuck the gun at the window. I plugged him. I emptied the gun into him."

The constable wanted the statement in writing, and Durelle suggested they sit down together in his home, away from the flashing police lights and the crowd that had gathered in the parking lot. Meanwhile, another officer was talking to Theresa in the kitchen. She told him she hadn't seen what had happened, and he instructed her to sit tight and not to speak to anyone. Durelle was in another room signing the statement. A few minutes later, Yvon walked into the kitchen and told Theresa, "I have to go to jail."

"He looked at me kind of surprised, because he didn't know what was going to happen," Theresa recalls. "I said 'Yvon, you have to go, but everything is going to be fine. You're going to jail tonight, but I will see you in the morning.'" By early Saturday morning, Durelle had signed two more statements, admitting that he shot Poirier but insisting that he was protecting himself and his family from a dangerous man. "He had been threatening me for a long time," Durelle told police in his final statement, taken shortly after two a.m. on May 21. "He wanted to kill me. I was jumping aside. He came goddam close. I wanted to do it. It was me or him. I'm smarter than he is. I will live longer."

An RCMP officer stayed with Theresa at home, drinking tea and chatting, answering the telephone and eventually taking it off the hook and wrapping it in a towel to muffle the buzz. Theresa was grateful for the company, but the officer's decision to stay with her wasn't altogether altruistic. The Mounties didn't want Theresa to speak to anyone until they were finished with Yvon, and in the early morning hours she signed a written statement twenty pages long. When the police officer left at six-thirty in the morning, Theresa asked her eighteen-year-old daughter Francine to drive her to the jail to be with Yvon.

McKenna couldn't take back what Durelle had already said, but his client would be making no more statements to police. McKenna also realized that Durelle wasn't holding up well in jail. He was gobbling Valium and antidepressants and was growing more distraught by the hour. "What we have to do now is get you out of here," McKenna told him before he left the interview room.

Yvon and Theresa didn't know what to think of their new lawyer, whose thin moustache only seemed to emphasize his youth. "When I first saw him, I thought he was too young," Durelle recalls. "I thought he was a kid. He was short, just a little guy. But when we called him, he came right away. He wasted no time." They decided that if Chief Allen believed McKenna was a good man, they would trust him do the job.

While McKenna projected only confidence in the interview room, he, too, was wondering whether he was ready for a case of this magnitude. He had never tried a murder case before, and now he would be defending one of his childhood heroes in what he knew would become one of the most celebrated murder trials in his province's history. "You couldn't be a New Brunswicker and not know Yvon Durelle," he says. "When you don't have a hundred TV channels and you're growing up in the country, you become focused on a few things, and in rural New Brunswick Yvon Durelle was a big story. I remember sitting on my father's knee watching Durelle fight. Those were moments of high drama."

When he left the lockup, McKenna pushed aside his fears and telephoned his partner, Denis Lordon, who was vacationing on Prince Edward Island with his family. Lordon immediately packed up and started driving back to Chatham. It went without saying that McKenna and Lordon would defend Durelle together. Before McKenna came to Chatham, Denis Lordon, a junior partner in his older brother Paul's firm, had been swamped with criminal Legal Aid cases. While the Lordons recruited McKenna to their firm in part because of his political aspirations, their more immediate concern was to find Denis some much-needed help.

McKenna's entry into the legal world of the Lordons was less than glamorous. Their law office on Henderson Street was a typical small-town storefront operation with plywood walls, worn carpets, battered desks and chairs. The office cried out for renovations, but the brothers were too busy in the courtroom to concern themselves with comfort and decor, which suited their working-class clientele just fine. McKenna spent his first few months in Chatham doing real estate and probate work before being turned loose in the courthouse to learn on the fly how to practice criminal law. In one of his first criminal cases, McKenna drove to Perth-Andover for a trial and found himself ill prepared for the Crown's procedural tactics. Because of his lack of preparation, he agreed to a statement of facts that resulted in what he later discovered was an unnecessary conviction.

"I vowed then that I'd never be beaten unless the case was overwhelming," he says. "I set out to learn all there was about criminal law, all the technical issues. I researched the law. I put together elaborate trial books. I might go into court twenty times a week, but when I walked in the Crown had to be ready because I was armed and dangerous."

For Denis Lordon, the firm's bright young graduate was a godsend. The two lawyers couldn't have been more different, but each seemed to complement the other as they strode into the courtroom in their black robes: Lordon, tall and angular, with a deliberate, brilliant mind, and McKenna, small and stocky, fast on his feet and doggedly determined. They were a true team; neither of them could have accomplished alone what they did together.

"It was a void that Frank filled quickly," Lordon recalls. "We did every type of criminal case you could think of. Neither one of us had a whole lot of time to whet our appetites on small cases. We got into the serious stuff very quickly. The Miramichi had a lot of crime, and there was lots of work."

Criminal law consumed McKenna's life. Every person who walked in the door was someone who needed his help. "I would never send people away," he recalls. "People would call in the middle of the night, I'd defend them. They wouldn't have any money, and I'd still do their stuff. I was everybody's soft touch. Every case was an ordeal to me. I just didn't want to lose for any of the people who had put their trust in me. I took them all seriously."

Miramichi Crown Prosecutor Fred Ferguson, a rugged veteran of the courtroom who has put the likes of serial killer Allan Legere behind bars, came to admire McKenna's work ethic. He remembers McKenna lugging heavy briefcases filled with files to the courthouse so he could work on other cases during breaks in the action, a time-saving strategy Ferguson learned to emulate. "He always came better prepared than anybody else, both on the facts and on the law," Ferguson says. "On top of that, you usually don't see someone who's a good student and also a great strategist. Trial strategy is where the lawyer can make a difference. It's knowing when to hold and when to fold. He always seemed to know when he was on the edge of trouble, and he stayed there but never fell over."

James D. Harper was the presiding judge at the Miramichi courthouse, an imposing grey stone structure that stands like a medieval castle guarding the highest point of land above the river. Before he was appointed to the bench, Harper was arguably the most talented criminal lawyer in New Brunswick, and he welcomed the challenges the eager McKenna brought to his courtroom. "We'd go at it toe to toe, and he just loved it," McKenna recalls. "He threw out case after case. I'd come up with some argument and he'd say, 'You're right, out you go.' It was a wonderful time."

McKenna and Lordon worked all their files together, studying Crown witnesses, deciding who would cross-examine them and who would lead the defence witnesses. David Cadogan, publisher of the *Miramichi Leader* newspaper, lived near McKenna and Lordon in the Riverside Subdivision, a neighbourhood of winding streets and new homes on a bluff overlooking downtown Chatham. The subdivision attracted the community's young professionals, who worked hard and played hard together as they raised their young families. When Cadogan was out for late evening walks, he would often stop by McKenna's bungalow to find the law partners in the living room, papers strewn on the floor, rehearsing for a trial, taking turns searching for holes in the other's arguments.

During these mock trials, McKenna trained himself as a public speaker. He found that he couldn't read prepared texts and make them sound natural and sincere, so when he addressed juries, he referred only to a few scrawled notes; later, he would give political speeches in the same fashion. "I just started saying what was in my gut and what was in my heart," he says. "That's why every speech for me is an adventure. I don't know what I'm going to say or how it's going to come out until I do it. I worry about them incessantly. I try to know as much as possible about the subject, so that when I speak whatever is in me will come right out. You could say it's winging it, but in fact it's twice as hard. It's more emotionally draining."

There would be many late nights preparing for Durelle's trial, but first McKenna and Lordon had to get their client out of jail. Theresa was concerned that Yvon was so heavily sedated that he might not be able to appear in court. "He wasn't going to be able to plead guilty or not guilty because he was just like a zombie," she recalls. "He had so many drugs in him that he couldn't even stay awake."

McKenna called Durelle's doctor and then spoke to the prison guards and ordered them to lay off the pills. On Tuesday, May 24, Durelle leaned on a cane next to McKenna and Lordon and pleaded not guilty to a charge of second-degree murder. The judge ordered him released on a $10,000 bond. Two days later, a group of Durelle's friends raised the money, and he was released. For now at least, he was going home.

———

Visitors who arrive in Baie-Sainte-Anne on New Brunswick's northeast coast today are greeted by a billboard adorned with a rough drawing of a young Yvon Durelle in his fighting crouch and the words, "Home of the Fighting Fisherman — Museum Ahead." The fishing village that Durelle put on the world sporting map consists of a collection of modest homes, boats and fishing gear stored in driveways, a grocery store, an arena, a peat moss plant and a white bungalow where the boxing legend has lived for more than three decades. In recent years, the bungalow has been renovated with wide halls, extra-large doorways and smooth floors that allow Durelle to walk easily through his home without stumbling.

In 1994, Frank McKenna's government granted the Durelles three thousands dollars to help them build an addition to house Yvon's boxing memorabilia. The walls of the museum are papered with photographs and newspaper clippings from his glory days in the ring. His British Empire light-heavyweight championship belt hangs on a hook. He helps guests try on the gloves he wore when he fought Archie Moore for the first time in 1958 for the light-heavyweight championship of the world, a fight pundits still rate as one of the top ten boxing matches in the history of the sport.

Durelle is a bear of a man, his hair thin and white and shaved short in a crewcut, his hands huge and soft. Sitting in his kitchen, he cradles his black miniature poodle, Scooby Doo, on his lap, making cooing noises and popping small pieces of orange cheese into its mouth. Theresa calls Yvon by his French nickname, Doux, which means mild or gentle. Theresa, six years younger than her husband, is youthful, petite and pretty, with short, grey-blonde hair, and she speaks with patience and deep intelligence. He watches her when she talks, allowing her to direct the course of the conversation. He rests his right foot in her lap, and she holds it gently in her hand. Durelle has a quick sense of humour, and in moments of lucidity he participates fully in the conversation. But his speech is garbled; he paid a price for his fame.

Yvon was born on October 14, 1929, a fisherman's son, the seventh of twelve children. When he was eleven, his father became ill and couldn't work. Yvon quit school, and he and his thirteen-year-old brother Ernie took to the water in a fishing boat to provide for the family. He started boxing in 1945, when his two older brothers returned from the war with a pair of gloves, and made his professional debut in the ring two years later. He worked in the woods in the winter, fished and fought in the spring and summer. He was a natural, a brawler and heavy puncher who was strong enough to take whatever punishment his opponents threw at him before he found the range to knock them down, usually with his jack-hammer right hand. "I never went to boxing school," he often said, pointing out that he took five punches for every one hard blow he landed on his opponents. During his years in the ring, he lost teeth and broke his nose, hands and ribs. Even at the highest levels, boxing in the fifties was far from a glamour sport. Durelle fought often and for little pay, drinking rum and water or brandy and orange juice in his corner between rounds to dull the pain.

Durelle always seemed to walk a fine line between triumph and tragedy. He fought the great heavyweight champion Floyd Patterson twice, losing both times. He became famous in the United States on June 14, 1957, when he fought the highly touted Tony Anthony to a draw in Detroit, a fight sports writers thought Durelle won hands down. In July, 1958, he won the British Empire light-heavyweight championship, defeating a rugged South African named Mike Holt. When he returned home, his eyes swollen and black, he treated his friends to a post mortem and a bout of drinking. He stayed sober, and late in the evening he was elected to drive to the bootlegger's to collect a stash of home brew. The car got stuck on a dirt road, so he asked everyone to get out and walk. When he was backing out of the road, Stanley Martin, Theresa's uncle and Yvon's best friend, slipped beneath the car. No one saw him fall. When they found him lying on the road, Durelle rushed him to the hospital, where he died.

On December 10, 1958, Durelle and Archie "Mongoose" Moore met at the Montreal Forum. In the first round, the underdog Durelle sprang from his crouch and knocked down the champion with a devastating right hand, then sent him to the canvas two more times before the round was over. In the eyes of sports writers at ringside, Durelle was robbed of the championship by a long ten-count after the first knockdown that allowed Moore to stagger back to his feet and survive the round. He put Moore down one more time before being knocked out himself in the eleventh round by the man who was considered to be the best pound-for-pound fighter of his day.

After the fight with Moore, Durelle's life began to spin out of control. His success in the ring ended the day he and four friends were out on Miramichi Bay in a power boat that overturned near Bay du Vin Island. Durelle swam four miles to shore to seek help for his friends, spending more than three hours in the ocean and emerging with permanent damage to his spine. He would never walk steadily again. The next year, when he and Archie Moore met for a rematch at the Forum, Durelle had to be helped into the ring. He could still throw punches, but he had no balance and no fluidity of movement. Moore knocked him out in the third round.

Yet Durelle kept fighting on his unsteady legs until, in 1963, after too many losses, his spirit and body broken, he retired from boxing. Back in Baie-Sainte-Anne, the circle of friends and hangers-on who had crowded around him when he was on top of the world faded away as quickly as his money and fame. He worked as a professional wrestler and as a game warden. He was hired by Oland's Brewery as its north shore representative but was dismissed because he gave away too much beer. And so he started fishing again until he and Theresa decided to go into business for themselves. They scraped together the money to build the Fisherman's Club on a vacant lot next to their home. They planned to run it with their own labour for a few years, then sell it and retire.

Their ambitions were modest; the club was a single-storey concrete block building that faced the road across a large gravel parking lot. They constructed a dance floor and bandstand in the centre of the room and set brown wooden tables and chairs on either side. They pushed a shuffleboard table against the two picture windows in the front wall. There was a bar at the back, a cold storage room, a cigarette machine and a juke box. Durelle mounted old black and white photographs from his fighting days on the walls. A large sign on the front of the building featured the trademark drawing of Durelle the boxer, his dangerous fists held just below his chin. Patrons came and went through two wooden doors, one in the front wall facing the parking lot and the other on the left side of the building.

On opening day, December 23, 1974, the Durelles wrote their liquor supplier a big cheque on an empty bank account, and by the time the holidays were over and the banks reopened, they had deposited more than enough cash to cover it. Every Friday and Saturday night they held dances with live bands. The Fisherman's Club was the only place in Baie-Sainte-Anne that served proper restaurant meals of steak, lobster, scallops and clams. Theresa looked after the money. Yvon greeted the patrons and played shuffleboard, and, on the rare occasions when a patron caused a disturbance, he would act as the club's enforcer. He didn't allow loud swearing in the club, and few drunks were reckless enough to mix it up with the Fighting Fisherman. When his regulars had had too much to drink, he would drive them home after closing time. For the most part, the Fisherman's Club was a peaceful gathering place — until Albain Poirier came along.

Durelle was released from jail on the condition that he stay away from the club. While he waited at home for his day in court, Theresa ran it herself, and his lawyers began to engineer a defence. McKenna and Lordon didn't have a budget to finance the comprehensive investigation such a complicated, high-stakes case demanded. They believed Durelle had killed a man but had acted in self-defence and therefore wasn't guilty of murder. Now they held his life in their hands. They also knew they were putting their careers on the line: if they lost, they would be blamed for taking on a case they were too inexperienced to handle; if they won, they would no longer be obscure small-town lawyers.

McKenna wrote a note to himself outlining potential trial strategies, his mind swinging back and forth between the technical legal defence and the emotional appeal to the jury. "How many of our witnesses gave previous statements? Must bring out 'the Fighting Fisherman from Baie-Sainte-Anne.' How about a chart with the location of our witnesses as opposed to theirs? How far can we go into Durelle's background? What is defence of property and other people?"

If the jury believed that Durelle reasonably feared for his life when he fired the gun, it had to return a not-guilty verdict. Self-defence is a complete defence for murder, but it is a risky legal strategy because it has no fall-back position, such as a lesser conviction for manslaughter. Durelle would be acquitted or he would serve life in prison. The problem for the defence was that Durelle had fired his gun five times in front of a couple of dozen witnesses, and it appeared from autopsy reports that the first shot, which entered Poirier's left eye and exited behind his right ear, was not the shot that killed him. The subsequent shots to the chest caused massive internal bleeding, and he died within minutes. If the first shot was justifiable, what about the four that followed? Hadn't the danger ended when he was shot the first time? What was Durelle's state of mind when he pulled the trigger?

The lawyers discovered that Poirier had been threatening Durelle and his family for some time. The shooting in the parking lot was just the final act in a much larger drama. "It became apparent early on that Poirier was a very dangerous person who was making serious threats to Yvon Durelle and his family," Lordon says. "It was a helluva position for Yvon to be in."

The lawyers sent private investigator Leigh Morehouse to Baie-Sainte-

Anne to scout for potential witnesses. When he reported back to the lawyers on June 10, 1977, the seeds of the defence's case were found in the
opening paragraph of his report. Yvon's nephew, Euclide Durelle, told
Morehouse that he was standing in the parking lot near the side door of
the club when he saw Durelle push Poirier into his car. He watched Poirier
speed across the parking lot three times, attempting to run down Durelle.
There was no question that Durelle feared for his life. An agile, younger
man might have been able to jump easily out of harm's way; however, the
neurological damage Durelle had sustained in the ring and the spinal
injury he had suffered in the boating accident left him unsteady on his
feet, especially in the dark on the rough gravel surface of the Fisherman's
Club parking lot. Euclide had watched his uncle stumbling frantically
as he tried to get out of the way of the car that was hurtling toward him
in the darkness.

Morehouse warned the lawyers that the investigation was going to be
frustrating. The man who was with Euclide, whose testimony would hold
more weight because he wasn't related to the accused, wouldn't talk to the
investigator. Other witnesses in the parking lot were avoiding Morehouse.
A woman who had been standing in the front window of the club said
she had already spoken to the police and wasn't going to get involved.
Everyone in Baie-Sainte-Anne was either at the club that night or knew
someone who was, but of the three dozen potential witnesses on the
premises, almost all were drunk or stoned. To make matters worse for the
lawyers and their investigator, the shooting had divided the community.
On the one side were those who labelled Durelle a cold-blooded killer,
on the other, those who believed Poirier had it coming.

By all accounts, Albain Poirier was a Jekyll and Hyde character, a great
friend one day and a dangerous and deranged man the next. Allain
Poirier, no relation to Albain, operated Al's Play Pen, a local hangout with
a hamburger counter, juke box and pool and ping pong tables. He told
Morehouse that one night he got into a dispute with Albain, who
punched him in the head, then kicked him in the stomach. When Allain
retreated, Albain came after him with a broken bottle. Allain ran into the
kitchen for his gun. He pointed it at his attacker and pleaded with him
to leave. It would take more than a loaded gun to deter this man when
he was in a rage, and Allain Poirier finally stopped Albain's menacing
advance by shooting him in the leg and shoulder.

Morehouse spoke with Albain's former girlfriend, who said she left him
after he tried to commit suicide by disembowelling himself with a large

butcher knife. As he writhed in pain, he smeared his blood on the walls and floor of their trailer, writing the word "dope" on the floor and marking a cross over the door. When RCMP Constable Terry O'Rourke arrived, he found Poirier "tearing at his stomach and crying out, 'You won't tap my phone. You won't open my mail.'" Poirier survived and recovered at the Campbellton mental hospital. The former girlfriend told Morehouse that Poirier was dangerous when he was drinking, but he was also like a small child who always demanded attention.

Nelson Durelle, no relation to Yvon, told Morehouse that he was out fishing lobster about a mile offshore when Albain Poirier motored along side him and accused him of stealing his traps. Nelson denied the charge. Albain threatened to ram him with his boat. Twice Albain backed his boat off and then sped forward straight at Nelson's twelve-foot wooden boat before turning away at the last second. When he was tired of his deadly game, he pulled out an axe and said he would chop Nelson's boat in half. He told the frightened man to go ashore, sell his boat and never come back on the water. Nelson was so terrified that he hadn't been on the water since that day. Witnesses like Nelson Durelle lived in fear of retaliation from members of the Poirier family.

"I find that the investigation of this affair is becoming tighter all the time, less and less people are willing to co-operate," Morehouse told McKenna and Lordon. "I try to explain to them just how serious this matter is, but most of them seemed to be quite unimpressed. They are just thankful it is not happening to them, and as most of them say it, 'I don't want no trouble with the Poiriers.'"

Working in an atmosphere of fear and mistrust, McKenna and Lordon spent the summer in Baie-Sainte-Anne searching for witnesses who hadn't already formed an opinion about Durelle's guilt or who weren't too afraid to testify for the defence. The lawyers became adopted members of the Durelle family, eating Yvon's famous ham cooked in wine and absorbing their stories in the kind of detail unexpressed in sterile police statements. Through these conversations with the Durelles and statements from reluctant witnesses in the community, the lawyers pieced together the story of the death of Albain Poirier.

The Durelles had known Poirier for years and at one time had considered him a friend. When Durelle was an Oland's salesman and Poirier was a bootlegger, Durelle had given him samples to try to encourage his customers to buy his employer's brand. Durelle had loaned him money and had visited him in the hospital when he was recovering from his suicide attempt. When the club first opened, Durelle had allowed him to eat meals and drink on credit. However, in the months leading up to the shooting, Poirier had started causing trouble in the club, and when Yvon tried to control him he had declared war on the Durelles.

Poirier would throw his beer in people's faces and start fights without provocation. One night he fell asleep on the floor and had to be carried outside. During the week before the shooting, he'd been thrown out of the club four times. When Yvon's son Paul removed him from the club one night, Poirier said, "It's your fuckin' father who told you to do this. Well, he's going to pay for it before the week's out."

After closing time on May 19, Yvon and Theresa looked out of the front window of their bungalow and saw Albain standing alone beside the road, throwing rocks in the ditch and flipping his cigarette up into the air. "Yvon was standing in the living room with the gun in his pocket because we were scared," Theresa recalls. "We felt like we were in a cage. There was nobody to help, nobody to call."

Shortly after one o'clock on the afternoon of May 20, 1977, Durelle called the RCMP detachment in Newcastle to report that he was having trouble with Albain Poirier and needed help. The Mountie who answered the phone told him he'd have to wait until Monday, when he could go to court and obtain a peace bond to keep him away from the club. Durelle reminded the officer that it was Friday. What was he to do during the weekend? Durelle recalls that the Mountie replied, "You'll have to take care of it yourself." The Mountie maintained at the trial that it was Durelle who said, "I'll have to take care of it myself." Regardless of which version of this conversation is accurate, there is little doubt that the police didn't take Durelle's pleas for help seriously.

"We asked for help," Theresa says. "We called the RCMP, and they did nothing. It was just as if they were scared of him, too. Maybe they thought Yvon could take care of it himself. It's true that you can take care of yourself if you have your fists, but when it comes to threats and you have a guy who is sick in the head, when you go somewhere and he is there, you were scared of him. When he started threatening us, we were scared to even go to bed at night."

About six o'clock on the evening of May 20, Poirier and another man arrived at the club. Durelle refused to serve them. Poirier asked Durelle, "How long have you had the club?"

"Two and a half years, and I intend to have it longer," Durelle replied.

"If this is the way you want it, then we'll have to do something about this place," Poirier said and then left. Durelle started crying and told Theresa to go home. If Poirier returned, he knew there was going to be a nasty confrontation, and he didn't want his wife there to witness it.

He called the RCMP again. He warned the officer on the phone, "Something will happen tonight. If you don't do something about this guy, you're going to have to come down later and pick up the pieces."

Shortly after nine p.m., soon after the band started playing, Poirier telephoned Durelle at the club and told him he had three days to get out of Baie-Sainte-Anne. Durelle could only mumble, "Eat my fucking shit," before hanging up. Then Poirier called back to tell him he had two hours to get out of town and asked him how many kids he had. "Yvon, tonight is the night," he said. "There is no more time to run." Theresa unplugged the telephone.

About eleven-thirty p.m., one of the bartenders turned to Theresa and said, "Oh my God, Albain is outside." Theresa started shaking.

Earlier in the evening, Poirier had downed a meal of fried clams and then started drinking hard. He swaggered into the club, clicking his brown leather cowboy boots on the floor, stuffing a package of Rothman's King Size cigarettes into his shirt pocket. Durelle pocketed the Smith & Wesson he kept in the till and met Poirier just inside the front door. He led Poirier outside, where he tried to reason with him one last time. "Albain, we've been friends a long time," he said. "I lend you money, I buy you drinks. I'm like a father to you. Why do you treat me like this?"

Poirier replied, "Times have changed, Yvon."

Durelle pushed him into his car, and Poirier said, "Get away from my car or I'll run you down."

"No, you won't, my friend," Durelle replied.

Poirier backed his car across the parking lot, crashing into a parked car, and then pushed the gas pedal to the floor, speeding toward Durelle in a spray of dust and gravel. Durelle stepped unsteadily between two parked cars. Through the front window, Theresa watched Yvon jump out of the way of Poirier's car and saw that he was holding a gun in his right hand. She ran to the bar to call the police.

Poirier backed up again, again crashing into a parked car. As he sped across the parking lot a second time, Durelle stepped up to the side of the car and reached in through the window on the driver's side, trying to pull Poirier out of the car. He couldn't maintain his balance.

When Poirier backed up a third time and drove toward Durelle again, Durelle aimed his gun at the driver's side window and pulled the trigger. Poirier slumped over on the seat. Durelle didn't know whether he had hit him or whether Poirier was reaching for a gun. He pulled the trigger four more times.

Theresa was standing inside behind the bar waiting for the police to pick up the phone when she heard the gunshots. When a Mountie answered she said, "Yvon just shot a man, I think, I'm not sure, I didn't see it, I'm almost sure. Hurry. Hurry." A minute later, Yvon walked into the bar and told Theresa to call the RCMP. He reloaded his gun and sat by the door, waiting for the police to arrive.

On the first day of the preliminary hearing, legendary Montreal criminal lawyer Frank Shoofy, the legal counsel for the fighting Hilton brothers of Montreal, among others, arrived in town. Boxing promoters in Quebec had pooled their money to hire him to go to New Brunswick and save their Acadian hero from the corrupt English justice system. Shoofy walked into the courtroom with a gaggle of reporters trailing behind him. He was dressed in a flashy salt-and-pepper suit, and the woman who clutched his arm was showing off more exposed skin than had ever been seen before on the streets of Newcastle. McKenna and Lordon, dressed in their black courtroom robes, turned to watch the commotion at the back. The presiding judge ordered Shoofy out of the courtroom and told him to ask his friend to put on some clothes.

Shoofy stayed in town for a couple of days, talking to reporters and posing for pictures. He offered to represent Durelle for no fee. Yvon and Theresa decided to stick with McKenna and Lordon. "Look, that guy Frank seems like a very smart guy," Yvon told Theresa. "I'll take my chances and go with him." Shoofy left town.

The trial began on September 12, 1977, with prosecutors Drew Stymiest of Newcastle and William Kearney of Fredericton presenting the

Crown's case before a jury of eight men and four women. Spectators and members of the media sat shoulder to shoulder on the wooden benches in the back of the courtroom. A crowd lingered outside on the stone steps and in the parking lot across the street, waiting for news of the biggest show to hit the Miramichi in years.

The prosecutors methodically set out to prove the murder charge, presenting the evidence of the police officers who arrived at the Fisherman's Club after the shooting and the medical examiner who performed the autopsy on Poirier. Then Stymiest began to lead witnesses who saw the shooting and recalled Durelle making unrepentant statements afterwards.

Bertrand Durelle, no close relation to Yvon, was drinking in his van when he saw Yvon push Poirier into the parking lot. He told the jury that he saw the car drive toward Durelle. He said he saw Durelle fire one shot at the car and then, as it veered to the right, run up and fire four more shots through the window.

In his cross examination, McKenna asked, "Is it your opinion that, if he hadn't moved fast enough, he would have been run over?"

"Yes."

"And then the car reversed?"

"Yes."

"And then drove forward again."

"Yes."

"And this time did Yvon Durelle again have to get out of the way?"

"Yes."

"Now, you know Durelle well. Is it safe to say that he's awkward on his feet?"

"Yes, that's true. He's had his problems."

"So it might be difficult for him to get out of the way?"

"Oh yes. I saw him stumble. He almost fell down."

Witness Cecil Lloyd told the jury that he remembered Durelle walking into the club after the shooting and saying, "He's dead. I emptied five cartridges in the son of a bitch."

When McKenna rose for cross examination, he paced up and down in front of the witness box, asking Lloyd if he could remember Durelle also telling him that Poirier had tried to run him down with his car. Lloyd said yes, he remembered that. McKenna pointed out that he had not included that part of Durelle's statement in his direct evidence.

"It slipped my mind," Lloyd replied lamely.

McKenna asked, "Were you and your brothers friends of Albain Poirier?"

"Yes," Lloyd replied.

McKenna sat down.

The Mounties who took the telephone calls from Durelle on the day of the shooting took the stand. RCMP Constable Jean Harrison had received a call from Durelle on the afternoon of May 20. Harrison said Durelle told him if he didn't do something, he would have to "take care of it himself," a crucial statement which implied that Durelle had planned to kill Poirier and didn't pull the trigger in a spontaneous act of self-defence.

"Constable, are you sure you didn't say, 'Mr. Durelle, you can look after that yourself?'" McKenna asked.

"No sir, I'm pretty sure I did not," the constable replied.

McKenna paused and continued to pace. He mused that Harrison was relating from memory what he heard more than three months ago. Suddenly he whirled to face the police officer.

"Can you repeat from memory the last five questions I've asked you here?"

"No," Harrison replied weakly.

"No further questions," McKenna said as he took his seat.

Constable Ron Gosselin told the court he telephoned Durelle after receiving a radio message shortly after six p.m. on May 20. He said Durelle told him that Poirier had threatened to burn down his club, that if the police wouldn't help him he would have to take matters into his own hands.

"He told me that if he comes back tonight he would kill him," Gosselin said, but the only action he took was to pass on Durelle's concerns to the other officers working the night shift.

McKenna asked, "Do you think it is fairly serious conversation?"

"Yes, it is."

"Pretty tough talk, isn't it."

"Yes, it is."

From the front row of the spectator's benches, a frustrated Theresa Durelle shouted, "If they had come, he would be alive today." Her cry became the headline in local newspapers the next day.

The defence opened its case by calling Yvon Durelle to the stand, a risky strategy, but McKenna and Lordon knew this was a high-stakes game to begin with. They would start with Yvon, putting the theory of self-defence clearly before the jury, and close with Theresa, who was far and away their best witness.

Durelle walked carefully to the witness box, leaning on his cane. McKenna made sure Durelle brought his cane to court, telling him he wanted him to stand up straight for the judge but knowing that the cane would emphasize Durelle's injuries to the jury.

"We went over his story several times," recalls Lordon, who would lead Durelle's testimony. "He had problems telling things in chronological order. We told him about the type of tactics the Crown would use in cross examination. I think by the time we got to the trial he was prepared. It was traumatic for him. It was hard to talk about it. For a person with such a violent reputation, he is really a sensitive person."

Durelle took the stand at one-thirty in the afternoon on September 15, and immediately started crying as he identified himself and referred to his wife and four children who were in the courtroom. When he regained his composure, he described his relationship with Poirier. "We used to get along," he said. "I loaned him a whole lot of money, as high as a hundred dollars. He would always pay me back. When he came back from out west, he was a changed person. He was a different man altogether. You couldn't talk to him anymore. It was like he was in another world." He suggested that Albain Poirier may have been involved in the death of his cousin, who had died in a boating accident. After the accident, Durelle said, several people had told him that Poirier was saying that he "got one Durelle and he's going to get another one."

Durelle broke down again when he started to speak about the shooting. Judge Ronald Stevenson called a recess, and when Durelle returned, having removed his jacket and tie, Theresa and his children had left the courtroom. He calmly told what had happened on the night of the shooting, stepping down from the witness box and grabbing McKenna by the shoulder to show how he escorted Poirier from the club.

New Brunswick poet and author Ray Fraser was covering the trial for the *Miramichi Leader* and would later write a biography of Durelle, *The Fighting Fisherman*. Fraser had been taking notes during the testimony of the other witnesses, but when Durelle started talking he put his pen down and just listened. "It was as though he had no sense that he was on trial at all but was there to play the crowd, as was usually expected of him," Fraser later wrote. "I realized his lawyers knew precisely what they were doing. For the more he went on the more you wondered if he was capable of a reasoned response in a critical situation, if he could possibly be held criminally responsible for what he had done."

Durelle remained calm under cross-examination from Kearney, at one point turning the tables on his questioner by asking, "I don't want to die. Do you want to die, sir?"

"No," Kearney replied.

"Well, I don't want to die," Durelle said emphatically.

Lordon was saving one question for his redirect at the end of Durelle's testimony. Before the trial, he had often asked Durelle why he had continued to box, even when, late in his career, doctors believed he had suffered such severe neurological damage that one hard blow to the head could kill him. To the question of why he would risk his life for boxing, Durelle had always replied, "It was either fight or starve."

"I thought that was a pretty amazing answer," Lordon says. "Here was a guy who risked his life every time he stepped into the ring." Lordon planned to ask the question and leave Durelle's answer with the jury as a stepping stone to their next witness, a neurologist. However, when he asked the question, Durelle replied, "I was a professional fighter most of my life, a damn good fighter. I loved to hit guys over the head. I used to look at their faces when I knocked them down — jeez, they had some funny expressions. I seen niggers turn white and whites turn black."

Lordon was stunned. "I just stood there," he recalls. "I couldn't believe he said it. I don't know why he said it. I'd never heard him say it before, and I've never heard him say it since. I had some questions in my back pocket that weren't really necessary to the story, but I jumped back with them rather than leave the jury with that."

Fraser recalled that when Durelle stepped down, everyone in the courtroom could feel that the jury was with him. "Here was a simple, befuddled and basically harmless man, who had been driven to an extreme," he wrote. "It was a remarkable feat alone to admit candidly that he got pleasure from inflicting injury on others and to come away looking as though it was the last thing he'd be inclined to do, unless he absolutely had to. What is not obvious in Yvon's projection of himself, unless you happen to study him very carefully, is that behind his apparent naiveness and rambling garrulousness, there is a kind of gypsy-like intelligence that functions on its own oblique terms. However he went about it, he was not likely to do his own cause harm."

McKenna called neurosurgeon Herbert Tucker to the stand, who said injuries Durelle sustained in the ring and in his boating accident would have left him unable to manoeuvre easily in the darkness of the parking lot faced with the sudden contrast of Poirier's car headlights. Tucker said Durelle had difficulties carrying out even basic motor functions; for example, he had to kneel down to put his shoes on. He said he had lost the ability to think rapidly and had poor short-term memory. He could remember details of his boxing career but had trouble recalling his telephone number.

Two of Durelle's children, eighteen-year-old Francine and twenty-three-year old Yvon Jr., testified about their family's fear of Poirier. Constable O'Rourke testified about Poirier's suicide attempt, and Daniel Allen described his encounter with Durelle the morning after the shooting. McKenna called witnesses from the club, who told the jury about Poirier's threatening phone calls and Durelle's calls for help to the police the day of the shooting.

Theresa performed admirably, telling the jury of the numerous threats to her family from Poirier and how her husband had sat in their living room the night before the shooting, crying and asking himself, "What am I to do, what am I to do?" She sobbed when she spoke of hearing Durelle and Poirier in the parking lot and her frantic telephone calls to the RCMP. "I don't know why they wouldn't help us before," she said.

On cross-examination, the prosecution made no headway. When Kearney asked Theresa why there was a revolver in the club, she replied: "For the protection of our club and for protection from guys like Albain."

In a thirty-minute closing address to the jury, McKenna's voice became choked with emotion when he asked, "What motive did Yvon Durelle have for killing Poirier other than self-defence?"

In less than an hour, the jury returned to the courtroom with their verdict: not guilty. As McKenna listened to Stevenson discharge the jury, his eyes filled with tears. Then he rose and shook Denis Lordon's hand. Spectators in the gallery began to applaud, but Durelle showed no emotion. He had misunderstood what had happened. He walked into a side room with his lawyers. Lordon said, "Yvon, we won. It's not guilty." Then Durelle dissolved into tears.

Durelle met the media on the courthouse steps. "I have the greatest lawyers in the world," he said. "They worked almost twenty-four hours a day for the past three and a half months. They done a job nobody else could have done." Durelle said he planned to sell his club, buy a boat and go back to fishing.

The Durelles stayed in Newcastle that night, and their friends celebrated late into the night. As McKenna drove home across the bridge to Chatham, he looked in his rear-view mirror and saw the flashing lights of a town police car. He pulled over with a sinking feeling in his gut. He had been drinking at the celebration party, he was likely over the legal limit, and, he figured, now that he had won his greatest victory in the courtroom, his career was about to end on a drunken driving charge. The constable walked up to McKenna's car and immediately recognized the lawyer. "Congratulations, Frank," he said. "You did a great job. Drive safely." Gripping the steering wheel with shaking hands, McKenna drove slowly home.

The Durelles, too, returned home, where they have lived peacefully since the trial, but they will never fully recover from the ordeal. "It's still hard for us because we have to live down here," Theresa says. "To us, it is still not finished. You are home and you live, but it isn't over. It will never be over. We're not good people, but we're not bad people. Since that time, Yvon has never been in trouble, but deep down you are always scared."

After the Durelle trial, McKenna and Lordon, two obscure lawyers from small town New Brunswick, became famous across Canada. Law firms from Toronto and Montreal started calling, asking "the guys who defended Yvon Durelle" to help them with their cases. Frank Shoofy would ask McKenna to work with him on a drug trial, an offer McKenna politely declined. In 1985, Shoofy was murdered in his office in what appeared to be a professional hit.

McKenna and Lordon would successfully defend other accused murderers, but none of the profile of the Fighting Fisherman. Eventually McKenna began to move away from criminal law into more lucrative civil litigation and insurance work. With the assistance of his friend John Barry in Saint John, he developed a large insurance practice, applying his work ethic to these new files. In one case, he was trying to find a way to convince a judge that a driver who had been drinking and had hit the back of a tractor trailer as he came around a curve couldn't have seen it coming even if he had been sober. McKenna had cameras mounted on a car and drove it around the curve at the same speed to show the judge what the driver would have seen before he died.

The more McKenna became involved in civil cases, the more of his work was done outside the courtroom. He loved the excitement of jury trials, but he also recognized its dangers for someone who worked so hard and was so driven to win. "Waiting for that jury to come it and having them pronounce on your client is literally life and death," he says. "I've never had an experience quite like it. The problem is that once you've tasted that adrenaline rush, you can never stop. You'll be as high as a human being can be without some foreign substance after one of those trials. But every high begets a low. You crash and your ordinary life becomes less meaningful. So then you seek out another high. You're always seeking another thrill somewhere to gratify you." McKenna recognized the addictive nature of criminal law and walked away from it, but eventually he would find that same high in politics.

While Crown Prosecutor Fred Ferguson's job may have been easier after McKenna left, he missed watching him work. "Nobody since then has done any better," he says. "We get lawyers from all over the province. We've had the best counsel in the province coming in here, and he still is, as far as I'm concerned, the best."

Two years after the Fighting Fisherman verdict, McKenna and Lordon visited the Durelle home in Baie-Sainte-Anne for Yvon's fiftieth birthday party. Late in the evening, as the guests grew more extravagant, Durelle brought out two pairs of his boxing gloves. His former lawyers tied them on. They began to dance around the room, pretending to spar. Then Denis Lordon, with his longer reach, stung McKenna with a couple of jabs. Suddenly the two fierce competitors were no longer smiling. McKenna stepped inside and banged Lordon with a couple of hard body shots to the ribs.

"The next thing you know, the two of them are just flailing at each other," recalls David Cadogan, one of the guests at the party. "It was a knock 'em down, pier-six brawl for about thirty seconds, a real good fight before people started to laugh and they broke it off."

McKenna may have helped to save Yvon's life in the courtroom, but ten years after the trial, when, as Liberal leader, he was heading to the polls against Richard Hatfield, Yvon and Theresa faced a dilemma. Richard Hatfield was a friend of Yvon's and had helped to smooth the way for his club's liquor license. Yvon didn't have any particular political affiliation, but he felt he owed Hatfield a vote. "We didn't want to hurt Hatfield because he was good to us," Theresa recalls. "We didn't want to hurt Frank because he was good to us. So what were we supposed to do?" They decided on a compromise. Theresa voted for Frank McKenna. Yvon voted for Richard Hatfield.

McKenna learned a valuable lesson. In the world of New Brunswick politics, he could take nothing for granted.

Frank McKenna's first media scrum after being sworn in as Premier, October 13, 1987.

5

SWEEP

Exercised hard, good diet, general work habits. Hatfield in
Arizona at a fat farm for two weeks. The campaign will start
on his return.
— *Frank McKenna, diary entry, January 6, 1987*

In the autumn of 1982, Richard Hatfield linked arms with voters,
spinning, gliding his way across the province toward his fourth term in
office. Even when the Premier travelled into Miramichi country, admiring
river banks blanketed in brilliant oranges and reds, it is unlikely that he
gave his future nemesis a second thought. Frank McKenna was just
another vulnerable Liberal candidate, learning to dance an awkward two-
step on the streets of Chatham. There, as in all small towns, the art of
politics required little more than a sturdy pair of shoes and an infinite
tolerance for the mundane.

Hatfield was moving through the political stratosphere. If he had an
election strategy, someone else was handling it. "I don't know if I hate
detail, but I avoid it if I can," he once said. Down at street level, McKenna
believed the answer to most of life's riddles could be found in the details,
and in his first campaign he would attend to all of them himself. He
knocked on every voter's door in his riding, recording pages of notes in
a long legal binder as if he were collecting the facts he needed to argue
a case in the old Miramichi courthouse.

"Met Wilfred Robichaud and wife. Non-committal. Had a German
shepherd dog that jumped up on me," McKenna wrote in his binder.

"Norman Lobban says that he is pissed off because he couldn't get
anybody on the grant to cut brush along the road.

"MacDonald. Appears to be leaning Liberal. Wife Davida may be a
Liberal. He is unemployed. She is interested in owning a home, and I
told her I would try to bring some materials out to her. She was David
Curtis's daughter. He was a notorious Tory, but he has since moved.

"Ken and Roland Dickson and Lawson and Carla Dickson. All said they would vote Liberal if I can look after getting a bridge in front of their house.

"Met Lloyd Wormell, who said he'd support me, along with his wife and two children. Also said we could get support from his mother and father and his sister Shirley and her husband Philip."

This sort of work appealed to McKenna's pragmatic soul; he would do what he needed to do to get elected, and if he had to endure a certain degree of indignity and pettiness on the doorsteps, so be it. If voters were lobbying for a new sidewalk in their neighbourhood, McKenna would take out a half-page newspaper advertisement supporting their position. If an elderly voter who intended to vote Liberal needed a ride to the polls, he'd ensure that a volunteer was parked outside with the motor running when the polls opened. None of his larger ambitions could be fulfilled if he didn't succeed in taking this first step into public life. Failure in the Chatham stronghold would destroy the foundation he had been carefully laying during his eight years on the Miramichi.

Voters in the disadvantaged neighbourhoods in his riding had been supporting the Liberals since Louis Robichaud's Equal Opportunity reforms offered hope that government could respond progressively to their needs. McKenna knew the election would turn on his ability to inspire these voters in small communities on the outskirts of the towns of Chatham and Newcastle with the promise that he, too, would become their champion after election day.

No community in the riding was more in need than Chatham Head, a cluster of families burdened by poverty situated across the river from the town of Newcastle. During the seventies, Chatham Head had earned an ugly reputation as the setting for gruesome crimes. Desperate and increasingly violent members of the community had started turning on their own. The sister of a priest had been murdered, stabbed fifty-seven times and robbed of her bingo winnings. An elderly woman had been robbed of her pension cheque and burned to death. A welding shop had been hit by a drive-by shooting. When McKenna arrived to campaign in Chatham Head, he found that his work as a passionate advocate in the criminal courts had preceded him.

"Half the doors I knocked on, the people went running back and said, 'Look Frank, I'll pay you what I owe you, you didn't have to come to the door,'" McKenna recalls. "I felt like I was a country doctor, like I had an obligation to help people." McKenna knew his reputation as a successful small town lawyer would win him some votes, but he also knew it wouldn't be enough to carry an election in rural New Brunswick, where who you are means at least as much as any natural abilities you may bring to the job. Frank McKenna's only natural advantage was his Irish Catholic heritage, but he wasn't a Miramichier and never would be. "You've got to live here for fifty years or so before you're considered a local," says Frank Kane, the Liberal MLA for Chatham from 1969 to 1982.

To compensate for his lack of birthright, McKenna had immersed himself in the economic and social life of his community. He and his law partners purchased land, developed building lots and subdivisions and built houses. He served three terms as president of the Greater Miramichi Chamber of Commerce, having drawn together the many parochial organizations along the river. He built and operated a general store, then founded the Chatham Downtown Merchants' Association, becoming the group's first president. The McKenna family attended St. Michael's Basilica. McKenna worked for the parish council, serving as project chairman for a $200,000 expansion of the church basement, and he sat beside the bishop at the head table at the official opening of the new St. Michael's Community Centre, an event covered by the *Miramichi Leader*.

In 1975, Christine Alice McKenna had been born, a sister for three-year-old Toby, and James Durward was born two years later. The McKenna family lived in a new bungalow in the Riverside Subdivision, where they attended neighbourhood parties and curled at the local club. McKenna played tennis, golf and old-timers hockey, and his daily jogging routine made him a constantly visible presence in the community.

David Cadogan, McKenna's neighbour, tennis partner and client, watched with interest as his friend prepared himself for a career in politics. The young lawyer saw to it that his name was mentioned as often as possible in Cadogan's newspaper. When McKenna won a civil case, he would deliver a copy of the judgment to the *Miramichi Leader* office. The overworked reporters at the community newspaper were grateful for these quick and easy news stories, and McKenna always made himself available for interviews.

McKenna's background as a farm boy and self-made man appealed to Miramichiers, who appreciated his unpretentious optimism. "Folks recognized that this was a guy who was not born with a silver spoon in his mouth," recalls his friend Rupert Bernard, who would later become mayor of the amalgamated city of Miramichi. "He was genuine and real, and he was accepted almost as one of them. Frank did an awful lot for a lot of people prior to being in politics. I guess when those IOUs are out there, in some cases, they pay their dividends."

McKenna had worked on the unsuccessful Liberal leadership bids of Norbert Thériault in 1971 and John Bryden in 1978, but as he sensed he was moving closer to his own day in the political arena, he avoided the internal wars that plagued the party during the late seventies and early eighties. At the contentious 1982 Liberal leadership convention, McKenna acted as chief returning officer, a position that kept him visible yet well clear of the fray. Doug Young emerged as leader of a divided party while McKenna walked away unscathed. "That was precisely the place for him to be," Cadogan affirms.

In unguarded moments, when McKenna told Cadogan matter-of-factly that he planned to become premier, the newspaper publisher would ask him to explain his political philosophy. McKenna would find himself at a loss for words; his agenda wasn't as easy to articulate as his ambition. Eventually, Cadogan came to understand that McKenna had the philosophy of a small mixed farmer, a man like Joseph McKenna, who looked after himself, worked at a dozen small jobs to make a living, and never once asked for a handout; who patched his jeans and boots, didn't waste a nickel, and never threw anything away. The politics of a small mixed farmer is the politics of self-reliance.

Cadogan also realized that his friend's memory was extraordinary. McKenna was able to recall recitations from school days in Sussex effortlessly, and he never forgot a face or a name, which he could invariably connect to a family and a hometown. He was building a network across the province, mentally storing information that he would retrieve time and again in public life. "I began to realize that his mind had a filing system far more organized that most people's," Cadogan recalls.

In the early 1980s, after more than a decade in opposition, Liberal riding associations were floundering throughout the province. Before McKenna arrived in Chatham, Rupert Bernard had been one of a handful of loyalists keeping the local association from collapsing. "There were lots of annual meetings of the constituency that you could have held in a phone booth," Bernard maintains. "Frank helped invigorate the party locally. I thought that was a very good thing because I was pretty tired from trying to hold it together for eight or ten years. He was like a breath of fresh air in this community."

In the spring of 1982, Frank Kane, an insurance salesman turned politician, grew tired of life in Opposition and announced he would retire before the next election, which was expected in the fall. When no one from the local hierarchy stepped forward to replace him, McKenna, thirty-four years old and president of the Chatham Liberal riding association, decided he was as ready as he was ever going to be. At his nomination meeting, he said he would strive to bring jobs to the Miramichi, where, depending on the season, half the population was unemployed. "Most important is what is happening to our young people," he said. "They have no jobs, no future, and perhaps most tragic of all, no hope. This is what the Conservatives have done." Every second car on the Miramichi had Alberta license plates, he said, "either leaving or coming back for a visit." The Chatham Liberal establishment considered this young outsider to be a long shot at best. "He didn't have a hope in hell in the next election, as far as anyone who knew anything was concerned," Julie McKenna recalls. "He just went out and started knocking on the doors."

When Richard Hatfield announced that voters would go to the polls on October 12, 1982, the Liberals were convinced that the Premier was vulnerable. A poll taken shortly after Doug Young defeated Hampton lawyer Joseph Day for the party leadership suggested that the Liberals held a substantial lead over the Tories. In the months leading to the election call, Young fashioned the Opposition's agenda in the image of his combative personality, relentlessly attacking and ridiculing Hatfield at every turn. The Premier didn't respond. He avoided the media, making impromptu visits to the province's summer festivals. Then he authorized a spending spree, promising 35,000 new jobs and $70 million worth of new government programs.

"The Conservatives drained the government coffers, enveloping the province in a haze to make voters forget the stagnant economy, unemployment, the deficit and other disagreeable realities that waited for them after the election," write Michel Cormier and Achille Michaud. "Hatfield and his ministers promised largesse throughout the province — public kindergartens, rent control, a second nuclear power station at Point Lepreau, mortgage assistance, grants for troubled industries."

The Opposition's campaign emphasized Hatfield's weaknesses rather than Young's strengths. While Young reminded voters that Hatfield's promises would be forgotten after the election, the Liberal message offered little to inspire voters. Moreover, Young appeared too greedy for power. "Hatfield and the media, including the knife-wielding portrayals of Young by *Telegraph-Journal* cartoonist Josh Beutel, reinforced Young's image as a man of ruthless ambition," writes Liberal commentator Don Hoyt. "There had just been too much trouble within the Liberal Party, too many innuendos about Young's motives and too little attention through the seventies to making the Liberal Party an organized, potent alternative."

On the Miramichi, Liberal prospects were as low as they had been in more than a decade. Cadogan openly supported McKenna in his newspaper columns, but he sensed that his friend was in political trouble. The federal Liberals were making noises about closing Canadian Forces Base Chatham, eliminating the 1,500 jobs that anchored the town's economy. "Richard Hatfield was doing his best to find solutions and was making all the political hay he could out of the mess," Cadogan recalls.

By election day, Hatfield was heading for a landslide victory and an unprecedented breakthrough in Liberal ridings in the francophone north. After the polls closed, McKenna paced in his Chatham law office, watching the election returns. With only the polls from Chatham Head left to report, he was trailing his Tory opponent, John Barry, a retired navy man with an impeccable record of community service who had campaigned as the underdog son of the Miramichi battling the ambitious come-from-away lawyer. Late in the evening, television election desks declared McKenna defeated, along with Liberal finance critic John McKay of Newcastle.

"I started drinking with each poll that I was behind," McKenna recalls. "I was absolutely ripped by the time they got to Chatham Head." While McKenna dulled his pain, one of his law firm's partners, Michael Bowes, continued to watch poll results as they came in.

"You're ahead, you're ahead," Bowes called out from across the room.

"I'm not ahead, I lost," McKenna replied. "Look at the TV, those people in Halifax said I lost."

"No, no, no," Bowes shouted. "Chatham Head has come in — you won big in Chatham Head."

Voters in Chatham Head supported McKenna two to one over Barry, pushing him over the top by eighty-one votes. In doing so, they changed the course of their province's history. "They are all God's children," McKenna says of his friends in Chatham Head. "They've been very good to me." McKenna's government would later order that the new Miramichi

Hospital be built in Chatham Head, drawing the formerly under-privileged neighbourhood fully into the new city of Miramichi and repaying an old political debt.

The news of McKenna's victory arrived slowly back home in Apohaqui. The day after the election, Olive McKenna telephoned the *Kings County Record* to inform the editors that they had wrongly declared her son defeated in his riding when in fact he had won. She acknowledged that their mistake was understandable, given the fact that the CBC had declared McKenna defeated, but she added that she was proud of her son and wanted the record corrected.

In the days following the election, Young announced that he would resign as Liberal leader, shouldering the blame for an election disaster that left the Tories holding forty-one seats, the Liberals twenty-two. When a television reporter asked McKenna if he had any aspirations to become Liberal leader, the new MLA for Chatham awkwardly glanced down at his shoes and murmured that he simply wanted to represent his constituents. It was difficult to mask his ambition, but he was trying to master the politician's art of speaking half-truths. The leadership was certainly on his mind.

Within days of the election, McKenna's friends were suggesting that he should be the next leader. Thomas O'Neil, a Saint John lawyer and a friend since high school, wrote to congratulate him on his victory: "Although the party has suffered a setback, I am confident that with a *new* leader things can be turned around." O'Neil, who graduated from the University of New Brunswick Law School a year after McKenna, had been waiting for his friend to make a political move since he landed in Chatham. "From day one, he stood out as a leader," O'Neil says. "I knew he had the ability to do the job, and I encouraged him over the next couple of years to run for the leadership."

In the months following the election, Arthur Doyle, a long-time Fredericton Liberal insider, began hearing a buzz around the name Frank McKenna. His friends in the legal community told him, "This guy is very ambitious, and someday he wants to be premier." Doyle didn't take them seriously. He listened to Hatfield's Justice Minister Rodman Logan demolish McKenna, who had been named Liberal justice critic, during a CBC radio debate, and he muttered to himself, "So they think *he's* going to be premier."

A year after the election, Doyle met McKenna for the first time at a Liberal meeting in Fredericton. "I saw him from a distance, and I remember going over and saying, 'Hi, Frank, my name's Art Doyle. We have mutual friends.' He was wearing a scruffy old sweater and a pair of khakis and wet, muddy shoes. He was looking at the floor most of the time." If this man was leadership material, Doyle had trouble seeing it.

However, as justice critic, McKenna began to make a name for himself in the Legislature and provincial media. When he received a leaked RCMP report about alleged election fraud in Saint John, he rose in the Legislature to read from police statements and call for a public inquiry. The police report suggested that in every municipal, provincial and federal election since 1978, Progressive Conservatives in Saint John had been putting the names of people who died between enumeration day and election day on voters' lists. According to the report, Tory organizers had obtained the names from funeral homes and then paid people to vote as many times as they could. McKenna read a sworn affidavit from a man who had been paid $500 to vote fifty times in the 1980 municipal election. He read a transcript of a taped conversation in which the participants in the scam were warned that under no circumstances were they to swear to their identities at polling stations. Hatfield dismissed the allegations as partisan muckraking, following his tried-and-true strategy of handling political corruption — deny and deny again until, miraculously, nothing seemed to stick.

The new Chatham MLA also attacked the Conservative economic agenda, stating that the policy of "budgeting for elections and then imposing extensive tax increases to pay for the next one is morally and economically wrong." His resource-dependent constituency was in trouble. Hundreds of Miramichiers lost their jobs when a wafer-board mill and a plywood mill closed, and hundreds more were laid off at local mines. While he attacked the Tories for ignoring the plight of his people, McKenna argued that it was wrong to depend on government alone to deal with unemployment. Rather, the province should create an atmosphere for new industry by developing an infrastructure that could support a diversified economy.

McKenna made the front pages of provincial newspapers by questioning Hatfield's creation of the New Brunswick Highway Patrol, which was replacing a number of RCMP detachments. By protesting that the province needed more, not fewer RCMP officers, McKenna reinforced the public perception that the creation of a new police force was Hatfield's political solution to his clashes with the Mounties.

Julian Walker remembers seeing McKenna, working late into the night in his office on the top floor of the opposition building, puffing on his pipe and returning phone calls. "He used the government system," Walker says. "He knew the housing program inside and out, that was a big issue in his riding. He'd be calling government agencies and getting whatever he could. He was a real digger." When he was finished with politics for the day, he'd pull out stacks of legal files and start dictating letters, practicing law well into the night. At times, McKenna's demands frustrated party researchers. "You could never do enough for Frank," Walker remembers. "He was young and brash, and he was going some-place."

The pace of McKenna's life grew more frenetic with each week on the job. He drove two hours to Fredericton on Tuesday mornings and returned home on Fridays to see his wife and children and keep his law practice afloat. "He would call from the road to check messages, driving like a bat out of hell with one hand, holding the phone with the other, passing cars, saying he'd just missed a transport truck," recalls Ruth McCrea, who was then an Opposition staffer.

Nevertheless, one young man's enthusiasm couldn't temper the in-sidious Liberal pessimism. Ray Frenette had agreed to be interim leader. No fresh leader was waiting in the wings, and all attempts to recruit high-profile outside candidates had failed. Hatfield was awash in political troubles, and the Liberals desperately needed to begin preparing for an election. Finally, Frenette reluctantly entered the race. "Party supporters came and twisted my arm, and I made the mistake of saying, 'Yes, I'll go,'" Frenette recalls.

At one of the first meetings of Frenette supporters in Fredericton, the group discussed the possibility that the leadership campaign would result in a Frenette coronation. When Frenette was asked if the caucus was with him, he replied that almost everyone was on side except Doug Young and a handful of dissidents.

"What about Frank McKenna?" Arthur Doyle asked.

"Who's he?" asked Bev O'Keefe, Frenette's campaign manager.

"Don't worry about him. Frank has offered to help me with the cam-paign," Frenette replied.

Indeed, McKenna had promised to support Frenette, but meanwhile Liberals in Chatham and insiders like Ruth McCrea were urging him to enter the race. When McKenna made it known that he was considering a run for the leadership, Frenette's backers commissioned a poll which suggested that, if an election were held the next day, Hatfield would win another majority. The poll went on to test the names of potential Liberal leaders on the basis of name recognition. Out of the five names tested, Ray Frenette placed first, with more than thirty per cent, and Frank McKenna dead last, with five per cent. The poll was presented to McKenna with some advice: politics is all about name recognition. See where Ray Frenette stands; see where McKenna stands. McKenna can't beat Richard Hatfield because nobody knows him.

Although McKenna would eventually understand the intricacies of polling, he accepted the poll's results at face value; he was convinced that his leadership bid was premature. He drove home to Chatham and told his wife and supporters what had happened. Julie McKenna was torn. For the sake of the family, as a wife and mother, she didn't want her husband in the race. Her mother had warned her about the dismal, lonely life of a politician's wife, and she was already living it. However, Julie McKenna has always spoken her mind, and so she gave it to her husband straight, the only way she knew how. She told him that, the way she saw it, the Liberal establishment, which had decided to anoint Frenette, was trying to keep him out of the race. "We thought they had skewed the poll," Julie McKenna recalls. "I got upset, and I said, 'You can't let them do that, you have to run.'"

The pollster had failed to ask a crucial question: out of those who recognized Frenette's name, how many would vote for him? Liberals in Chatham were of the opinion that if Frenette ran against Hatfield, not only would they lose the election, but their promising young member would lose his seat. However, McKenna had already promised to support Frenette, and to enter the race would mean going back on his word. "It was really bothering me," he recalls. "For me, mental stress is much worse than anything else, and it's always about issues of integrity, always about issues of morality. The issue wasn't whether I'd win or lose. I assumed that if I ran I would probably lose because I'd be running against the establishment."

Finally, he decided to run, thinking it might be the only way to save his seat. "It came right down to that," he says. "I wanted to be in politics. I wanted to make a difference. I felt that even running and losing would give me enough profile that I would win my seat. What was tearing me apart was that I had told Ray Frenette I would support him. I could not dishonour that." McKenna went to see Frenette to tell him he would run, but only with his blessing.

"Frank came into my office to tell me he was running, and I told him,

'Please do,'" Frenette recalls. "He said, 'I know you are going to run, and you are probably going to beat me,' and I said, 'No, I'm willing to bet you any dollars that you are going to beat the pants off me.' The Liberal party had been through three or four leaders, and all of a sudden there was this fresh face with no baggage. He was clean and young and a very articulate anglophone. Do you think the people, the Liberals, would support somebody that had been there for ten years? And a francophone? No way."

Soon after he entered the race, McKenna travelled to Bathurst to ask Fernand and Aldéa Landry to join his campaign. One of McKenna's weaknesses was that he was a unilingual anglophone from the south who wouldn't easily convince Acadians to return to the Liberal fold. The Landrys were old friends; he admired their legal and political acumen, and they personified the young Acadian intelligentsia whose support McKenna needed. Aldéa Landry, a fiery young lawyer, had already told McKenna that, should he ever decide to seek the leadership, she would back him with all her considerable energy. Her husband Fernand, a thoughtful and patient man, wasn't so sure he wanted to support a green anglophone lawyer over an Acadian veteran, and in fact he wasn't sure he wanted to become involved at all. He had already given a lot of his time to the party and to politics. He was practicing law, trying to earn a living, and he knew he would pay both a personal and a financial price for joining McKenna's team. But Landry could see in McKenna the energy the party needed to win. And he had promised himself that if he ever became active in Liberal politics again, he would position himself at the centre of the action, where he could bring dedicated professionalism to the process, something that he believed had been sorely lacking during the party's years in the political wilderness. Fern Landry would become McKenna's closest friend and political advisor. His level-headedness was an antidote to McKenna's impatience; whenever McKenna prepared to plunge straight ahead, Landry always checked to see where he might land. The Landrys educated McKenna about the history and aspirations of the Acadians, and their constant presence at his side legitimized his candidacy in the north.

Soon after McKenna launched his campaign, Harrison and Wallace McCain decided they should meet the new contender. The McCain brothers were Liberals, although they had been friends and supporters of Richard Hatfield, who grew up in Hartland, just down the St. John River from their Florenceville home. "Dick Hatfield was a very powerful and potent Premier, and I liked him," Harrison says. "He couldn't help it if he was a Tory. He used to be a guest at my home for meals, and I liked him just fine. He did a good job of managing the province."

Their political activism, however, was in the Liberal direction. When Pierre Trudeau was seeking the federal Liberal leadership, Wallace had been his campaign manager in New Brunswick and Harrison had been his chief fundraiser for the Maritimes. The brothers were also married into the Liberal establishment, Harrison to former Liberal premier John McNair's daughter Marion, Wallace to Liberal Senator Margaret Norrie's daughter Margaret. As the Liberals prepared to choose a new leader in the spring of 1985, the McCains believed it was time for Hatfield to go, and so they called McKenna and asked him to stop by for a chat.

For his part, McKenna had no intention of making a trip to Florence-ville as a supplicant. "When they wanted to get together with me, we turned that down," he recalls. "Our attitude was, 'Look, we're not going to be beholden to anybody. I am not going to walk in, cap in hand, to the McCains. That's the old way of doing it.' And I didn't. As it turned out, I saw them in their office, but it was because we were heading up the St. John River valley to Edmundston."

The McCain brothers worked out of adjoining offices at their head-quarters overlooking the St. John River. They left the door between their offices open, and as they worked they yelled back and forth, phones rang wildly, and the air turned blue with the four-letter words they were notorious for hurling about. When McKenna arrived, he was ushered into Harrison's office, where Wallace joined them.

Harrison recalls that they were "favourably impressed" by the young politician. "I felt he would be a breath of fresh air to the party," Wallace recalls. "I liked the way he talked. He seemed to be confident."

They promised McKenna several thousand dollars, and then Harrison asked McKenna about his plans for the campaign. As McKenna outlined his strategy, Harrison realized he needed help. He didn't have staff with enough experience to run a successful campaign.

"You need John Bryden," Harrison said.

"I agree, John Bryden is the best, but I can't get him," McKenna replied.

Harrison said, "Is that so?" He picked up the telephone, placing a call to John's younger brother Rod Bryden. John was working in Toronto as the chief executive officer of Rod's company, Paperboard Industries Corp.

"Rod, we need John to run the campaign for Frank McKenna. We hope to make him premier," Harrison said. "Now, will you let us have him or not?"

"We had him within an hour," Harrison recalls. "John Bryden got Frank elected. Without Bryden, he wouldn't have made it."

Bryden remembers the day when Harrison McCain called his Toronto office. "John, Jesus Christ, a young man just left my office, and he's the man," he barked as soon as Bryden lifted the receiver. "He's rough, he's some goddam rough, but I think he's the man. You've got to come down here and run this campaign."

Bryden told McCain he was trying to run a company and make some money. "Money, Jesus Christ, you can always make money," McCain said. "You got to come down here and take this young fellow over. I think he's gonna be good, but he's rough, he's rough. He needs your help."

Harrison McCain may have believed he had John Bryden within an hour; however, Bryden insists he made no firm decisions until he discussed the situation with McKenna. The silver-haired, steely eyed Bryden, a self-made man remarkably similar to the new Liberal contender, wasn't one to allow his arm to be twisted by anyone.

Bryden had grown up on a small mixed farm beside the Northumberland Strait. He was an academic prodigy, graduating from Mount Allison University and then travelling to Philadelphia to pursue his doctorate in philosophy at the University of Pennsylvania. Before completing his degree, he returned to New Brunswick, graduated from law school, and became Deputy Minister of Justice in the final year of Louis Robichaud's government in 1969. When Richard Hatfield was elected Premier in 1970, Bryden resigned and announced his intentions to seek the leadership of the Liberal Party. In 1971, he finished just a hundred and sixty-two votes behind Robert Higgins. Bryden ran in the 1974 election and lost. In 1978, he sought the leadership for a second time, this time finishing fifty-three votes behind Joseph Daigle on the first ballot in a six-candidate race, only to lose by 364 votes on the third ballot.

Bryden returned to politics in 1979 as executive director of the Liberal Party to help Daigle prepare for the next election, then quit in disgust in 1980 when the leader was ousted. "I refuse to be party to or in any way appear to be associated with a blatant and callous power grab attempted within the Liberal Party," he declared, after summoning the members of the press gallery to the steps of the Legislature. As far as he was concerned, at that moment he had burned his bridges in New Brunswick politics.

Now, four years later, he was being asked to return to the fray, and to his surprise he felt the competitive fire returning. His unrequited political ambitions could be fulfilled through McKenna, who as a student had articled at his Fredericton law firm and who, in so many ways, appeared the mirror image of his younger self.

"In 1971, I believed that what the Liberal Party needed was a new, bright, energetic young leader who didn't have baggage, who would be able to look forward, not back, and I believed I was that person," Bryden says. "When it came to 1984, I realized that I was no longer the bright, young, capable, energetic person the party needed. Frank McKenna was my sense of what the party needed in 1971, translated into Frank McKenna instead of John Bryden."

Bryden met with Frank and Julie McKenna at a Fredericton hotel, where they talked for about an hour about the fundamentals of launching a leadership bid. "Frank was like a sponge, just absorbing everything," Bryden recalls. McKenna formally asked Bryden to manage his campaign. Bryden said he wasn't sure he was the man for the job. He saw McKenna's greatest strengths as not only his youth and his energy but also the healthy distance he had placed between himself and the Liberal wars. New Brunswick voters were as disillusioned by Liberal infighting as they were by the scandal-plagued Hatfield administration. Bryden feared McKenna would lose his political advantage by bringing an old warhorse on board. "I carried the scars and the experience and the liability of all of that," Bryden says. "I was involved in most of it, and the part I wasn't involved in, people would say I caused anyway." He asked McKenna to speak to a number of Liberals whose opinions he valued to find out what they thought about Bryden's running his campaign. A week later McKenna called Bryden back to say he had made the calls and wanted him to manage his campaign all the way to the premier's office.

Bryden agreed and turned his attention to the chaotic team McKenna had already patched together. "We had every hanger-on that you could imagine walking in and taking over," McKenna admits. "All of these people were my friends. I just couldn't tell them to get lost." McKenna couldn't say no to anybody, Bryden recalls. "He has this need to be loved."

McKenna called a meeting at his office in downtown Fredericton to introduce his new manager to his campaign workers. Bryden arrived to find McKenna and his group of aspiring managers seated around a table. "Frank finally bit the bullet and said, 'I've asked John, and he's agreed to be my campaign manager,'" Bryden recalls.

Bryden took charge, and as his first order of business asked the workers to remove a stack of empty beer cases from the entrance to the headquarters.

"It was a party," Bryden says. "It was fun. But when you bring the Bible thumpers in from Carleton County and the first thing they're presented with is empty booze cases, it doesn't go down very well."

John Bryden and Fern Landry took over all of the thousands of decisions involved in managing volunteers: who would occupy which office, who would best accomplish which tasks. "It was just driving me crazy for the first few weeks," McKenna recalls. "I have always been a control freak until I really trust somebody, then I say, 'Just take the whole thing.' From then on I was at the end of a phone line, gone campaigning. John Bryden really brought a lot of order to chaos. He was decisive and strategic, and he is a gentle leader. Without creating a lot of excitement, he just makes things happen."

Bryden became the field general, Landry the conciliator. "If you got a phone call from John Bryden, you were in deep shit," McGuire recalls. "If things had to be smoothed over, Fern phoned." Far from saddling the campaign with political baggage, Bryden, with Fern and Aldéa Landry, brought instant credibility to the campaign. In Fern Landry, McKenna had a friend and confidant, in Bryden, a political mentor. Under Bryden's tutelage, McKenna began to mature as a politician. "John Bryden taught Frank, 'Make a goddam decision,'" Francis McGuire says. No decision is perfect, Bryden told him, but if he was going to lead he had to be decisive.

Bryden was pleasantly surprised by McKenna's political instincts. "He has a natural warmth for people," Bryden observed. "He is very much self-contained, and you never really know whether what has just happened is a spontaneous outburst or whether he's been planning it for weeks. However, the effect of his campaign style in a crowd or in a small room is personal and direct."

As the convention approached, it became clear that McKenna was going to defeat Frenette handily. At the eleventh hour, Frenette's handlers convinced him to deliver his bitter, stinging attack on McKenna as just another young, inexperienced lawyer who would lose to Hatfield. "Oh yes, I regret the speech," Frenette says today. "I knew it was the wrong speech to give at the time. But my handlers felt that there was no prize for second place, and we had to shake people into recognizing that they were making a mistake. But my feeling was that we couldn't do that, no speech would do that. He would have beaten me two to one, and I knew he was going to beat me two to one. The way it was put to me was, 'Look, we're $35,000 in the hole here, and we don't know how we're going to deal with this.' I was a person of very, very limited means. When they said, 'Somebody's going to have to pick this up,' I felt an obligation to do as they would like. I said, 'Look, I'll deliver the speech, but I think you are making a big mistake.'"

In a final blow to Frenette, the night before the convention, Allan Graham, an eighteen-year veteran of the Legislature and a formidable fundraiser and organizer, had defected to McKenna's camp. "It's going to be overwhelming for Frank and the unity of the party," he told CBC Television on the convention floor. "I feel we have the makings of a new premier. We need a Frank McKenna, we need another Louis Robichaud to bring the party back."

Doris McKenna remembers that her older brother was overwhelmed by the hype at the convention. As she sat beside him in the stands after he arrived, he turned to her and said, "What am I doing here?" His sister Rosemary held a cardboard sign on which she had written, "Hi, Dad," a message for Joseph McKenna, who was too crippled to make the trip to Moncton. He stayed on the farm in Apohaqui, watching his son's big moment on television.

Frenette should have trusted his instincts. During his speech, he watched his supporters drop their placards and move to the McKenna side of the floor. "I knew, listening to that speech, that it wasn't Ray Frenette, and I knew that it would end up with my getting almost a unanimous convention because it so isolated and marginalized the Frenette campaign," McKenna recalls. "It was just kind of a general conclusion: we chose the right guy and now let's get on with it."

Members of his campaign team did not feel so serene. Aldéa Landry, who was doing commentary in the Radio Canada booth upstairs, wept openly. Downstairs, McKenna's advisors retreated to a motorhome they had parked inside the arena. David Cadogan recalls entering the motor home to find members of the McKenna team bouncing off the walls. The Miramichi delegation demanded vengeance. "They were worked up into a frenzy," Cadogan recalls. "Some of them would have liked Frank to punch Ray in the mouth. To them that would have been an appropriate response."

The Liberals were facing the possibility of another divided convention. McKenna turned to his Acadian conciliator to handle the crisis. "It could have been disastrous," Fernand Landry recalls. "Some people in our group were awfully upset. Some people had smoke coming out of their ears. I argued in favour of making the first step and going to see them. It was obvious by then who would win. I said, 'Look, sure, it was a hard go and tough today emotionally, but let's keep our cool and go see those people and have them on our side. We're winning.'"

While the delegates were voting, Landry met with Frenette and his organizers and negotiated the concession, which he knew would be projected live on CBC Television. Frenette would come to McKenna, and he would be received warmly when he arrived. Frenette was more than willing to co-operate. "I also knew that, after it was over, I would give him my full support. After the twelve years we were together, I never changed giving him my full support and loyalty."

Five minutes before the results were announced, Frenette walked across the floor to McKenna, where he was greeted with a bear hug. McKenna embraced each member of the Frenette campaign team. "Thanks for coming over, boys," he said. "We'll be calling you."

Back in Chatham after the convention, Julie McKenna recalls meeting John Creaghan, one of her Tory cousins, in the days following the convention. "I don't know why Frank wanted to be the leader of this party," he said. "You're never going to win, ever."

"Well, things change, John," Julie McKenna replied. In fact, things did change, and quickly.

———

The Hatfield government in its fourth term had lost its way. Within weeks of taking office in 1982, the spending spree had been scrapped in favour of a program of economic austerity that Hatfield refused to apply to his personal conduct. "Hatfield seemed like a heavyweight champion who had successfully defended his title one last time and was basking in his glory before retiring," Cormier and Michaud write. "He was frequently absent from the house and cabinet meetings, he appeared to have lost interest in provincial affairs, and he was less careful about his public image. While his government forced the public to make sacrifices during the recession, Hatfield continued to make trips to New York and Montreal at the expense of the party and the province."

The Premier who once had made New Brunswickers proud had become an embarrassment. At the federal Conservative leadership convention in

Ottawa in June, 1983, CBC television cameras captured an overweight Hatfield, his stomach bulging out of a tight purple t-shirt, dancing awkwardly on the convention floor. Later that month, when the Prince and Princess of Wales visited New Brunswick, Hatfield managed to transform a public relations coup into an international scandal. When the Premier rose to toast Charles and Diana at an official dinner in Saint John, he tactlessly made reference to their marital problems. "Your Royal Highness, the Princess of Wales, we have heard and read the lies, today it was wonderful to meet and know the truth," he said. The British tabloids pounced on the story. The *News of the World* suggested Hatfield had been drunk and published its story under the headline: "Hatfield embarrasses royal couple with his bizarre behaviour." The *Mail* reported, "The Premier, age 52, a bachelor and notorious eccentric known as Disco Dick, has even outclassed the princess."

In the fall of 1984, when Queen Elizabeth visited New Brunswick, Conservatives prayed that a few days of pomp and circumstance would salvage their leader's faltering public profile. On September 25, 1984, Queen Elizabeth and Prince Philip landed in Fredericton. Hatfield met them at the airport and while he was there told the airport manager to make sure his suitcase was placed on the royal plane before the Queen flew back to Moncton. Hatfield would need to change clothes before that evening's state dinner.

In a speech to the state dinner in Moncton, the Queen praised New Brunswick's bicultural harmony under the leadership of her host. "The French and the British at first fought over this land, but their descendants learned to live here in harmony and to have a common purpose," she said as Hatfield beamed in the audience. But even while the Queen was praising Hatfield's crowning political achievement, his political destruction had begun at RCMP headquarters in Fredericton. During a routine search of Hatfield's suitcase before it was loaded on the royal plane, in an unzipped outside pocket, a police officer had found a brown envelope containing a package of marijuana. After the Queen left New Brunswick, RCMP officers visited Hatfield to ask him to explain the envelope. Hatfield denied the drugs were his and said he had no idea how the package got there.

The story broke in the Fredericton *Daily Gleaner* on October 20, 1984, under the explosive but deliberately vague headline, "Senior N.B. politician under drug investigation." The story did not name Hatfield, but it said a drug seizure had been made while police searched luggage that was destined for the royal plane. Two days later, Hatfield confirmed publicly that marijuana had been found in his suitcase and repeated his implausible denials. On October 26, Hatfield was formally charged with possession of marijuana.

Hatfield's trial began January 28, 1985, before Andrew Harrigan, chief judge of the Provincial Court. Crown prosecutor David Hughes tried to show that Hatfield's suitcase was in the hands of authorities from the moment it was dropped at the airport, and thus the drugs could not have been planted as Hatfield's lawyers maintained. He called witnesses who suggested that Hatfield was nervous that day, asking the whereabouts of his suitcase as if he had suddenly remembered he had left his drug stash in the pocket. The defence team suggested that the drugs had been planted, possibly by a television reporter who had been making inquiries about the drug seizure the day after the package had been found in the Premier's suitcase. Harrigan decided that the defence theory was plausible and acquitted Hatfield, offering the embattled Premier the benefit of the doubt — a judgment rarely extended to everyday drug users.

The scandal didn't end with Hatfield's acquittal. During the trial, two dogged reporters, Michael Harris of the *Globe and Mail* and Julian Beltrame of Southam News, had stumbled onto the story that four former St. Thomas University students had visited Hatfield's home in January, 1981, where they said they shared drinks, marijuana and cocaine. Then the Premier had flown three of them to Montreal on the government plane and put them up at the Queen Elizabeth Hotel at taxpayers' expense. The story about the students and their strange journey exploded across news wires on February 3, 1985, three months before McKenna was elected Liberal leader. At that moment, the tumultuous love affair between New Brunswick voters and Richard Hatfield ended.

"When he was found with drugs in his baggage, the whole province was abuzz with rumours, and we certainly got our share," recalls Julian Walker. As justice critic, McKenna's advice was to stand back and let Hatfield self-destruct. "His advice to Ray Frenette was to leave this be, don't gore him while he's down," Walker says. "That was Frank's instinct, and I think he was right."

In Fredericton, Hatfield had disappeared, and his ministers and bureaucrats were engaging in open warfare that spilled over into brown envelopes delivered to the Opposition offices. "There was a time toward the end when I remember a press conference Hatfield had," Walker recalls. "It was after the story broke about taking kids to Montreal on the government plane, and Hatfield said 'I'm a gregarious person,' the famous quote. I can remember feeling, the jig's up, there's no way he's going to get over this."

From the moment McKenna won the leadership, he directed the energies of the Liberal office toward preparing for an election. "It was like we were getting on with our lives," Walker recalls. "They could do what they wanted, but we were not going to talk about Hatfield. Frank talked about his vision, he talked about New Brunswick. The work was extremely detailed and exciting."

———

Back in Apohaqui in September, 1985, seventy-seven-year-old Joseph McKenna's arthritic pain became so intense that he finally went to see his doctor, who recommended hip replacement surgery. On October 7, McKenna visited his father in the Moncton Hospital. The next day, he received word that Joseph McKenna had died of a pulmonary embolism. "With farmers, there's no such thing as stopping," McKenna says. "They die when the farming stops. Their work is their life." He travelled home to bury his father in the Catholic cemetery in Sussex, then, still privately grieving, returned to the campaign trail, always living the work ethic he had inherited from his father.

McKenna was becoming a stronger campaigner by the day; however, Landry and Bryden wanted to refine the Liberal advertising and communications strategy that had served them so badly in the past. Guy Thibodeau, the executive director of the Liberal Party, began searching for a bilingual communications expert who also knew something about polling, and he recommended that they hire Francis McGuire, who was working in Ottawa in the office of Quebec Liberal MP Raymond Garneau.

McGuire was born in Halifax, the son of a Nova Scotian of Scottish heritage and his war bride from Paris. The family moved to Montreal when Francis was a child, and he didn't learn English until he returned to the Maritimes to attend high school at the Halifax Grammar School. There he was handed the first book he had ever read in English, *Paradise Lost*. He struggled through high school and then went on to graduate from Dalhousie University with a Bachelor of Arts. He continued his studies in French at the Institut d'études politiques in Paris before graduating with a master's degree in international studies, trade and economics from Johns Hopkins University in Washington, D.C. McGuire's career had allowed him to gain an understanding of the cultures of Ottawa, Quebec and the Maritimes. He had been a special advisor to Lloyd Axworthy when he was Minister of Employment and Immigration and responsible for dispersing job creation funds to Atlantic Canada. He had worked for Transport Canada and Canadian National Railway, and he had been an advisor to the Council of Maritime Premiers. In the summer of 1985, the thirty-three-year-old political animal began working part-time for the McKenna team. In December, McKenna flew to Ottawa and, during an extended breakfast meeting at the Four Seasons Hotel, convinced McGuire to come to New Brunswick full-time in April, 1986.

A team was forming around McKenna. Aldéa Landry became party president and Fern Landry and John Bryden were named co-chairs of the campaign. McGuire, Thibodeau, Walker and Andy Scott, a former leader of the Young Liberals, the jacks of all trades on the election team, called themselves the four horsemen of the apocalypse.

As his first order of business, McGuire set out to refine McKenna's image. The unilingual McKenna would attend the Memramcook Institute outside Moncton for intensive French lessons; six months later, McKenna was able to travel throughout the province and converse with people in both languages. In McGuire's view, McKenna also needed to look more like a premier. "We got him a proper haircut," McGuire recalls. "He's got this big square head. It looked like a box. We went to the barber shop, moved the part and shortened it up so it didn't look like a hood. Frank was saying, 'Gee, I had to pay fifteen dollars for this haircut.' I said, 'That's the world you're living in, so get your head around it.'"

The tattered lawyer's suits, wrinkled khakis, frayed shirts and thread-bare sweaters had to go. At Bryden's request, Arthur Doyle, a dapper conservative dresser, met Frank and Julie McKenna in Saint John one evening for a secret after-hours shopping spree at Jack Calp's, which he deemed the best men's clothing store in the province. Before they arrived, Doyle briefed the legendary haberdasher Norm Calp about what clothes to show the Liberal leader. He was to be offered only dark suits, white shirts, striped ties and black knee socks. Doyle stood off to the side and either shook his head or nodded his approval when McKenna picked out his wardrobe.

"I was pretty frumpy," McKenna admits. "I looked at this as an indignity I had to endure to get where I wanted and do what I wanted to do." He recalls that young Liberal activist Paul Zed would often complain about the way he dressed. "Zed would just say, 'Give me that tie. Jesus, Frank, what am I going to do with you?' And he'd take his tie off and put it on me and say, 'Now, doesn't that look better?'"

McGuire hired Bathurst artist Charles Thériault to create a home-grown advertising campaign. New posters emphasized McKenna's physical strength. "We did two things explicitly," McGuire recalls. "We showed his big, thick woodcutters' neck and his big, huge milking hands. We wanted people to see his hands, particularly in contrast to Hatfield's. A lot of the imagery was purely physical. He was thick and wide and that became part of it — he's a working man. He's an intellectual lawyer and all that, but he works. That's the image, but that's also who he is."

"They would take two days to shoot a thirty-second ad," McKenna recalls. "You'd sit there for hours. Later on I just couldn't take that bullshit anymore. I was always glad when the campaign was over because I'd get to go back to work and I'd be in total control of the environment."

McGuire was also determined to correct McKenna's deficiencies as a public speaker. Julian Beltrame had written that McKenna tended to sound "like Donald Duck" and was more of a yeller than an orator. McGuire took McKenna to Montreal to take voice lessons from a retired opera singer. "He couldn't breathe, and therefore he couldn't pause correctly," McGuire says. "And he'd keep on waving his hands in front of his face. He was too rapid-fire. He started techniques of breathing, speaking slowly and learning how to stop at punctuation marks. He really had tremendous control over his body. In two days he learned to breathe, he learned elocution, how to stand."

After his trip to Montreal, McKenna carried a laminated card in his pocket to remind him to speak slowly, use his diaphragm to breathe, keep his hands down and always think of the message before he started speaking. At Bryden's insistence, he also dropped the flowery clichés and mixed metaphors that had infected his speeches and become a running joke among political commentators. His seventy-page response to the Throne Speech in April, 1986, which Bryden still considers the worst political speech he has ever heard, included such McKenna gems as, "Our country is not a melting pot, our province is not a melting pot — we have woven many colourful threads in a great tapestry and that is not a cause for foot-dragging and hand-wringing, but joy and celebration," and "We must race toward this mother lode of wealth, the way a thirsty traveller hurries to a spring of fresh water." When questioned by reporters about his use of language, McKenna responded, "You live by the sword, you die by the sword. I like that style." Like it or not, Bryden shut him down, and McKenna learned his lesson.

During the trip to Montreal, McGuire bluntly told McKenna that he needed to know his physical needs. When did he like to sleep? Did he need an afternoon nap? Did he usually have a bowel movement in the morning? Did he need to be alone with Julie five times a day or once a week? "I went back to Ruth McCrea and said, 'I asked Frank a bunch of important questions, so here's the structure of the day from now on,'" McGuire says. "We organized the campaign around his physical schedule."

At the Tories' annual convention in November, 1985, Hatfield survived a call from dissidents within his party for a leadership review, he attacked McKenna, and he reminded delegates that, above all else, he knew how to win elections. Hatfield seemed to determined to go to the polls; he would only leave the premier's office when voters threw him out. As Dalton Camp would say, in politics "sometimes there are worse things than losing." After the leadership review, McKenna told Canadian Press reporter Chris Morris that "only very naïve people are expressing the view that Richard Hatfield might be a pushover." In an interview with the *Globe and Mail*, McKenna said he feared Hatfield was sick but not dead. "There are a lot of markets where the media doesn't penetrate in any meaningful way," he noted. "There are some parts of the province that rely on the Quebec press rather than the New Brunswick press. We don't have a French-language province-wide daily. We're split up into regions where there are completely different thought processes."

Privately, McKenna admired Hatfield. "He had a lot of class in many ways," he says. "I always thought his failures were often failures of effort. I've always taken the view that Bricklin is something that should not be criticized. That was a noble effort to punch beyond our reach. You can't fault him for that. My work was a lot more disciplined. I would never come to a meeting late. I would never miss a meeting. But Hatfield would often not show up for appointments. He didn't go to cabinet. In my own value system, it was a terrible insult not to return a phone call or to miss a meeting or not to be present when you are scheduled to be present. Philosophically, he represented a more liberal view of New Brunswick than his constituency would support, and I always admired that. He was ahead of the wave. His inclinations were very liberal. I admired him for being a free spirit."

As McGuire polished McKenna's image, Hatfield dodged the media, following Camp's advice to "ignore the thundering herd." In his *Telegraph-*

Journal column, Don Hoyt noted the growing contrast between the two leaders. McKenna was open and accessible, as Opposition leaders tend to be, but he was also showing the media he was a man of substance. "McKenna demonstrates an in-depth knowledge of the matters he's dealing with," Hoyt wrote. "At his last press conference he gave one reporter a quick lesson in how the 'complex' equalization formula works. Hatfield, on the other hand, often acts as if he had been passed his formal statement and a one-page briefing paper to read on the elevator taking him from his second-floor office to the press conference one storey down."

Hoyt also noted that Hatfield had never been able to master French and depended on simultaneous translation to take questions from French reporters. McKenna had mastered his second language to the point where he was able to respond to reporters in French.

On February 10, 1986, Liberal candidate Roland Beaulieu faced Conservative Charles Fournier in a by-election in Edmundston, the riding that had been ruled by Jean-Maurice Simard until he was appointed to the Senate in June, 1985. This bellwether riding had chosen the government side for the past fifty years.

"The only safe seats left for Hatfield are in francophone New Brunswick, and this is the safest of the safe. If we win this, it would mean we have captured the Tory *Bismarck*," McKenna said. Then, borrowing the words of former heavyweight champion Joe Louis, he added, "It would mean Hatfield can run, but he can't hide." McKenna poured his energy into Edmundston, vacationing there with his family and making more than two dozen campaign swings through the riding. He knocked on three hundred doors and mailed three thousand Christmas cards to voters in the riding. Beaulieu won by 1,801 votes. The Tories came within 123 votes of losing their hundred-dollar deposit by failing to capture half as many votes as the winner.

The Edmundston disaster confirmed Hatfield as yesterday's man. While the Liberals ran a campaign choreographed from a central office, Hatfield insisted on running without modern polling or a strategy; these political methods offended his ideas about how democracy should work. "I'm probably a nineteenth-century liberal," he said. "That's why I hate what is happening to the mechanics of politics. It doesn't allow a person to come up to you and say, 'I've got a problem.' I still believe that what democracy is really about is protecting one person, not the majority. I hate polls. I speak for the minority, and the ultimate minority, of course, is the individual."

From the moment Francis McGuire arrived in New Brunswick, McKenna embraced the kind of politics Hatfield so despised. McKenna's "Agenda for Change," as Bryden christened the new Liberal platform, emerged from the work of McGuire and pollster George Perlin.

"We brought about twenty people around the table, anglophones, francophones, people from each region, and came out with some hypotheses," McGuire says. "You'd spend a two-day think-tank session on what policies were better, and you'd get everybody all over the map, total disagreement. George and I would always laugh because we would go away and do the research and come back and say, 'Now that we've done the research on the hypotheses, here's what we've found,' and every time we did it, the twenty people around the table would all say, 'I told you so.' And we're saying, 'Holy shit, they really didn't start there at all.' It started to create a team."

In March, 1986, Perlin delivered a report that helped to set the agenda for McKenna's ten years in the premier's office. The report was Perlin's interpretation of a baseline poll that involved lengthy surveys of a thousand New Brunswickers clustered in five areas — Saint John, the south and southwest, Moncton, the northeast, and the independent-minded Madawaska County.

Perlin reported a Liberal lead in every region and in both language groups, a lead that bridged every social divide. Voters expressed widespread negative feelings about Hatfield, and Tory loyalty was breaking down. "The issue of Mr. Hatfield's premiership is clearly settled," Perlin wrote. "Voters generally believe Mr. McKenna would do better, but this is still probably more a function of their low regard for Mr. Hatfield than any clear perception of what Mr. McKenna represents. The *Hatfield* government has been defeated; the objective now is to ensure the defeat of the *Conservative* government."

Moreover, the poll revealed that the political climate had been poisoned; people no longer trusted politicians or public institutions. Sixty-seven per cent expressed a low estimation of the competence of political leaders; seventy-two per cent doubted the integrity of politicians; eight-two per cent expressed concerns about the level of trust that could be placed in politicians; ninety-three per cent expressed a lack of confidence in their ability to influence government.

"The general pattern reflects a broader sentiment of disenchantment with politicians and politics that *cannot* be explained simply by opinions about Mr. Hatfield," wrote Perlin, who for years had been tracking trends of declining public confidence in political institutions. "Among many members of the sample, the belief that politicians are dishonest, untruthful and untrustworthy is linked to a perception that government is ineffective and that the average person has little control over the political process." Perlin advised McKenna to avoid political rhetoric, exaggerated policy proposals and personal attacks on Hatfield.

McKenna followed Perlin's advice, along with a Machiavellian twist devised by McGuire. "Frank was trained that every time you see a microphone, you say, 'I refuse to talk about Mr. Hatfield's problems,'" McGuire says. "If someone asked, 'What do you think of this tie?' McKenna would respond, 'I refuse to talk about Mr. Hatfield's problems, that's a really nice tie.' The campaign plan was as simple as can be, just repeat it, repeat it and never say anything else."

On the economic front, Perlin reported that fifty-seven per cent of the sample group said New Brunswick's economic situation was getting worse, and eighty per cent said it was getting harder for average families to achieve the standard of living they wanted. Half of the sample said some part of their family income came from government payments other than family allowance.

Perlin exposed widespread attitudes of dependence on a government few people trusted, what he would call a kind of "dependency syndrome." For example, if it were found that not much more could be done to create new jobs in New Brunswick, fifty-five per cent of the people interviewed said they would choose social assistance and stay in the province rather than move to other provinces to find work. At the same time, many people suffered from deep insecurity and believed that esteem for New Brunswick had eroded in the rest of the country.

"The overriding preoccupation of New Brunswickers, regardless of any social cleavage, is unemployment," Perlin wrote. "In spontaneous response to the question 'What do you think is the most important problem facing New Brunswick today?' sixty-five per cent gave unemployment as their first response and an additional nine per cent mentioned it as a second or third response. This substantial level of agreement in response to an open-ended question of this kind is very unusual.

"Unquestionably, the central issue in the campaign must be unemployment," he continued. "The best approach to the problem, given in particular the mood in the political culture, is to be candid. The public's views of the causes of economic disparity suggest that some frank discussion of the fact that New Brunswick needs to think about the development of new kinds of resources and products that are less affected by the costs of penetrating distant markets would be understood. Attention could be drawn to the increasing importance of the service sector in the economy and the fact that there are services which can be sold in distant markets through new communications technologies. Attention could also be drawn to the potential for developing and marketing such products as computer software."

The themes expressed in Perlin's first report would define the leadership of Frank McKenna. However, Perlin, who has known McKenna since he was a graduate student at Queen's University, maintains that pollsters shouldn't take too much credit for a politician's success. His reports merely reinforced what McKenna understood instinctively. "What the research did was give him confidence that he was right, and that it was important," Perlin says.

Although McGuire agrees that Perlin's conclusions allowed McKenna to follow his instincts, he observes that, before the first baseline survey, McKenna's plans to transform New Brunswick society were vague and poorly defined. After receiving Perlin's report, he was convinced that pursuing the province's destiny meant changing people's attitudes, restoring their confidence in themselves and in their public institutions. Modernizing the economy meant diversification and training workers for the new world of information technology. The province was being swept into a period of profound global economic upheaval. Free trade, the mechanization of traditional resource-based industries and the information revolution would change New Brunswick society forever. McKenna told New Brunswickers that this transformation was an opportunity, not something to fear. He assured them that they now had an ordinary man, a farm boy turned leader, who would show them the way.

McKenna was determined to make New Brunswickers once again believe that the spectacular and the grand were possible, that they could form a community based upon a single economic impulse — a vision of a better society that W.S. MacNutt argued had been slipping away since Confederation. In 1986, McGuire remembers meeting in the boardroom on the top floor of the Opposition offices with McKenna, Bryden and

Landry to plan their agenda. The conversation turned to the fact that New Brunswickers had descended deep into a valley of self-doubt. "Our most important goal was to change the psychology," McGuire says. "We had to make New Brunswickers think they could be winners. And that was the basis of everything that happened after that. That became the overwhelming challenge."

———

The Liberals had been expecting an election call in the fall of 1986. When it didn't come, they spent the next year refining their strategy. In January, 1987, McKenna and his advisors travelled to Boston to meet Massachusetts Governor Michael Dukakis, who would later become an unsuccessful Democratic presidential nominee. Dukakis was credited with engineering the "Massachusetts Miracle," transforming a resource-based economy by attracting new high-tech industries. "Certainly we felt a great deal of sympathy for the philosophy behind your approach — strong government and personal leadership in helping the private sector rise to the challenge," McKenna wrote in a January 28, 1987, letter to Dukakis. The governor had hired a commissioner of economic development to work in his office, reporting directly to him, a strategy McKenna adopted as part of his platform.

Meanwhile, the real election race was being fought at Liberal nomination meetings, wide-open, raucous affairs that attracted thousands of delegates. There's nothing like the scent of victory to energize a political party. In the riding of Memramcook, half the eligible voters came to the convention as card-carrying Liberals. By the time the election was called, there were 180,000 registered Liberals in the province out of 450,000 eligible voters. Before the election was called, McKenna commissioned Donald Savoie to prepare a transition plan, a thick document McKenna carried with him on the campaign trail.

Finally, on August 29, 1987, the last day Richard Hatfield could remain in power without creating a constitutional crisis, he called an election for October 13. It would be a forty-five-day campaign, the longest allowed by New Brunswick law, giving Hatfield every possible opportunity to pull a political rabbit out of his hat. "In politics, you can't take any chances," Hatfield joked with reporters on the first day of the campaign. "I consulted numerologists and astrologers. I checked my biorhythms. I called the lobster fishermen and the duck hunters."

At the Liberals' opening news conference of the campaign, held in the Miramichi Room at the Beaverbrook Hotel, reporters asked McKenna what he planned to do about patronage. McKenna said that, while he agreed the patronage of the Hatfield years had been excessive, he wasn't going to be able to eliminate such an entrenched cultural and political tradition. For the next three days, newspapers carried stories about McKenna's refusal to stop patronage. McKenna's communications guru wasn't concerned. Long ago, McGuire had learned not to read headlines literally. When he was working for Lloyd Axworthy, the Winnipeg *Free Press* ran screaming headlines about patronage in his boss's riding. An angry Axworthy asked McGuire what he was going to do about the negative publicity.

"I said, 'Yeah, and every person in Winnipeg is saying, Fuck those Quebeckers, I got a piece of the pie, too. You'll get elected forever, so stop complaining.'

"I remember John Bryden coming in and saying, 'Jesus, Francis, you're in charge of communications, what are you going to do about this?'

"Every time someone writes an article like this, I'm going to send him a hundred bucks," McGuire replied. "This is gold. Bring it on, this is exactly the story we want." The stories were a big flashing light saying that Frank McKenna was telling the truth. "That was a great start to the campaign," McGuire says. "The media were saying, 'Hey, with this stuff on patronage, maybe Hatfield can pull it out.' I was saying, 'This is it, Hatfield is done.'"

Inexplicably, the Conservatives were focusing their campaign on their embattled leader, running television and radio ads with the Premier speaking to voters in long soliloquies. "I felt like throwing away my advertising and buying some of their ads," McGuire recalls.

The Liberals hired a bus and decorated it Liberal red, a mobile bill-board that carried the leader throughout the province on carefully planned routes that had been test-driven several times by campaign workers with too much time on their hands. On the first day of the bus tour, McGuire ordered that the schedule be followed rigidly. If the bus was to leave at 9:03 a.m., then it was to pull away at that moment. If members of the media were left behind, so be it. McGuire assigned two trail cars to pick up stragglers.

"First they said, 'Yeah, sure, we've heard that before,' then they said 'Holy shit, these guys are actually leaving without us,'" McGuire recalls. "I was hoping we'd leave five or six behind the first time to really make the point. We wanted them to think, 'These guys aren't kidding. They're organized and they're serious.'"

Despite how certain he was of victory, McKenna maintained his intensity throughout the campaign, rising early every morning to jog before boarding the bus. "I always had this lingering sense that Hatfield would rise from the dead, I had that kind of emotional reaction, but my rational self said, We're going to win this thing and win it pretty big," McKenna recalls. "I just couldn't believe everybody was lying to me, and the field we had was so good, so strong."

Canadian Press reporter Chris Morris, who travelled with Hatfield, was stunned by the open disgust voters expressed for the Premier. "It was traumatic, I've never seen anything like it," she recalls. "He would hold out his hand to shake hands with people, and if they even took his hand, they would wipe their hand afterwards. It was terrible. Horrible. They would just turn and walk away when they saw him coming. I've never covered a campaign like it."

On the other hand, the McKenna campaign was moving from strength to strength. "McKenna was obviously having a wonderful time," Morris says. "People were happy to see him, they were happy to take his hand. But he could have been a yellow dog, really, it didn't matter who he was, Hatfield was in such terrible shape. He had overstayed his welcome."

As election day approached, John Bryden commissioned a few scattered polls and found the Liberals were leading even in the safest Tory seats. "I asked, 'If we're winning these seats, where are we losing?' I couldn't find anywhere. I became convinced that we could win them all. That's what I began working toward in the last week or so." For two and a half years, Bryden had worked night and day to prepare for the election. On election day, he found himself at loose ends, so he wrote letters of appreciation to his campaign workers and staff and then drove around Fredericton delivering them by hand to kill time.

After the polls closed, McKenna was back in Chatham, watching the election results roll in with his family and his friend David Cadogan. Early in the evening, it was obvious that the Liberals were winning in a landslide, and McKenna started getting dressed and preparing to address the province. As he rushed past the television set, CBC suggested there was the possibility of a sweep. "He just froze for a minute," Cadogan recalls. "He turned dark red as the enormity of the thing swept over him. He was stunned and overwhelmed by the results. Then he gathered himself, turned on his heel and left the room."

In Hartland, a fragile-looking Richard Hatfield emerged from his brother's white saltbox home to concede an election in which he had lost his own seat. Only two of his candidates were still leading in their ridings. "I simply want to say how much I have loved the last seventeen years of serving the people of New Brunswick," he told reporters. "I'm very sorry, as leader of the party, and I accept full responsibility for the significant defeat of our party. The people of this province wanted change, and they got change."

The curling rink at the Miramichi Exhibition Centre in Chatham was jammed to the rafters and decorated with signs declaring the Miramichi to be "McKenna Country" — in celebration of a newly adopted native son. Only Tory street fighter Percy Mockler still hung on to his seat in Madawaska South, with several polls still left to report. McKenna plunged into the crowd, his campaign theme song "The Walk of Life" by Dire Straits blaring over the cheers of the crowd. Dressed in a blue suit with a red carnation on his lapel, trailed by Julie and Toby, McKenna pushed his way to the stage and declared, "You are looking at the happiest man in all of New Brunswick."

As he addressed the crowd, still referring to his victory as a "strong majority" and expressing his condolences for candidates for both parties who had gone down to defeat, CBC Television flashed the news on the screen that it was a Liberal sweep. After expressing respect for Richard Hatfield and gratitude for his service, McKenna stepped back and smiled. "We are witnessing the dawning of a new era," he said. As the crowd chanted his name, a man near the stage shouted, "We got fifty-eight."

"We got fifty-eight?" McKenna asked. He winced, paused for a moment, and appeared almost embarrassed by the magnitude of what had happened before turning back to face the crowd with a broad smile. Toby McKenna, who was standing on stage, remembers his father appearing more nervous as more Liberal names were posted on the board. "You must be excited, this is a sweep," Toby said. "Actually, I'm not," his father replied. "This isn't what I expected at all." Still thinking as a tactician, McKenna was convinced that the lack of opposition would mean trouble for his party. Four years down the road, voters might be so anxious to restore a political balance in New Brunswick that they would punish the Liberals.

"The no-opposition was just another issue to deal with. 'Hadn't thought of that one, put it on the list,'" says McGuire, who was coordinating media interviews in Chatham on election night. "There was no euphoria at all.

It was kind of weird. I didn't feel much from Frank or Fern or anybody else. We were all working. There was no day off."

Moments after his victory speech, McKenna was interviewed live by the CBC's Barbara Frum on *The Journal*. She was interested, not in McKenna's unprecedented victory in New Brunswick, but in his position on the Meech Lake constitutional accord, about which McKenna had expressed reservations during his time as Opposition leader. Opponents of the Accord were already rallying around McKenna as their new champion.

"Are you going to try to change the deal?" Frum asked bluntly.

McKenna, appearing fatigued and unsure of how to handle a live interrogation from one of the best in the business, only said that he wanted to make improvements to the deal to ensure a "strong national identity for Canada" and to protect the rights of the francophone minority in New Brunswick.

When McKenna's plane landed in Fredericton, RCMP cruisers escorted him to the banquet room at the Fredericton Inn, where the crowd picked him up and passed him over their heads to the stage. At 7:25 the next morning, McKenna arrived at the office and started conducting media interviews, thereby sending a message that he would bring a new work ethic to the capital city. However, eager as he was to begin navigating a new economic future for his province, Frum's interview had been a warning shot across his bow. Frank McKenna would soon be thrust into a crisis of conscience that would define his place in Canadian history and dominate his agenda during his first term in office. He would also soon learn that, although he had painted the province Liberal red, New Brunswickers were as far from dreaming a common dream as they had ever been.

Frank McKenna and Brian Mulroney.

6

RETURN TO ACADIE

Mulroney looked across the river at Quebec and said, "All this will be lost if Meech fails."

— *Frank McKenna, diary entry, May 27, 1990*

In the novel *Pélagie-la-Charrette*, Antonine Maillet tells the story of a resolute band of Acadians who in the late 1700s returned home after living in exile in Georgia. Only those who held their tongues survived *le grand dérangement*, Maillet writes. When the people of Acadie crept back into their homeland, they remained silent, a hidden society, before they cautiously allowed themselves to be heard once again. According to Maillet, "In 1880, a hundred years after the return from exile, on tiptoe, in by the back door, Acadie stepped out into the front yard to sniff what the weather was and to get news of the family." She continues, "From all the creeks and all the bays and all the islands, they perked up their heads and cocked their eyes open. And that's how they came to rediscover each other."

Pélagie-the-Grouch calls out, "Bestir yourselves, you bunch of flabby asses! No one here's going to spoon-feed you or tuck you in bed. Come out of your holes and take your place in the sun. The wild geese are back from the south, time to start turning the earth again and casting our nets into the sea. Come out, you lazybones, the weather's veered to fine."

In the fall of 1987, a century after they stepped out of isolation, Acadians were on the final leg of a long journey toward equality and a political legitimacy that would ensure a future for their language and culture. Louis Robichaud had offered them a promise of equal opportunity. Richard Hatfield had fulfilled Little Louis's promises and welcomed Acadians into mainstream provincial politics. But the aspirations of Acadie were crumbling along with their champion. For years, Hatfield had restrained the formidable anti-French forces in his party. Now Conservative dissidents were turning to a new anti-bilingualism party. In 1986, members of the right-wing Christian Heritage Party, along with the Association for the Preservation of English in Canada, formed a Maritime chapter of the Confederation of Regions party based in New Brunswick. "There were always tensions with those people under Hatfield, but the discipline of power kept them in the party," says Dalton Camp. "When the party lost, they fell out."

In Hatfield's final years, the Tories had begun the process of revising the Official Languages Act, introduced by Louis Robichaud's Liberals in 1969. A comprehensive report recommending the expansion of official bilingualism and documenting the state of bilingualism had been prepared for Hatfield by Bernard Poirier, an architect of the original act, and Michel Bastarache, a constitutional lawyer who would later become the first Acadian appointed to the Supreme Court of Canada. Among other things, the report contained the results of a survey exposing the depth of intolerance among anglophones who resented Hatfield's recognition of the needs of Acadians. This survey demonstrated just how fragile the Tory peace had become. Without a strategy to cool the simmering tensions, Hatfield decided to release the thousand-page report and ordered that public hearings be held in the fall of 1984.

The hearings degenerated into disgraceful exhibitions of bigotry. On the Miramichi, an opponent of official bilingualism threw an egg at a member of the panel. In Moncton, a session ended in a melée of insults, a shouting match between English and French. Acadians were humiliated. The final report on revisions to the Official Languages Act was tabled in the spring of 1985 and left to gather dust by a government concerned only with political survival.

A child of the English south, Frank McKenna had grown up mimicking the view of his neighbours that "those goddam French get everything." However, at the University of New Brunswick Law School, he made friends with impressive Acadians such as Fernand and Aldéa Landry and began to see the story of Acadie in a more sympathetic light. When he began practicing law on the Miramichi, he frequently travelled into the heart of Acadie, where he found a rich culture that he deemed worthy of great admiration. In Fredericton, he found the ugly expressions of outrage by anglophones offensive. There was a perception that French was being forced on the public service. There was a perception that you had to speak French to get promotions. There was a perception that more money was going into the north than into the south. Few of these perceptions had anything to do with reality. McKenna had no sympathy for anglophones who voiced these opinions and who openly expressed their irritation to public servants who didn't speak perfect English. "Acadians experienced these slights every day of the week, every hour of the day," he notes.

At first glance, militant anglophones saw McKenna as one of their own, a simple English farm boy from Apohaqui. Surely he wouldn't sell them out the way Richard Hatfield had. However, their farm boy was learning to speak French and attending northern festivals, immersing himself in Acadian culture. His key advisors and cabinet ministers were Acadians, whose intellect and political determination he respected. "As time went on, they came to the conclusion that I was cut from the same cloth as Louis Robichaud and Richard Hatfield in wanting to protect the rights of the two linguistic communities and to ensure equality of access," McKenna says.

He would have preferred to spend his first term calming cultural tensions at home. However, as McKenna struggled to resolve Richard Hatfield's most contentious piece of unfinished business, the journey of Acadie became linked to the survival of the country.

Hatfield made his final stand on the national stage on April 30, 1987, when he attended a First Ministers' Conference at an estate overlooking Meech Lake in the Gatineau Hills of Quebec. On the agenda were a series of amendments to the constitution. After a ten-hour session, the premiers and Prime Minister Brian Mulroney emerged from a conference room with a deal to amend Canada's constitution, this time with the agreement of Quebec, an accord they claimed would heal the wounds of Pierre Trudeau's "night of the long knives" in 1981. "What you have now is a whole country as opposed to part of a country," Mulroney announced to reporters. "I am profoundly convinced that, as a result of today's discussions, the bonds of Confederation will be strengthened and the unity of our people will be enhanced."

As details of the deal emerged, Acadians began to express grave reservations about the document Hatfield had signed. The accord would allow Quebec as a distinct society to *preserve* and *promote* the language and culture of the French majority, but allowed francophone minorities only to *preserve* their language and culture. Simple preservation, in the view of Fern Landry and other Acadian leaders, would result in assimilation and certain cultural death.

"Our position on Meech was the result of a lot of thinking on the part of the francophone advisory committee," Landry argues. "Meech Lake went against traditional Liberal views on the relationship of the two linguistic communities in Canada. Meech was clear — there were a majority of francophones in Quebec and a minority of anglophones, and Canada was a marriage between Quebec francophones and anglophones in the rest of the country. The constitution from then on was to be interpreted in that light. We wanted the concept that was portrayed by Meech changed to reflect the fact that there were significant francophone minorities across the country and a significant anglophone minority in Quebec."

Acadians had no intention of becoming second-class francophones behind Quebeckers. "We had a lot of debates with people in Quebec," Landry reports. "I must say at times it would have been easy to become emotional because their perception was very self-centred, and it was obvious that they weren't thinking about francophones outside Quebec." Opposition to Meech was a question of cultural survival, and surely after their long struggles Acadians had a right to assert themselves as a people.

McKenna began to state publicly that he had reservations about the accord and would seek changes to the document when he was elected premier. No one paid much attention to the young leader of the Opposition in New Brunswick. The country did pay attention in May, 1987, when Pierre Trudeau broke three years of silence to publish a scathing essay in *La Presse* and the *Toronto Star* denouncing the new constitutional accord. "Those Canadians who fought for a single Canada, bilingual and multicultural, can say goodbye to their dream," he wrote. "We are henceforth to have two Canadas, each defined in terms of its language."

Like so many other young Canadians in the late 1960s, Frank McKenna had fallen under Trudeau's spell. He had worked for the Liberals in the 1968 campaign and had introduced Trudeau when he spoke at the University of New Brunswick Law School in the early seventies. McKenna accepted as faith Trudeau's vision of Canada as a country that maintained a balance between the rights of individuals and the protection of minorities. As McKenna absorbed Trudeau's carefully timed intervention, he knew that in a matter of months, when he took over as premier, he would be asked to stand either with Trudeau or with the new vision of Canada championed by Brian Mulroney.

On June 2, 1987, Mulroney and the premiers gathered in Ottawa to finalize a legal document that expressed the agreement reached at Meech Lake. Mulroney opened the meeting by addressing Trudeau's criticisms, saying, "He still thinks he is governing this country." Author Andrew Cohen reports that Mulroney continued to attack Trudeau until an impatient Richard Hatfield interrupted to say, "Look, will you forget about him." According to Cohen, as the meeting dragged on into the night, British Columbia Premier Bill Vander Zalm expressed a need to catch his flight home; Mulroney promised a jet to fly him back when the meeting was over. Hatfield interjected with a grin, "Perhaps you'd give me the jet? There's a marvellous party going on in New York this evening."

On the morning of June 3, 1987, Mulroney announced that a constitutional text had been negotiated to bring Quebec back into the Canadian family. "It was a time for healing in this land," Mulroney said. "We all hoped someday to be able to set aside our differences and work together to accomplish a common destiny as Canadians." The deal was to be ratified by all ten provinces by June 30, 1990.

Back in New Brunswick, McKenna's election strategists worried about the political implications of the accord. On June 8, 1987, Julian Walker wrote a memo to McKenna suggesting that Hatfield might use Meech Lake to make the Liberals appear weak. "Our position on Meech Lake to date is, in a word, 'reservations,'" Walker wrote. "This has carried us for more than a month, but I believe time is running out when this can serve us any longer." He recommended that McKenna take a firmer stand. He suggested several options but preferred a statement such as, "We oppose Meech Lake in its present form and will be seeking amendments to make it an acceptable document."

A decision to fight the accord to the bitter end was what most old Liberals would prefer, Walker noted. However, that option had "grave implications for an election campaign and the early part of a governing term. We will be sure to fight the campaign on the accord, even if Hatfield waits until fall. We must be prepared to take on nine premiers and the Prime Minister when in government." Walker added with remarkable political foresight, "Destiny may take us down this road, but I doubt it is in our political interest to do so, and probably we don't have the political will to do so."

The main political danger, Walker warned, was to do nothing and allow Hatfield to label McKenna as too weak to take a stand or, even worse, allow the Tories to recognize the flaws in Meech Lake and propose amendments to deal with the concerns of Acadians. "I believe a firm, moderate and progressive response can put to bed, once and for all, the complaint about us 'not taking a stand' and put the icing on your election victory," Walker wrote.

On June 23, 1987, Hatfield asked the New Brunswick Legislature to refer the accord to the Law Amendments Committee for public hearings. If Hatfield recognized the inherent flaws in the accord for Acadians, he was politically astute enough to know there was nothing to be gained by exploring the details of the document. He played down the significance of the accord, insisting that it simply reflected the reality of Canada and responded to the "defect" of the 1982 patriation of the constitution in the face of Quebec's dissent. Heeding Walker's advice, McKenna rose in the Legislature to clarify his position. Liberals welcomed the plan to bring Quebec into the constitutional family; however, the details of the document needed to be revised. First, the accord eroded the concept of a strong federal government. "Throughout our history, a strong national government has been in the best interests of all Canadians," he said. "It has certainly been in the best interests of the less wealthy provinces of this country. The government of Canada must not be hamstrung in continuing to deliver quality programs of benefit to all Canadians."

He then turned to his most significant objection. "The fundamental character of Quebec is recognized in the accord," he acknowledged. However, he went on to say, "The fundamental character of New Brunswick should also be recognized. In the constitutional accord, francophones outside Quebec receive inadequate recognition of their essential rights. I believe that the Parliament of Canada has an obligation to *preserve* and *promote* the rights of francophones outside Quebec, and I will be encouraging the addition of wording to this effect." He added that, as Premier, he would protect New Brunswick francophone rights in the constitution, with or without Meech Lake, by seeking an amendment to the constitution that expressed the province's essential character as a bicultural society.

When closing the debate, Hatfield warned that changes required the unanimity of all provinces and the Parliament. Hatfield noted that he had already attempted to improve the wording on minority rights, but that his proposals had been rejected at the bargaining table. Afterwards, although he continued to speak in support of Meech Lake, he failed to put the accord to a vote in the Legislature.

In August, 1987, as McKenna prepared to appear before the Special Joint Commission on the Constitution in Ottawa, Walker wrote another memo to McKenna suggesting that he stop offering gratuitous words in support of the accord. "We needn't be so positive about the 'spirit of

Meech Lake,'" Walker wrote. "For most people in this province, Meech Lake was a deal cooked up hastily with a lot of horse-trading over a long, long night and not to be viewed as any sacred sacrament."

On August 25, 1987, McKenna appeared before the commission in Ottawa. He began his presentation by insisting that changes to the accord could be made if they met certain criteria. "First, any amendment must not nullify the principles agreed to in the accord. If we are to survive as a nation, we cannot go on indefinitely with one province politically isolated outside of the constitution and the constitutional process. Second, any amendment should further advance or clarify the rights of Canadians. It is disturbing to Canadians to hear that groups or regions may be abandoned in this process."

After making his arguments for a strong central government, McKenna returned to his main theme. "I believe that our constitution must recognize the obligation of Parliament to promote the existence of both linguistic groups throughout our nation. To only preserve a minority is to condemn it to eventual assimilation. Surely this is not the collective destiny we intend for our country. The principle of equality of the two official languages and the two linguistic communities is the fundamental characteristic of our province."

"It seems to me you are a possible threat to the accord," MP Charles Hamelin said, challenging the young leader.

"It seems to me I am also a possible source of comfort to many Canadians who feel improvements can be made," McKenna replied without missing a beat.

Two days later, Trudeau appeared before the commission, solidifying his position as the spiritual leader of the anti-Meech forces. When McKenna buried the Hatfield government in October, he was embraced as the one politician in Canada who had the political power to defend Trudeau's vision of Canada.

After the election, McKenna assembled his team in the premier's office. The most difficult decision he had to make was whether he would choose Fernand Landry or John Bryden as his deputy minister in the premier's office. "It became obvious to me that John had very substantial skills, but the demands of a bilingual New Brunswick were such that, especially with an anglophone premier, we should have a deputy minister with a strong respect and competence in French. And also Fern had some important skills that would have tended to complement me. He had good people skills, a gentleness and an ability to work with people, where John Bryden's strengths would have tended to parallel my strengths. My feeling was that Fern was a better choice."

While McKenna had great respect for Bryden's organizational skills and political toughness, he saw in Fern Landry the man he needed at his right hand. Bryden had taught McKenna how to make decisions, and his protégé had learned his lessons well. Landry reluctantly agreed to give McKenna four years in the premier's office, and when McKenna announced the appointment, Bryden returned home to his farm.

On October 28, 1987, McKenna noted in his diary, "Depressing day. John B. left in a huff. Ruth gone home with a headache. Everybody is obviously unhappy." When *Telegraph-Journal* columnist Don Hoyt reached Bryden by telephone, Bryden insisted he wasn't disappointed by Landry's appointment. "I didn't want the job," he said. "I hope to stay close to the Premier and Fern, but I really do want to return to the private sector." On October 31, the day Hoyt's column was published, McKenna wrote, "Story re John B. not bad. Simply indicates he wants to return to the private sector." Eventually, Bryden returned to the premier's office as the industrial commissioner.

With Fern Landry soothing ruffled feathers in the office, McKenna appointed Aldéa Landry Minister of Intergovernmental Affairs and Deputy Premier and handed her the Meech Lake file. He was confident she would bring the passion of her heritage to the job. Born in the tiny Acadian village of Ste-Cécile on the island of Lamèque in the northeastern corner of the province, Aldéa Landry had absolute faith that McKenna was on the verge of fundamentally transforming the character of the province. In November, 1987, when McKenna made his first appearance at a First Ministers' Conference in Ottawa, Aldéa Landry found herself sitting directly behind McKenna and beside her husband, who passed her a note that said simply, "It's a long way from Ste-Cécile to here."

McKenna convinced McGuire to stay on as Aldéa Landry's deputy minister. In that position, McGuire returned to familiar territory. When he was working for Quebec MP Raymond Garneau in Ottawa, he had been embroiled in the debate within the federal Liberal Party about the nature of a constitutional deal that could accommodate Quebec. McGuire advised McKenna that what Quebec had gained at Meech Lake couldn't be taken away, but he believed the accord could be improved to address New Brunswick's concerns.

"We started with a basic strategy not to rip down what had been proposed but to add to it to fill the gap," McGuire says. However, when he took McKenna's proposals to Ottawa, federal officials appeared uninterested. "I think their view was, 'We'll give them a few more transfer payments and we'll shut those boys up. We'll handle Frank McKenna.'"

Aldéa Landry was equally discouraged by the initial response from Ottawa. "They were just patting us on the head and saying, 'You're going to pass Meech Lake, you cannot *not* pass it,'" she recalls. "It don't think they were listening to what we were saying: that there had to be some changes, otherwise it would not pass in New Brunswick."

Meanwhile, Ottawa began sending messages that, without McKenna's support of Meech Lake and free trade, about which the new Liberal government was also expressing reservations, New Brunswick would suffer economically. On October 22, 1987, John Bryden attended a meeting in Saint John with federal officials at which he was warned that there would be no multi-billion-dollar Canadian patrol frigate contract for the Irving family's shipyard unless New Brunswick agreed to support Meech Lake and free trade. "We, of course, said we weren't prepared to compromise on a question of principle," McKenna noted in his diary.

On November 5, 1987, when McKenna travelled to Quebec City to attend the funeral of former premier René Lévesque, he met briefly with Premier Robert Bourassa to express his concerns about Meech Lake. He recorded that Bourassa suggested "separatist forces would be aroused if Meech Lake wasn't signed." Bourassa responded to his concerns about the apparent lack of consideration for women's rights in the accord with, "You can't please the women, forget it."

A week later, Bourassa met in Moncton with the leaders of the Société des Acadiens et Acadiennes du Nouveau-Brunswick to discuss Meech Lake. Emerging from the meeting, he announced to reporters that Acadian leaders no longer opposed the accord. After several confusing days of media speculation about where Acadian leaders stood, the Société announced its support for the new constitutional package. As the debate over the accord intensified across the country, McKenna found himself in the odd position of taking a more militant stand on minority language rights than the leaders of the Société des Acadiens et Acadiennes.

"It was a blow because their support was needed for us to convince Bourassa to open the Accord," McGuire says. "Once Bourassa got Acadian support, his position became more entrenched. We felt that we had the real support of the majority of the Acadian population, even if we hadn't gotten the elite, so we took the populist track."

Looking back on these early days in the premier's office, McKenna believes he was betrayed by political naïveté. He was convinced he could make a reasonable case on its merits and withstand external pressures. "Not in my wildest dreams could I have ever anticipated the extraordinary events that made things impossible," McKenna says. "There was a juxtaposition of events that I never could have anticipated. My mistake was not being mature enough to realize that there will always be events outside a person's control."

In March, 1988, Trudeau waded into the debate again, testifying for five and a half hours before the Senate. He urged senators to send Meech back to the House of Commons with amendments, and then an election could be called. "Let the people decide," he said. "If the people of Canada want this accord, and that is not beyond the realm of possibility, then let that be part of the constitution. I, for one, will be convinced that the Canada we know and love will be gone forever, but then Thucydides wrote that Themistocles's greatness lay in the fact that he realized Athens was not immortal. I think we have to realize that Canada is not immortal; but if it is going to go, let it go with a bang rather than a whimper."

As Meech Lake opposition gained momentum, the national media started to notice McKenna. L'Actualité featured McKenna as "L'enfant terrible du lac Meech," a man who held the constitution of his country in his hands. "If the Meech Lake Accord unravels, McKenna will probably be the catalyst," wrote Andrew Cohen in Saturday Night magazine. "Until McKenna, the critics had no standard bearer. There was now a premier who hadn't signed the accord and who had — or so he could argue — a mandate to change it."

McKenna made for a compelling profile because, unlike most first ministers, he was educated in constitutional affairs. He was no Trudeau, but he had studied political science at Queen's and he had worked for Allan MacEachen in the Privy Council office. Cohen found McKenna as cool as the currents of the Bay of Fundy; he saw McKenna maximizing his leverage by deferring a final decision on the accord. "Of course the real question is whether McKenna will kill the deal. Will he have the courage to say no? Will he risk the antipathy of Quebec, which will forever blame him for thwarting its aspirations? Will he resist the blandishments — and the punishments — of an angry Brian Mulroney? Realpolitik says he will relent; the Premier and the province suggest otherwise."

Cohen predicted a campaign of aggressive persuasion in the form of federal largesse waved under McKenna's nose. Two days after McKenna endorsed the free trade deal, he noted, Ottawa announced that the Saint John shipyard had won the second phase of the frigate program, although everyone denied a *quid pro quo*. The New Brunswick position on free trade had been forged after a series of tense debates within the Liberal caucus soon after McKenna was elected: the new Premier would support the deal and oppose the national Liberal position. However, at the same time, the province was lobbying to bring the frigate program to Saint John. As soon as cabinet made its decision to support free trade, McKenna walked down the hall to his office to telephone Brian Mulroney to tell him New Brunswick's position, which he knew the Prime Minister would immediately use to embarrass Liberal leader John Turner. During the conversation, McKenna recalls Mulroney saying, "Coincidentally, we've just reached an agreement on the frigates, and all of the frigates are going to Saint John."

McKenna immediately felt uncomfortable. "I'm thinking, 'You don't need to tell me that in this conversation. The two are not related.'"

In the end, McKenna says, the suggestion that Ottawa was trying to buy his co-operation on Meech Lake with federal money has been embellished. Punishing Atlantic Canada was a losing political proposition in the long run, and both Mulroney and McKenna knew it. As David Peterson often said jokingly to McKenna, "The trouble with you Atlantic premiers is, when you get bought, you don't always stay bought."

"Mulroney was pretty good to Atlantic Canada," McKenna says. "I personally don't think he was trying to buy me off. Even after Meech went down and he would have every reason to associate me with its demise and also to be angry at me, he was always very reasonable." Still, the Prime Minister and federal officials would often remind McKenna of the power they held over his province to disperse or withhold money. McKenna noted in his diary on September 21, 1988, that Mulroney had telephoned him and, in the course of the conversation, appeared interested in helping find highway construction money. He and his wife Mila had driven across New Brunswick several years earlier and found the roads the worst in Canada. "Feels that the Government of Canada must do something with us," McKenna observed. On Sunday, September 25, 1988, McKenna recorded in his diary that after he returned home from an outing to build a duck blind with his son Jamie, Mulroney had called to tell him he was very sympathetic to New Brunswick's need for money to rebuild the Trans-Canada Highway; he would try to make a deal. "Says he understands New Brunswick."

While Ottawa may have believed it could easily push a have-not province back into line, it failed to take into account the growing spirit of provincial pride in McKenna's office. "We were basically getting hard-lined by the PMO, Mulroney and others, who said, 'Guys, we don't have to deal with you, and we've got all these financial levers that we can use to make you squeak,'" McGuire says. "What they didn't understand was that we had adopted this economic philosophy of saying, 'We will never depend on federal transfers for anything of real significance.' So the traditional card that they had played on Robichaud, Hatfield and others didn't play any more."

"We may have been a poor province, but we didn't want a handout," Aldéa Landry says. "We wanted to be self-sufficient. This was a very different message than they had been accustomed to. It was all part of building pride with New Brunswickers that we can do anything, it doesn't matter our size or our wealth. This was a province that had am-bitions within the country and wanted to become a leader."

At the same time, Acadians were also rejecting the traditional view that their interests were just as well represented by Quebec francophones as by the anglophone majority at home. "It began with the feds saying, 'We'll handle New Brunswick, Quebec, don't worry about it,' and Quebec saying to us, 'We're really committed to francophones outside Quebec, you can trust us to defend your rights,' and us, particularly in the person of Aldéa, very strongly saying, 'Fuck you,'" McGuire recalls. "Fern was being more diplomatic but just as strongly saying, 'No, we're not having Quebec speak for us.'"

As far as McGuire was concerned, New Brunswick, as Canada's only officially bilingual province, could stand up to Quebec without conceding moral ground. "Fern and I would walk in and sit down with Quebec officials, saying in French, 'Listen, let's talk straight here. You guys are putting this guilt trip on anglophones and you're bamboozling them. As the basis for our discussion, we're French, too, and we don't have to take that shit from you.' And the guys would always start laughing. Quebec beautifully played the poor-little-Quebecker routine, but they couldn't play it with New Brunswick. We'd say, 'Hey, we're officially bilingual, you're not.'"

While New Brunswick continued to assert its case in meetings in Ottawa and Quebec, political events continued to raise the stakes and transform the nature of the debate. On December 16, 1988, Gary Filmon, the new Conservative Premier of Manitoba, introduced a resolution in the Manitoba legislature to pass Meech Lake, a decision that would have left

McKenna once again as the only dissenter. Two days later, Robert Bourassa announced he would invoke the notwithstanding clause to override a Supreme Court of Canada's ruling that had declared Bill 101, Quebec's French-only sign law, unconstitutional. "Although Quebec's action had nothing to do with Meech Lake, the symbolism was devastating," Cohen writes. "When Bourassa moved to suspend fundamental rights, he lost whatever goodwill the accord had fostered." The next day, Filmon withdrew his resolution to pass the accord. "I believe the decision made yesterday by the Government of Quebec to restrict minority language rights in that province violates the spirit of the Meech Lake Accord," he said. Sharon Carstairs, leader of Manitoba's Liberal Opposition and a zealous opponent of the accord, added that "democracy can only function when the majority concedes some of its privileges and its rights to the minority, be it the English-language minority or the French-language minority."

In early January, 1989, McKenna took a ten-day vacation with Julie in Mexico. He noted in his diary that he ran five miles each day on the beach and worked out in the exercise room. He ate well, didn't smoke and didn't drink alcohol or coffee. While this may seem more like a Spartan initiation ritual than a vacation, McKenna knew he would need all his reserves of strength in the months to come.

A Meech Lake dissident of a different character altogether was emerging in Atlantic Canada. The watchers of the constitutional file in the premier's office in New Brunswick knew that the direction of the debate would change radically with the ascent to power in Newfoundland of a tough, cerebral, inflexible constitutional lawyer named Clyde Kirby Wells. Fern Landry had warned senior officials in Ottawa that it appeared Wells was going to be elected in Newfoundland. It would be in their best interest to meet with Wells, he advised, before the new player had put himself in a position from which it would be impossible to retreat. "We warned them that there were elections coming in Newfoundland," McGuire recalls. "We kept on warning them, telling them they had to move quickly. We weren't asking for things that fundamentally challenged what Quebec wanted. Clyde Wells was a very different kettle of fish. In our case, we were saying, 'We can live with what is in there for Quebec, but we have to have our demands met too.' Clyde was fundamentally opposed to the spirit and concept of Meech."

In April, 1989, Wells won a majority government in Newfoundland, defeating the tired remnants of Tory Brian Peckford's regime. Peckford had passed Meech Lake in the House of Assembly, but by the time Wells took office he had already outlined his objections to the accord and promised to rescind its approval when he formed a government. Ottawa would wait until a First Ministers' Conference in November to acknowledge Wells's position on Meech Lake. In the meantime, Wells hired Deborah Coyne, a Toronto legal scholar and critic of the accord, as his advisor on constitutional affairs. Whereas McKenna was surrounded by smooth political operators like McGuire and Landry, Wells had anchored his Meech Lake team with an ideologue even more inflexible than he was.

Ignoring Wells and Filmon, Mulroney and his advisors decided they would work through the New Brunswick Premier to find a resolution to the constitutional impasse. They recognized that McKenna was, above all, a pragmatist and that, from the beginning, he was the one Meech Lake dissenter who seemed willing to search for solutions. To the dismay of Coyne, who disparaged what she considered New Brunswick's lack of fortitude, McKenna transformed himself into Canada's constitutional conciliator. "Our position in substance didn't change at all," McGuire says. "Our role changed dramatically, went from black to white." For the next year and a half, McKenna's diary entries reveal days dominated by the Meech Lake debate in an endless string of secret meetings and telephone diplomacy. The process of reforming Canada's constitution had moved underground into the old boys' world of heavy-handed backroom manoeuvring.

McKenna recorded on January 12, 1989, that he had met with Senator Lowell Murray, the interprovincial relations minister, a former aide to Richard Hatfield, who had attended St. Francis Xavier University with Brian Mulroney. "Told us Filmon's decision to pull plug on Meech Lake was a complete surprise to them. Mulroney had called Filmon that weekend to congratulate him on the speech that he gave in the Leg. on Meech Lake. A day later, GF says he's pulling the plug. Obviously feds aren't happy."

On February 26, McKenna met with Mulroney at 24 Sussex Drive. Mulroney was angry with Filmon and warned McKenna, "Don't ally yourself with that guy." On May 25, McKenna spoke with Bourassa about Meech. The Quebec Premier indicated that he had received more than he asked for in the accord, but retreat was no longer an option, and if Meech wasn't ratified, he would be pushed toward sovereignty association. "He said, 'I'm not a young politician. I must worry about my place in history,'" McKenna wrote in his journal.

While Mulroney's chief negotiators, Lowell Murray and Norman

Spector, the cabinet secretary for federal-provincial relations, made their rounds of the provinces, the New Brunswick negotiators were unclear about how a solution was possible when Ottawa insisted that Meech Lake had to pass unchanged. As negotiators, they had boxed themselves into a tiny corner; all they could tell the provinces was take it all or take nothing. "We were trying all kinds of desperate ways, saying, 'Look, guys, this isn't going to sell, this is no way to do business, let's find a way out,'" McGuire recalls. "Lowell Murray and Norm Spector were intransigent, saying, 'This cannot change, period. If we open up a comma, the deal's finished.' In my view that was bad strategy because, among other things, as long as you said that to Bourassa, he would be nuts to be any weaker. They thought they'd scare everybody by saying, 'I'm going to hold my breath until I die.' Well, they died. It was that simple. The foundation was rotten. The strategy just stunk."

On January 8, 1990, McKenna met with Murray. They discussed the possibility of introducing a "parallel accord" in New Brunswick that might let Ottawa squeeze out of its tight little corner. "Invited me to try and sell to Manitoba and Newfoundland," McKenna recorded. "I declined. Federal responsibility. Will carry on informal talks however. Very negative sense to meeting. No extending deadline. No other solutions."

Three weeks later, McKenna travelled to Ottawa to meet privately with Mulroney. According to McKenna's diary entry, Mulroney suggested during an intense two-hour conversation that New Brunswick could win some concessions through a parallel accord. McKenna's support for a parallel accord would help neutralize the influence of Liberal leader Jean Chrétien, who was expressing concerns about Meech. "Filmon can then sign on," McKenna wrote. "Would isolate Clyde. Doesn't think Clyde will pull the plug. Hates Chrétien. Talks about incessantly." McKenna noted also that Mulroney said he was planning to help fund New Brunswick highways and was "squirreling money away." The Prime Minister added that he would try to shield New Brunswick from the cuts in the next federal budget.

On March 5, 1990, McKenna held a secret meeting with Murray and Spector at Fern Landry's home in Fredericton to launch a desperate Meech Lake salvage mission. New Brunswick would introduce Meech Lake and a companion accord in the Legislature. The companion accord would address some of the issues raised by Meech Lake's opponents. Ottawa would guarantee the entrenchment of "Bill 88," a constitutional amendment entrenching the equality of French and English in New Brunswick.

"We introduce Meech and parallel accord," McKenna wrote in his diary after the meeting broke up. "Would pass Meech if parallel accord passes. Ottawa would act surprised. After a day, they would endorse, introduce in the Parliament of Canada and call public hearings in several provinces. Momentum would build and Ont. would support, PEI and NS would support. Man. and Quebec would be asked by Mulroney not to shout it down too quick. Give it a chance. Quebec would be the final province on board. We work on Chrétien, editorial boards, opposition parties and interest groups. We do Bill 88 at the same time. I agree. Must be done within two weeks. Only way to save the accord and prevent the breakup of Canada."

On March 14, a week after the parallel accord had been drafted, Mulroney telephoned McKenna at 11:40 p.m. and woke him up. The Prime Minister was leaving for Mexico the next day. "Said everything was ready for Wednesday a.m.," McKenna wrote. "He said that he would deliver Filmon and Bourassa. Already had two very tough conversations with Bourassa. Said Robert sometimes makes tough decisions himself. Said guy on the Rock is crazy. PM said he is still squirreling money away for the TCH."

McKenna met with Chretién in Montreal on March 19 to discuss the Meech rescue plan. "Somewhat supported but felt we didn't go far enough," McKenna recorded. "Said he would try to say positive things. Would call Wells and Carstairs. Would try to mellow out Trudeau. Cordial meeting. He is very egocentric. Convinced his good standing in Quebec is proof Quebec accepts his vision. Says it depends whether Bourassa is a separatist or a federalist. Concedes there is a very real chance of the former."

Before releasing the contents of the companion accord, McKenna spoke to newspaper editors and francophone leaders to prepare them for his announcement in the Legislature. Acadian leaders were pleased with his plan to entrench New Brunswick language equality in the constitution outside of the Meech Lake deal, he wrote on March 20: "Jean Chrétien called several times. Doesn't feel we have gone far enough. Talked to Sen. Murray early Tuesday a.m. Says Bourassa is a coward and with enough pressure he will fold like a house of cards in two or three days. PM to call Bourassa and Filmon and Quebec business leaders."

The next day, McKenna rose in the Legislature to make a motion to adopt the Meech Lake Accord on the condition that other provinces support his companion accord, a parallel accord that would resolve ambiguities about women's rights, establish the right of Ottawa to promote, not just preserve, linguistic duality, put native issues on the table for the next round of constitutional talks, and require public hearings on future constitutional amendments. "What we need now are strong hands and cool minds and an unwavering determination to find a solution," he said. His legislative duties complete, McKenna drove immediately to the airport, where he boarded the government plane, the constitutional travelling salesman setting out across Canada to market the new deal.

David Peterson and Nova Scotia Premier John Buchanan endorsed McKenna's resolution. Mulroney played his role in the public charade, telling reporters the companion accord was a New Brunswick initiative. He promised only to introduce it in the House of Commons so that it could be examined by an all-party committee, which was to report on May 18, thirty-six days before the Meech Lake deadline. "I have not endorsed Mr. McKenna's proposals," Mulroney said, which was legally true but substantially false. While reporters may have dutifully swallowed Mulroney's denials of collusion on the McKenna resolution, federal Environment Minister Lucien Bouchard didn't buy the "superb coordination" of events in New Brunswick and Ottawa. He had heard about the McKenna plan while he was on government business in Vancouver and was enraged that he hadn't heard about it in advance. When he finally obtained a copy of the companion resolution, he became convinced that it undermined the substance of the accord.

The supposedly random events had unfolded too smoothly for Bouchard's liking. "On March 21, the McKenna resolution leaped out of the hat," Bouchard writes in his autobiography. "The next day, in a televised address, Prime Minister Mulroney welcomed this great contribution to Meech's rescue. On March 23, he tabled the resolution in the House of Commons for federal study. It was a brilliant improvisation, neutralizing Trudeau's brutal attack, transforming Clyde Wells into a quarrelsome politician, and putting the renegotiation of Meech on the rails."

Meanwhile, Wells and Filmon argued that McKenna's proposal didn't address their most substantial concerns: in particular, it failed to propose an acceptable formula for Senate reform, an issue that McKenna had never championed. However, Bourassa stood firm in his position that Meech had to be ratified as it stood before any further amendments were considered. Therefore, the day after McKenna introduced his plan, Wells started the process of rescinding his province's approval of the accord.

The rescue mission's momentum had flagged even before Meech took a final body blow. On May 22, Bouchard quit the Conservative Party, saying he could no longer tolerate what he considered the erosion of the promises Meech Lake offered to Quebec. A House of Commons committee, led by Tory Jean Charest, had proposed a series of constitutional proposals to be discussed at future First Ministers' Conferences, and the situation for Bouchard had become intolerable. In a letter of resignation to Mulroney, he made it clear that McKenna's demand for equality of language rights in New Brunswick was unacceptable for a Quebec nationalist. "I was astonished last week in Europe to learn that the [Charest] report proposed twenty-three modifications as a basis for discussion at a future conference of first ministers," he wrote. "Several affect the essential nature of the accord. I am thinking of the levelling of Quebec society's distinctive character by inserting in the same clause the equality of New Brunswick's anglophone and francophone communities."

McKenna heard the news of Bouchard's resignation while he was attending a budget think-tank meeting in New Brunswick. He wrote that evening, "Bouchard resigns. Everybody shocked. My lowest point. Talked to Peterson and Devine. Both working on it. Talked to Clyde. He accused me of insulting him. Left me more depressed than ever."

Five days after Bouchard's resignation, McKenna met with Mulroney; the Prime Minister appeared haggard and disheartened. "Spent a lot of time on Bouchard's resignation," he wrote in his diary. Mulroney "said it was a story of great treachery. Looked across river at Quebec and said all this will be lost if Meech fails." Mulroney had reopened old wounds, remarking that there had been an all-party agreement in Manitoba but Filmon had "fucked it up. Brian said he would call a First Ministers Conference and put the two premiers on trial before the nation. Don't be caught with them. History will prove them great traitors to Canada. Very important to try and recognize the reality in Quebec. Mood is terrible. Mulroney said he was giving extra $ to NB because we're bilingual. Said he was at his best with Filmon — the best he's ever been."

The Prime Minister was preparing McKenna for the endgame in his lamentable Meech Lake strategy. On June 3, 1990, Mulroney invited the premiers to Ottawa for dinner. Mulroney would later tell *Globe and Mail* reporters that this eleventh-hour pressure cooker had long been part of his plan. A month earlier he had told his closest advisors that he had chosen the day when the premiers were going to start meeting. "I said, 'That's the day I'm going to roll all the dice.'"

With the country now suffering from what the national media had diagnosed as a "constitutional crisis," the first ministers gathered in a conference centre in a renovated railway station in Ottawa. On June 4, after a day-long negotiating session, McKenna walked out of the meeting room, huddled for a moment with the Landrys and McGuire, and then emerged to meet the wall of reporters waiting outside. He said he was prepared to endorse the Meech Lake Accord. He had decided that Ottawa's assurances and undertakings for future discussions, which he had long maintained were not enough, were the best he could negotiate. He urged the other holdout provinces to follow his lead. To hard-line critics of the accord like Carstairs, Wells and Coyne, McKenna had proven himself to be a spineless sellout who had caved under federal pressure. Where was the old McKenna who had the courage to stand alone in opposition to the accord?

What appeared to be a sudden collapse of will was, in fact, another step in McKenna's new, choreographed constitutional dance. "The strategy for many months was done hand in hand with the government of Canada," McKenna says. "The parallel accord and the last bargaining sessions and the timing of our interventions and everything was all very carefully scripted with Ottawa." After day one, McKenna was on side; Wells and Filmon were isolated and, in Mulroney's eyes, "on trial" before the nation.

Why did McKenna, a determined and competitive man, agree to a complete retreat on Meech Lake, knowing he would lose face and be publicly ridiculed by the very people for whom he had been a champion? Months of federal pressure had not broken his spirit, but it had shifted his perspective. McKenna's concerns over the substance of the accord now paled in comparison with his overwhelming fear that the country would collapse if Meech Lake failed. He had been vanquished by the apocalyptic warnings of Mulroney and his advisors. "The process put such a price on failure that we reached the conclusion that it was better to lose face," McKenna says. "The gunboat diplomacy that had been carried out had carried such a high risk of failure that we had to find other means of resolving our issues, and so we were prepared to accept softer solutions than we would have earlier on. We ended up swallowing more than we would have."

Ultimately, McKenna's hasty endorsement was for nought. The talks in the old railway station stretched into the seventh day. For the premiers and their advisors, the process was exhausting. The sessions officially began at nine a.m.; however, Fern and Aldéa Landry, McGuire and McKenna held their first meetings of the day at six a.m. and worked straight through a series of bargaining sessions and debriefings until at least midnight. As the week went on, the participants became more exhausted, more susceptible to persuasion. McKenna, who had accepted the role of conciliator, was particularly vulnerable to the process. While Clyde Wells would later remark, "camaraderie impairs judgment," Ottawa reporter Susan Delacourt wrote, "McKenna slides easily into the boys' game of politics, the locker-room mentality, the snapping towels type of camaraderie among politicians."

Fern Landry recalls McKenna's patience wearing thin only once. There was a debate in the meeting room about the wording of future discussions on minority language rights, focusing once again on the elusive word *promote* that Quebec had so much trouble accepting. Bourassa wouldn't agree with the concept of promoting minority language rights inside or outside Quebec. McKenna left the meeting room to consult with a tired Landry, who was waiting with the scores of other advisors in the outer rooms of the conference centre.

"Frank, no, no. I don't think that they're right, and I don't think that francophones in New Brunswick or Manitoba or elsewhere are less Canadian citizens than francophones in Quebec," Landry said. "I can't accept it."

McKenna snapped, "You're being very helpful," turned and walked quickly back into the meeting room.

"He never got upset with me, ever, except that time," Landry says. "I could see that he was tired, and he was a little bit emotional."

On the seventh day, the first ministers agreed that there would be a national commission on Senate reform and a future meeting to discuss amendments to protect minority rights. Mulroney had a deal, with the caveat that Wells had only agreed to put the deal to a vote in the House of Assembly. Outside the meeting room, McKenna linked arms and danced with Mulroney cabinet minister Benoît Bouchard. "Bouchard, a consummate performer, was dancing the steps of a Quebec folk dance; McKenna was hopping about in the steps of an old Scottish folk dance," writes Delacourt. "Miraculously, the two steps worked together. It was the last time for Bouchard that French and English would work in such perfect step."

When he met with reporters, McKenna made a point of thanking Aldéa Landry for her work on the Meech Lake file. Overcome with exhaustion, Aldéa wept quietly as McKenna spoke. "He had no particular reason to thank me," she says. "I was just there doing my job like anybody else, but I think that I represented for him part of the reason why he had fought for changes to Meech Lake, for the francophones and Acadians of New Brunswick. To me that was very touching. The underlying message was that I represented in my own little way the reason he had fought to have changes to Meech Lake."

The celebrations were short-lived. Back in the Manitoba Legislature, Elijah Harper, a New Democrat and Cree Indian, refused to cast his vote to create the unanimity Filmon required to introduce the Meech Lake Accord without the normal two days' notice. On June 15, while the accord was dying in the Manitoba Legislature, New Brunswick's all-Liberal Legislature approved it. Eight days later, Clyde Wells cancelled a vote on the accord in the House of Assembly when it became clear not only that there wasn't going to be a vote in Manitoba before the deadline, but also that Ottawa appeared willing to extend the deadline in Manitoba but not in Newfoundland.

Meech Lake was dead, and Frank McKenna felt enormous guilt over the role he had played in its demise. For weeks he would lie awake at night, replaying events in his mind, suffering more anxiety than he had ever experienced in his life. "I have to share responsibility, and it weighs heavily on me," he told Andrew Cohen. "I don't think any of us has done a great deal of honour to the country."

He found some solace in conversation with David Peterson, who had become a close friend during the crisis. "There are some people who blame Frank for it, and if Frank could play that part of his life again, he would probably do it differently," he says. "That being said, I have not one criticism. I think the things he said were not unreasonable. Wells was the problem. Frank is reasonable. Wells is not reasonable. When it came down to it, Frank was there, and he was there in spades. Frank is not a hypocrite. He doesn't have a hypocritical bone in his body."

The Prime Minister shared Peterson's assessment. While Mulroney would continue to blame Clyde Wells for the failure of Meech Lake, McKenna remained a friend and confidant. That summer, while McKenna was attending his mother's seventieth birthday party at his sister Doris's home outside Sussex, the phone rang. It was the Prime Minister's Office calling. McKenna picked up the phone and stretched the cord into the bathroom, where he could close the door for privacy. For an hour, he tried to console a dejected Mulroney. Finally he opened the bathroom door and called Olive McKenna to the telephone. Mulroney wished her a happy birthday and apologized profusely for interrupting the party. Olive was thrilled. When McKenna rejoined the family, Doris asked, "Who was that?"

"That was the Prime Minister," McKenna replied.

"Well, I hope it wasn't too important, because we're on a party line," Doris replied. McKenna blanched, then returned to the party.

As far as McKenna's constitutional advisors were concerned, he had won a victory for Acadians. The province and Ottawa would proceed with plans to entrench New Brunswick's language equality in the Constitution. Robert Pichette, an Acadian writer and former advisor to Louis Robichaud, maintains that McKenna has unfairly been labelled the gravedigger of the Meech Lake Accord, when in fact he was responding to the concerns of the leaders of the Société des Acadiens et Acadiennes, who then sold him out. "The leaders of the Société des Acadiens et Acadiennes had very large egos, inflated by their naïveté and lack of political sense and experience," Pichette says. "When McKenna rallied to the Meech Lake Accord he also made sure, to his eternal credit, and in the spirit of Louis J. Robichaud and Richard Hatfield, that linguistic rights in New Brunswick would be enshrined in the Constitution. It is sadly ironic and unfair that McKenna's bold role would be misconstrued within the Société des Acadiens et Acadiennes at the time, and by sovereignists in Quebec, because it suited their political agenda."

New Brunswick was the only province to emerge from the ruins of Meech Lake with constructive constitutional changes. For McKenna, this belated victory offered little consolation. "I spent the rest of my political life trying to be a leader in finding a solution, in some way perhaps to balm my tortured soul," he says. "I always felt my country could have been destroyed because of my lack of foresight. The mistake I made was not realizing that, in trying to deal with the Constitution of Canada, there is no such thing as a perfect solution, that sometimes you have to accept whatever's on the table, with all its imperfections."

He would also question his Liberal faith, in particular his arguments in favour of a strong central government, which in theory helped Atlantic Canada but in practice tended to be wasteful and unresponsive. With or without Meech Lake, he was learning that Ottawa was going to do what it wanted, including slashing regional programs and transfer payments. He was learning just how hard it was to govern a have-not province under the thumb of a strong central government.

In the wake of Meech Lake's failure, McKenna was also questioning the sacred primacy of the Charter of Rights and Freedoms. Perhaps in some instances collective rights were as important as individual rights. "The role of government, its right to manage the affairs of the nation, was being compromised by some of the increasingly radical interpretations of the charter," he says. "I came to practical conclusions that were less religiously attached to the Charter of Rights." McKenna would tell reporters he found himself from time to time looking "almost a little wistfully" at Quebec, which had managed to forge a sense of collective identity. "Yes, individual rights are important, and yes, the Charter of Rights was an enormous accomplishment. But let us not worship at that altar to the exclusion of a sense of identity." McKenna would never again see himself as a Trudeau Liberal.

He would continue to champion Acadian rights, but more quietly. Donald Savoie recalls McKenna rising to address a fundraiser in Toronto for the Université de Moncton. As he stood at the podium, he paused before he began speaking to ask if there were any reporters in the room. When he was assured there were not, he proceeded without notes to give a passionate speech in defence of Acadie. The speech, says Savoie, was one of the most remarkable political performances he had ever witnessed, and by the time McKenna stepped down, the Bay Street crowd was musing about the possibility that this young New Brunswicker might become Prime Minister one day.

What would Frank McKenna say about Acadia only in a room with no media present? Today he answers without hesitation. "We have to recognize that hundreds of years ago we made a horrific mistake in trying to destroy a culture. We should feel a great sense of awe that Acadians returned and, in the toughest of geographical settings, created this great culture and sense of industry and economy. This would only continue if the country recognized its obligations to Acadians and supported their institutions. As a province and as a country, we are richer by far for having these equal communities. It is a mark of our civility as a country and as a province that we can live side by side and respect each other and respect the right to keep your culture and your language, to live and love and learn in that language."

At the time, McKenna feared speaking one phrase that might be splashed on the front pages of local newspapers, increasing French-English tensions once again. He was determined to heal his province's deep divisions without a confrontational public campaign.

When McKenna announced that voters would go to the polls in October, 1991, optimistic members of the press mused about the possibility of another sweep. The Conservatives had been resurrected under the able leadership of Dennis Cochrane, a former school administrator, but the financially and spiritually bankrupt party was a long way from returning to power. NDP leader Elizabeth Weir was campaigning hard just to win her seat in Saint John. The only unknown was the political strength of the Confederation of Regions Party, whose folksy white-haired leader, Arch Pafford, was preaching anti-bilingualism as his only policy of substance.

The CoR membership was made up largely of disgruntled Tories like Ed Allen, a seventy-one-year-old former Hatfield cabinet minister. "I concluded that official bilingualism was too costly and that my home was no longer in the Tory Party," he said. Candidate Greg Hargrove, a thirty-two-year-old pipefitter, announced, "Assimilation is not a bad word in my book." Referring to his Scottish heritage, he added, "My people did it — they used to speak Gaelic."

CoR's strength was unknown because the party wasn't showing up on the polling radar; people weren't willing to admit to the pollsters that they intended to vote for the anti-French party. McGuire, Bryden and other members of the McKenna team were driving blind. However, veteran Canadian Press reporter Chris Morris had covered enough campaigns to sense the stirrings of a protest vote. The McKenna government had been conducting a review of bilingual services in all departments, and grumblings about an Acadian takeover of the civil service swirled through the hallways of Fredericton office buildings. In the ridings around Fredericton, where a large proportion of the uneasy civil servants resided, the CoR message found a home.

"I live in the country, I'm married to a guy who is generally perceived as right wing, and I could hear from my neighbours that they were giving CoR a lot of credence," Morris recalls. "But whenever I talked about it to certain other reporters who were very close to the premier's office, they would attack me. 'Don't be so stupid, there's nothing to it, and you shouldn't be encouraging that kind of talk.' It was that pointed.

"Right up to election night, those same people, who had been on the McKenna campaign bus, were predicting another sweep. I can remember sitting there with another reporter from the Toronto *Sun*, and we took bets. I said I thought CoR was going to take at least a half dozen seats." Local reporters laughed at Morris's predictions. "They told this guy from the *Sun*, 'You just can't listen to her. It's going to be another sweep for the Liberals, McKenna has done it again.'"

Paul Kaihla of *Maclean's* rode the bus with McKenna on the final leg of the campaign when the Premier was joined by his wife and children. "The twelve-hour days in close quarters while travelling New Brunswick's bumpy roads did produce an intimacy among the Premier's advisors and the press," he wrote. "As the bus rolled towards one of the final events, McKenna, his children, campaign workers and reporters danced together unabashedly in the aisle as the sound system blasted rock music hits."

The dance ended abruptly on election night. The Liberals won an overwhelming majority, but it was far from a sweep. The Confederation of Regions Party had formed the official opposition, winning eight seats, five of them in the ridings surrounding Fredericton. Dennis Cochrane brought two members with him to the Legislature, including former Hatfield loyalist Jean Gauvin, who had defeated Aldéa Landry in Shippagan. Elizabeth Weir won her riding of Saint John South. The Liberals found little consolation in the defeat of CoR leader Pafford in his riding of Newcastle, which bordered McKenna's stronghold in Chatham. The CoR Party had finished second in eighteen ridings and captured a remarkable thirty per cent of the anglophone vote.

"CoR was a creation of Mulroney, Meech, and Quebec. This was a language issue," McGuire says. "The Tories were unwilling to accept the anti-French, anti-Quebec mantle, absolutely to their credit. They staunchly refused to let them in. Mulroney's presence played a role. People hated him. 'Goddam Quebecker, a Frenchman, doing all this for Quebec. Bill 101, when they invoked the notwithstanding clause. Look at those Frenchies just beating up on the English.' We should have seen it coming."

Ray Frenette believes CoR's support was a response to the government's aggressive moves to expand official bilingualism within the civil service. "We were moving just a little too fast on the language issue," he says. "When people see that any given policy of government might take some jobs away from A and transfer them to B because of language, you're going to have people reacting badly."

No one seemed to know what to say on the government plane as McKenna flew with his wife and advisors from Chatham to Fredericton for a victory party. Julie McKenna broke the heavy silence to say that she felt ashamed to be a New Brunswicker. McKenna's communications director Maurice Robichaud recalls that the night was particularly traumatic for francophone members of the McKenna team. "We were trying to build something positive and something constructive and valuable for both communities in New Brunswick, and to see a party that was just driven to tear it apart saddened us," he says.

"The results brought home to us our greatest failure," McGuire says. "We all felt a real sense of personal failure. The ultimate goal was to have both communities share the same dream. That was it. In 1991, at that point, we had failed."

McKenna, who smiled a brave smile at his victory party, was in fact overwhelmed by a sense of dread about the future of his province. In one night he saw Aldéa Landry defeated by "Vroom Vroom" Gauvin, the notorious former Hatfield minister who spent his car allowance on a white Trans Am, as well as the emergence of an Official Opposition whose primary goal was to deepen the province's cultural divide. "It was one of the saddest nights of my life," he recalls.

McGuire, the strategist, immediately turned his attention to rectifying the problem. The cascading national events had pushed them away from the agenda that had been so clearly defined by pollster George Perlin in 1987. "We couldn't win on the language issue, and we had to get it off the map," he says. "The constitutional issues had put it there, and we had to get it off."

Four years earlier, George Perlin had defined political leadership for McKenna. "Leadership is reaching across the barriers that divide groups in our society and showing people how, in their daily lives, they have the same concerns and the same goals," Perlin wrote. "It is getting people to look beyond the things that divide them and getting them to work together to achieve their common goals." A clause in a legal document, no matter how carefully worded, would never unify a people long divided. "I always thought that our issues were absolutely identical. We wanted a place to live where we could enjoy a good quality of life. We wanted to work. We wanted a better life for our children," McKenna says.

The issue of *Maclean's* magazine that reported the angry rise of CoR in New Brunswick featured on its cover the story of Constitutional Affairs Minister Joe Clark's plan to pick up the pieces of Meech Lake and create a new package that Canadians would accept or reject in a referendum. McKenna would find himself intimately involved in this project, but never again would he stray so far from home.

Frank McKenna, January, 1993.

7
THE HUSTLER

Hectic day at office. Very discouraging. Paper is choking us.
Worked until 11:30 p.m.
— *Frank McKenna, diary entry, November 2, 1987*

Start 7:30. Going to do it right.
— *Frank McKenna, diary entry, November 3, 1987*

Robert Bourassa died. Long days and long nights.
— *Frank McKenna, diary entry, September 26, 1996*

Frank McKenna doesn't stay long in one place. Even in the evenings when he's relaxing after a long day on the road, you'd probably find him in his hotel room sitting in front of the television in a worn grey sweatsuit, channel surfing with one hand, smoking a Cuban cigar and doing a crossword puzzle on his lap with the other, all the while deeply involved in a conversation with whoever else is in the room. And that's down time.

In June, 1990, near the end of Brian Mulroney's roll-the-dice week, when McKenna found himself closeted with an exhausted group of first ministers in the National Conference Centre in Ottawa, he decided he would take part in the country's constitutional negotiations and deal with another outstanding file at the same time. He had heard through the grapevine that the Montreal Canadiens franchise was on the verge of choosing a new location for its American Hockey League farm team and that Fredericton was one of the cities in the running.

Fredericton and its too-often-empty Aitken Centre on the University of New Brunswick campus needed the economic and spiritual boost of a professional hockey franchise. As McKenna turned away from the Meech Lake file to consider the Baby Habs, it occurred to him that he had the Premier of Quebec in the same room. During a break in the talks, he cornered Robert Bourassa and asked him if he had a relationship with

Serge Savard, the general manager of the Canadiens, who also happened to be one of McKenna's hockey heroes. Bourassa was only too happy to talk about something other than the gut-wrenching issue of Meech Lake. Yes, he said with a smile, he did have a contact: his bodyguard was a former hockey player who knew Savard. The bodyguard got Savard on the phone, then put McKenna on the line. McKenna told Savard he wanted the Canadiens in New Brunswick and would do what he could to make it happen. What could Savard say? The future of the country was hanging in the balance, and he had two premiers intervening in the matter of his decision about where to locate his farm team. Predictably, Savard decided that the Baby Habs would settle in Fredericton.

During those final trying days of the Meech Lake debate, McKenna had retreated for a moment into the more comfortable role of political hustler. In fact, the whole Meech Lake debate had been terribly distracting for him. It was time to get back to work. Stripping off his suit jacket, rolling up his sleeves and just getting things done was in fact what he did best. It was time to pick up the pace again, to regain the momentum he had when he first stormed into the premier's office in the fall of 1987.

In the weeks following the election, the new premier's energy had permeated the capital city. Bureaucrats and members of the press gallery were relieved to have him there. The memories of Hatfield's spectacular political crash had fouled the quiet riverside city, and the wreckage had to be hauled away, the streets cleaned. Despite the fact that the Liberals were governing without opposition, the press willingly gave Fast Frank the longest honeymoon in New Brunswick political history.

"There was so much to write about, so much positive stuff, because Richard Hatfield was just awful towards the end," recalls Chris Morris. "Richard rarely went to the office, he could hardly drag his ass into the Legislature. And then there's Frank coming, just bouncing down the street at seven-thirty in the morning, bursting into the office and turning on the lights in the Centennial Building."

For long-suffering reporters in Fredericton, the new regime felt like the first shirt-sleeve day after a long hard winter. The affable Hatfield had turned icy cold in the years before his fall, and he didn't care that reporters despised him when he marched past them without so much as acknowledging their presence. McKenna always returned telephone calls from reporters and often invited them into his office to conduct interviews; he had learned from experience on the Miramichi that if he helped reporters do their jobs, they'd more often than not return the favour in subtle ways.

"You'd call over to the premier's office sometimes to get a quote or a comment, and half the time Frank would answer the phone himself," Morris says. "It was really lovely to have that kind of openness and access. We all appreciated it after so many years of having no contact at all."

The new Premier put the city on a new schedule. He set his alarm to ring about ten minutes before six in the morning. He listened to the news while he was shaving, left home about six-thirty, walked to work and arrived a few minutes before seven, an hour before the day officially began. He ate a bowl of cold cereal and drank a cup of Postum at his desk (he was too wired in those days to handle coffee), read the newspapers and started returning phone calls to people he knew were early risers. Before the receptionists came to work, he answered the phones and handed out messages to his staff as they trickled in. Cabinet meetings were scheduled for eight on Thursday mornings (Hatfield had held cabinet meetings at three in the afternoon); reporters could interview McKenna and members of his cabinet if they staked out the corridor outside the cabinet meeting room by seven-thirty. McKenna made sure bureaucrats saw the new work ethic first-hand. He rode the public elevators instead of the private lift Hatfield preferred. He ate lunch in the government cafeteria. When the Legislature opened, he applied his new schedule there as well, beginning sittings at eight in the morning and working members until late in the evening. The Premier's office on the second-floor of the Centennial Building, a glass and concrete rectangle a stone's throw from the legislative complex, was always lit up until late in the evening. Reporters started calling the building "Frank's 7-11." Soon, civil servants in all departments started arriving at work earlier, filling government parking lots by eight o'clock. Without saying a word, McKenna sent a clear message: Wake up, there's work to be done.

The Premier had always worked hard; therefore, on the one hand, he was simply imposing his own habits on the public service. On the other hand, his schedule was inspired by political strategy, like almost everything he did. "If everyone had to get up early to work, they wouldn't be out late at night," Francis McGuire says. "The 7-11 government didn't allow much time for people to get into trouble." The devil finds work for idle hands.

McKenna was also living the ethic of his youth. When he made his first appearance on the national stage at the First Ministers' Conference in Toronto in November, 1987, he caused a stir among national reporters because he arrived at the opening reception on time and alone, circulating among bureaucrats and journalists while the other premiers remained in their hotel rooms with their handlers, carefully planning fashionably late entrances. By the time the other premiers arrived, McKenna had left. It never occurred to him that he should be anything but punctual. He also insisted on carrying his own suitcases, and he alarmed police security personnel by stepping out for a morning jog without telling them where he was going. When he addressed the first ministers, he said his government didn't want Ottawa to throw more money at New Brunswick's economic problems. "What we want is to work, the opportunity to work, to create opportunities," he declared.

Six months after he swept all fifty-eight seats in the 1987 election, McKenna set the tone for his government's relationship with the national business establishment in a speech to the Canadian Club in Toronto. He structured his speech as a response to a *Saturday Night* magazine article by John Fraser entitled "A Modest Proposal Concerning the Atlantic Canadian Problem." Fraser, the magazine's editor, had presented a satirical plan to relocate the population of the region. "It is time everyone in Atlantic Canada cleared out and moved on," Fraser wrote. "The compassionate solution is a comprehensive relocation of the entire population. Humane common sense, as it turns out, is also sound business sense. In embracing the bottom line in Atlantic Canada, we will be saving countless tax dollars as well as eliminating the most vexing and enduring social problem in the country."

McKenna acknowledged that Fraser had written these lines tongue-in-cheek. Nonetheless, he said, the story reinforced the widely held misconception that Atlantic Canadians were lesser partners in Confederation. "There seems to be a sense in some places that we come to the table of Confederation as suppliants on our knees, as beggars looking for crumbs instead of having the right to sit and enjoy the full banquet," he said. He told his audience that his government intended both to lead the country in eliminating deficit financing and to work tirelessly in strengthening the economy of Atlantic Canada. "We know that through the years we have received handouts and transfer payments and that we've become very dependent on them," he admitted. "And in some ways we're not so much the beneficiaries of that dependency, we're the victims. What it has done is perpetuate a cycle of dependency, where more and more people are supported by fewer and fewer, and where the will to work and the will to invest and the will to take risks has been knocked out of us."

He intended to break this cycle, to invest in education and training and to restore dignity to his people by putting them to work. "We want to take the future into our own hands," he said. "We know that we are not going to become equal to our Canadian brothers economically by relying on handouts and dependency, transfer payments and welfare payments. What we ask from you is that you give a good, solid look at us; we ask very simply for your investment, your business, but not your charity."

McKenna measured people's worth by their ability to produce results, and he was impatient with himself and with those around him, including the civil service. "Frank wanted things to be accomplished," Francis McGuire says. "He had the view, 'I'm only here for ten years, and so I'm not wasting any time. I've got a lot of things to do.' And those who didn't deliver didn't last. Frank was really quite ruthless. Give him credit for bringing in a good team of deputy ministers, but the deputy minister who couldn't get things done was gone. He would tolerate your arguing with him, he would tolerate your saying, 'This is wrong.' We would have real solid fights that would last for months. As long as the points were valid, that was fine. But you better deliver. The day I stopped moving jobs and getting things done would be the day I was gone. Jean Chrétien and people like him have a sense of long-term loyalty. Frank has that and understands that, but there are very real limits to how much non-performance Frank can take, and it's not much. That's the hard part of Frank."

While McKenna would still suffer great anxiety about wounding people around him for the good of the mission, he learned to do what he needed to do as he became more committed to the agenda and more decisive in his leadership style. "I used to get absolutely stuck in the mud whenever an issue involving a relationship would come along," McKenna recalls. "I really hated hurting anybody's feelings. It bothered me terribly. Then I started doing those things with less fear. If you are going to move forward, you have to sacrifice some of these relationships."

Nowhere did McKenna demand results more than from his economic development staff, established in the premier's office and modelled after Michael Dukakis's Massachusetts Miracle team. After the 1987 election, McKenna handed John Bryden, his economic development commissioner, a mixed bag of goods. On the surface, the province was riding a five-year wave of economic growth. The cyclical forestry sector, the province's largest employer, was on a high in the wake of rising pulp and paper demand. The Saint John Shipyard bustled with activity, employing two thousand people to complete Ottawa's multi-billion-dollar patrol frigate contract. Mines were prospering. The new salmon aquaculture industry in the Bay of Fundy was showing promise as a major creator of jobs.

However, there were ominous signs that this booming economy would soon falter. Although the province's unemployment rate was dropping, at thirteen per cent it was still above the national average. New Brunswick's population had stagnated to the point that there was little evidence of an echo generation in the New Brunswick demographic — children born after 1980, following the baby boom and baby bust generations — a factor that would profoundly hinder the province's economic growth. Donald Savoie points out that "the reverberations would be felt in virtually every sector, from health care to educational facilities and of course in the province's work force." To make the economic forecast even worse, New Brunswick was experiencing a significant brain drain as the highly educated moved away, mainly to Ontario, and, as a result, the province lagged far behind as the national economy embraced information technology industries. Furthermore, New Brunswickers were far too dependent on government, Savoie notes. By 1987, twenty-two per cent of personal income in the province came from government transfers, the highest percentage of any province except Newfoundland. The province relied on these transfers for about forty per cent of its revenues at a time when the federal government was sending out warning signs that transfers were going to be cut. On top of all this, McKenna inherited an annual deficit of $368 million and a debt of $2.5 billion. Bryden was charged with transforming the province's economy without the benefit of government spending.

With the appointment of Bryden, the Premier's inner circle was nearly complete. However, because Francis McGuire was mired in the constitutional swamp, McKenna needed someone to deal with communications. He had learned from McGuire that in politics, image is everything. If he was going to transform New Brunswick, he needed to create a buzz about his government. Changing people's attitudes and creating optimism were his first priority, and to achieve these objectives, he needed to engage the right communications director and to work that person hard.

He found Maurice Robichaud, a thirty-four-year-old communications officer, in Canada Post's head office in Ottawa. Hiring Robichaud was a bit of a long shot, and certainly at the time no one realized what a treasure they had discovered. Robichaud's family was from New Brunswick, but he was born in Ontario and studied at French schools in Toronto and Mississauga before specializing in languages at St. Thomas University and the Université de Moncton. Robichaud was working for the New Brunswick government in a tranquil Natural Resources job early in 1987 when he landed his job with Canada Post. Before he left town, he bumped into his friend Julian Walker in the parking lot of a grocery store. "I understand you're leaving to move to Ottawa," Walker said. "It's really a shame, you should stay here. We're going to win the election whenever it's called, and we're going to need some good people like you to help us out." Robichaud, who had never been involved in politics, thanked him for the offer but said he had a different career path in mind.

In the spring of 1988, Robichaud returned to New Brunswick to attend an unpleasant meeting in Sussex about a planned reduction in postal services in the farming community. He had some time to kill in Fredericton, so he stopped at the Centennial Building to visit Walker, who again suggested he consider coming back to New Brunswick, giving him a copy of the Agenda for Change election platform to read. Impressed by McKenna's ambitious plans, Robichaud decided to fly down for an interview, and he spent a day in the Premier's office being grilled by every member of the team — John Bryden, Fern and Aldéa Landry, Ruth McCrea, McGuire and Walker. McKenna dropped by for a moment to say hello. Robichaud seemed like a perfect fit — sharp, gregarious and perfectly bilingual. With a name like Robichaud, how could he go wrong in New Brunswick politics? Robichaud accepted the job with the naïveté of a career bureaucrat, not realizing that he had agreed to work for a man whose energy would consume his own.

"I didn't know what I was getting into," Robichaud says. "It was a far, far higher-charged environment than working in the civil service. The Premier was driven all the time. He didn't quit, he didn't lay off for a second. Some people fill space in time; he tries to get as much done in the time that's available to him." Robichaud soon learned his new boss had an insatiable appetite for information and retained more of it than anyone else, challenging his staff members constantly about files he often knew more about than the point person on the issue.

Robichaud was the antithesis of the rapid-fire, urbane McGuire. A thin man with angular features, he often appeared fragile and slightly bedraggled, the type of man with whom reporters identified. Members of the press gallery called him "Moe," and he made a point of getting to know the life stories of his colleagues on the other side of the fence. He was also honest with reporters, choosing to level with them rather than toss out bold-faced lies. However, beneath his soft demeanour, he was — and remains — as competitive and unrelenting as they come. He was slow to adjust to the pace of McKenna's world, and during his first few months the premier and McGuire contemplated letting him go. By the time he hit his stride, there was no more effective government communications officer in Canada.

McKenna recruited the final member of the team during a visit to the Université de Moncton, where he was introduced in perfect French by a student named Steven MacKinnon. After his speech, McKenna approached the student and asked how a young man with a name like MacKinnon spoke such perfect French. MacKinnon explained that he was a political junkie from Prince Edward Island and had chosen to learn French and study in Moncton. McKenna hired him to be his personal assistant; he would work with the Liberal caucus and travel with the Premier.

The Premier of New Brunswick, especially holding a fifty-eight-to-nothing majority, wielded an enormous amount of power. McKenna knew his agenda would live or die in his own office, and it was up to him to keep his young staff motivated. While members of his cabinet would play important roles in the government, the drive and energy was generated Monday mornings when he, Fern Landry, McGuire, Robichaud, MacKinnon and Ruth McCrea assembled at his round table. "It's a great day," McKenna would say, looking at his bleary-eyed knights. "What's everybody so glum for? What's going on? Cheer up. It's great to be alive. It's a great place to be, and there's so much to look forward to. I've been working all weekend. I've got a whole agenda."

Robichaud recalls staring in dismay at the piles of paper stacked in front of McKenna and wondering how he did it. He himself had finished his seventy-five hour work week on Friday, had gone out for a beer, headed home and collapsed to spend some time with his family and friends. For McKenna, work had never stopped. Being Premier, he liked to say, was like drinking from the end of a fire hose. The flow of information saturated every moment of his life. McKenna would start flipping through his pages. "Francis, I read through this report, and I'm telling you, I think your department can do a lot better than that. Maybe we need to get a meeting together. Ruth, will you arrange a meeting? Steve, we've got to do something with the caucus there, we've got a bit of an issue with the Saint John caucus. And Moe, a couple of short snappers here."

The Premier's leadership produced a highly motivated, intensely loyal group. One of the team's strengths was the consistency of its message. "It was like good football," McGuire says. "Everybody knew the game plan. Frank has a very systematic mind. He likes ideas, but then he likes people to come around and put the system together. This was highly choreographed. Everybody understood their role."

Fernand Landry recalls the first time McKenna went on vacation. Landry chaired the Monday morning meeting and told the staff they would all be slowing down for a week. Then faxes from McKenna started to arrive, and his requests kept the office hopping. When McKenna returned the following Monday, he had filled several notepads with dozens of ideas that he wanted to start on right away. "There were never two or three priorities, there were a hundred priorities," Landry recalls.

John Bryden used to say that McKenna drops all his marbles on the table and then expects everyone else to pick them up. "He's got a memory like a computer," Landry says. "He remembers details and follows up on things that most people would forget. He had no system. He would pull these little notes out of his pockets and never miss anything."

McKenna didn't always remain so cheerful as the week progressed, but he refused to descend into cynicism, whereas MacKinnon, who was idealistic, impatient and impulsive, often expressed frustration about how slowly the agenda for change was progressing. They'd be driving through northern New Brunswick, and MacKinnon would mutter, "This is hopeless. We're never going to be able to bring jobs up here." McKenna would grit his teeth and turn on his young assistant. "You may think that, but just watch me," he'd growl.

Members of the Liberal caucus felt fortunate to have McKenna as leader; however, he didn't always bring them along intellectually, and at times his impatience would transform him into a bully. He enjoyed being challenged, but if his challengers didn't have their homework done, he'd flatten them mercilessly and move on to something else. And when the caucus or cabinet couldn't agree, McKenna would carry the day on faith. The running joke among members of the McKenna cabinet was, "Eighteen to one? We have a consensus."

Soon after he arrived in Fredericton, Robichaud discovered that he was working for a man who was fascinated by the possibilities of communications. At least once a day, McKenna would stop by Robichaud's office for an update. "What's shaking, Moe? What are you hearing? What are the press saying?" For a media handler, McKenna was a dream client. He understood what reporters needed, and he happily gave it to them. If he was stung by a story — and, being extremely thin-skinned, he often was — he never held a grudge. Yesterday's news was history. He rarely paused to look over his shoulder.

With McKenna's blessing, Robichaud expanded his influence beyond the premier's office and began to redefine the province's image. He hired the eminent New York image consultants Lippincott and Margulies Inc. (whose clients included Coca-Cola Co.) to produce a report on how New Brunswickers viewed their province and how the province was regarded nationally. Robichaud turned to the New York firm because he wanted an unbiased report from a company with no vested interest in the outcome of the study. McKenna supported Robichaud's decision despite its $250,000 price tag. After conducting polls inside and outside the province, Lippincott and Margulies concluded that, from the inside, New Brunswickers had a pitiful image of their home, and that from the outside New Brunswick was seen as a beautiful place but an economic basket case.

Even worse for McKenna's job creation agenda, outsiders viewed the province as one of the worst places in the world to do business, Francis McGuire told *Canadian Business* magazine. "In focus groups, when you mentioned New Brunswick, what came to mind were places like the Ozarks or the backwoods of Arkansas." The message New Brunswickers had been receiving from their political leaders had been that they were destined to be poor and hopelessly dependent. "The solution to every problem involved going to Ottawa to look for a handout," McGuire said. "We wanted to change that."

The Lippincott and Margulies study received poor reviews at home. The Tories, the NDP and the media questioned why McKenna had hired a New York firm while he was telling New Brunswickers they needed to start making it under their own steam. Why wasn't a home-grown firm able to do the work just as well? What did hiring Lippincott and Margulies have to do with self-sufficiency? Novelist David Adams Richards wrote that he couldn't understand why McKenna "ever needed a consulting firm from New York to tell us what our identity should be." Moreover, a New Brunswick logo created by Lippincott and Margulies designers had been rejected and replaced by a logo drawn by staffers at Communications New Brunswick, a fact critics homed in on as proof that the whole New York marketing study had been a boondoggle.

After these mixed reviews, Robichaud decided that he needed to do a better job of coordinating how the government as a whole dispensed information. On the one hand, he wanted to keep reporters busy working on good-news stories. On the other hand, McKenna's activist government was planning fundamental changes that the public needed to hear about from the government first, before the opposition started spreading its own version of events. The fifty-eight-to-nothing Legislature was making some hard decisions to bring government spending under control, and McKenna wanted people to know there was reason to be optimistic. The goal was self-sufficiency. If the reality was somewhat different from the message, no one was going to say it out loud.

"We all knew that the vision would not be realized by the time we left office, and it probably won't be realized for decades yet, but it encapsulated everything that he stood for. It said to everybody, 'This is where we're going,'" Robichaud says. "We're driving this little go-cart around the planet, we're not going to make it around the planet with this little go-cart, but that's where we're headed. We didn't acknowledge to ourselves, nor did we acknowledge publicly, that we weren't going to get to the end of the line, that we weren't going to become self-sufficient by the end of it, but that's where we were taking people."

When there was positive news, Robichaud promoted it shamelessly. Managing the news not only helped the government but also simplified the lives of reporters in the press gallery, who were looking for stories, preferably easy ones, which would satisfy their editors and producers from day to day. "It became clear to me that there were all kinds of things going on at cabinet that were announceable, that were being announced on a Friday at three p.m. or on the same day as a major highway accident, and the story would get totally blown off, or sometimes the story wouldn't even get written about. But Monday to Friday, reporters were there, saying, 'What am I going to write about today?'" Robichaud recalls. As the communications plan took shape, Moe came to be seen by the press as a colleague rather than an adversary. If they would help him with his agenda, he would help them with theirs. "My own disposition is that I'd rather make friends than enemies, rather have peace than war," Robichaud says. "That's my nature. I'm competitive, but I believe in fair play. I understood early on that they had a job to do, and if I could work with them, overall they might be happier. Why did I need to have a confrontational situation between what they did and what I did? I was frustrated sometimes by what they did, but I suspect that they were equally frustrated by what they perceived as stonewalling on my part."

In the press gallery, Chris Morris saw the Lippincott and Margulies study as a turning point in government communications, the point at which the McKenna government's door of open and free access for reporters slammed shut. McKenna would still be available for interviews, but the message was more tightly controlled. "They developed a system that was amazing," she recalls. "Some would call it strong-arm, but basically it involved very strong manipulation of the message to the public, very tight control on what got out and what was said and how things were handled. Mo was the personification of the McKenna technique. He was the gatekeeper. He was the one we had to deal with, and it became very frustrating at times.

"They were kind of intimidating because you knew if you did a story they didn't like, you'd hear about it. They'd call and directly confront you about it, they'd go to your editors and complain about it. Some might call that bullying. I think we saw a shift in the civil service, too. People became much more circumspect about what they said and who they said it to. You saw the whole development of spin doctors for every department. You couldn't go directly to the deputy ministers anymore – they'd tell you to call the spin doctor, and then ultimately they all had to go through Frank's spin doctor."

Meanwhile, Morris recalls that Robichaud appeared to have successfully cultivated relationships with key reporters in the press gallery who would generally repeat whatever "Moe said" without question. These reporters forged a special connection with the Premier, and in the process, Morris believes, they lost their objectivity. "The machine just kept grinding out this stuff," she says. "New Brunswick was open for business. You couldn't mess with that. McKenna had a lot of popular policies, and he really sold them well."

While it may have appeared to reporters that Robichaud was managing the news, the Premier himself was directing the agenda. "Frank was very much the communications planner, not only for himself but for the entire government," MacKinnon recalls. "Moe was an incredibly good soldier, but Frank was the general. Frank would vet every speech, he would vet every announcement. Moe would say, 'Here are the four or five things we have to announce,' and Frank would plan them and say, 'Well, I want that on Tuesday. Do this on Friday because *L'Acadie Nouvelle* doesn't publish on Saturday. Why are we doing this on Tuesday, and why is the press release going out at ten-thirty, not eleven?' Frank was the master of his government and the master of his day-to-day communications."

By the spring of 1989, McKenna had decided that his economic agenda had stalled. His office of economic development was unable to influence the direction of the bureaucracy. John Bryden had moved on after a year to become the chairman of the New Brunswick Liquor Corporation. McKenna was impatient. He wanted jobs for New Brunswickers and he wanted them right away, but at the same time he was imposing increasingly tough restraint measures on government spending that did little to create a sense of optimism. The recession of the late eighties had started to take its toll on New Brunswick's resource-based economy. Five thousand forestry-related jobs had disappeared as a result of a downturn in the market and increased mechanization in the woods. Mines were laying off staff or closing altogether. The only bright spot was the patrol frigate program in Saint John, a recession-proof industry that was pumping $200 million a year into the provincial economy. However, the 1997 end date for the program was looming. The time to take decisive action had long passed.

McKenna decided to play a more direct role in economic development. When he had visited Michael Dukakis in Boston, the governor had told him how he had been his state's chief cheerleader and how he had personally escorted busloads of business executives on tours through the state. "Massachusetts was considered to be a hotbed of innovation, and they had a strong information technology economy," McKenna recalls. "I didn't know all of the ways in which it would be carried out, but I felt that the pulpit of the Premier's office would be helpful in economic development."

McKenna asked Francis McGuire to put the job creation program back on track. According to McGuire, "Frank realized, 'This isn't working, this isn't clicking. I'm driving the car and I'm turning the wheel, but this wheel's not connected to anything.'" McGuire told the Premier he would do it, but he needed the clout of a more traditional bureaucratic position. In April, 1989, in the middle of the Meech Lake fiasco, McKenna appointed McGuire Deputy Minister of Economic Development, moved his office up to the fifth floor of the Centennial Building and dissolved the commission in the premier's office.

The first thing McGuire did when he moved into the Department of Economic Development was to send back the new office furniture his predecessor had ordered and retrieve an old desk and chair out of government storage. The last thing McGuire wanted was for McKenna to arrive for his first meeting in the new office to discover that he was spending public money before he had attracted one job to the province. The Premier had also set an unwritten standard. After he was elected, McKenna had refused to renovate his own office. His only concession was to remove a mildewed couch from the Hatfield era and replace it with a battered conference table from storage. The nasty blue carpet wouldn't be replaced, even after its most noticeable feature was a hole worn through to the floor.

McGuire shared his boss's sense of urgency and determination. His attitude was, "We're only here for a short time. Let's get this done. You don't think I can do this? Give me a week and I'll prove to you I can." He was a deputy minister, but not in the fashion of Julian Walker, now deputy minister of environment and a civil servant who no longer practiced politics. McGuire would remain a member of the Premier's inner circle, attending Monday morning meetings, helping to plan both the economic and political agenda. He also continued to work on the constitutional file when the premier needed his expertise. The civil service knew McGuire carried the authority of the Premier. A loyal soldier, he remained one of the few who dared challenge the premier intellectually. "We'd have great debates," McGuire recalls. "He gets stubborn. He'd say, 'What's the matter with you? I'm the premier.' I'd say, 'I don't care. Prove to me I'm wrong on any of these points.'"

"Francis has a very sharp mind, one of the most agile minds I've ever come across," McKenna says. "People in the department still talk about him, his ability to infuriate the public service because he had so much clout and so much energy, and he was very aggressive. But he has a very nice personal style about him that allowed him to get away with the exercise of power."

When McKenna grew impatient with the slow-turning wheels of

government, he would invariably seek McGuire's help. In a meeting discussing strategy for the 1991 election, their conversation turned to the dormant tourism industry. "I'll take that, why don't you give it to me?" McGuire said.

After that election, McKenna restructured the bureaucracy to create the Department of Economic Development and Tourism. McGuire started to plan changes the way he started all his projects, by polling. He found out what tourists wanted, which wasn't what the province was offering. Tourists wanted vacation adventures presented to them in an easy-to-understand package. In 1994, the government purchased seventy thousand acres of land from the Hearst Corporation to build the Fundy Trail, which McKenna opened in June, 1995. He had pursued the initiative since the day he toured the coastline with millionaire philanthropist Mitchell Franklin. "One day with Mitchell, and I was sold," McKenna told reporters as he stood beside Franklin at the official ceremony on the bank of the Big Salmon River. Franklin spoke that day of the millions of New England tourists within a day's drive of New Brunswick, a lucrative market that McGuire felt he was unable to tap until 1996. In that year, tourism revenue would exceed $700 million, almost double the amount realized at the end of the Hatfield administration.

It wasn't until after the 1991 election that McGuire's economic program started to gain momentum. "The first years were kind of figuring out what we could do," he says. "We really didn't have much of a game plan." He likes to tell the McKenna economic story in two phases — the early years of working on the province's image, and the job creation phase that began in the second term. "After the 1991 election, we really decided to get the constitutional stuff off the table," McGuire says. "After that, it was pure, solid years of economic policy."

In 1991, McKenna announced to a skeptical caucus that the key to the transformation of the New Brunswick economy was information technology. "When he came up with his idea of technology and the new information age, some of us in cabinet were wondering, Where the hell are we going with this?" recalls Ray Frenette. "As it developed, all of a sudden we realized that he was right. Information technology would not only provide new jobs for New Brunswick, but it would also bring our two peoples closer together because of our language ability."

Bernard Richard, who joined the crowded Liberal back benches in 1991, recalls his first day in caucus, when he heard the Premier talking about the opportunities of technology and felt the skepticism of his colleagues. "He was absolutely convinced this was an area where we should invest," he recalls. "And he convinced all of us that it was important to get New Brunswick to the forefront of information technology."

As McKenna transformed himself into New Brunswick's chief salesman and job hunter, he spent less time dealing with the day-to-day governing of the province in the Legislature. He abdicated his responsibilities as the head of government to the man who had emerged as his chief lieutenant, Ray Frenette. The Premier put Frenette in charge of the Legislative Assembly as government house leader, a job the political veteran accepted and executed with style and finesse. "Frank didn't like the Legislature," Frenette says. "He saw his position as the chief executive officer in charge of making New Brunswick what it should be. He thought he could do much more on the telephone from his office or on the plane to Toronto and Ottawa and Los Angeles to create business activity in the province. The Legislature for him was a necessary evil. He'd stay for Question Period, and then he'd leave me in charge of steering the business of government through the House. I loved it."

In 1987, McKenna could count the number of active files in the Department of Economic Development on the fingers of one hand, and he realized that his economic development officers were under-challenged and uninspired. When McGuire moved into that department to light a fire under the staff, McKenna started trying to influence them as well, telephoning them directly or dropping by their desks, hounding them about progress on their files. Over time, they would become more aggressive about attracting business to the province. But no matter how inspired they became, the public service tends to be process-driven. Changing a culture in which moving paper along a line is a large part of a person's job takes time and patience, both of which, in McKenna's case, were in short supply.

To assist him on his job-hunting crusade, McKenna had found one civil servant who was an exception to the rule. When he dissolved the premier's economic development office, McKenna asked Charlie Harling to stay behind as his personal economic development advisor. Harling, a former Hatfield civil servant, could match the premier's intensity stride for stride and speak like a corporate pitchman. "We watched the way he operated on some files, and we liked his style," McKenna recalls. "After a while we became inseparable. He turned out to be an absolutely superb closer. I talked to him at least every day, either a phone call or a visit. We wanted to get the deal done, signed, and on to the next file. That's what he brought to the table."

Harling, who was recruited by Fern Landry to work under John Bryden, recalls the first day he met the Premier. "He walked into my office unannounced, introduced himself, talked about his vision and where he wanted to take the province, and immediately wanted to know what deals I was working on. He wanted to create jobs and improve the economy as fast as we could."

Harling's job was to find potential targets and close deals. When he came to the Premier's office from the job protection division where he had been working, Harling brought one file with him. CP Express & Transport was exploring the possibility of setting up a back-office operation in Moncton, where the economy had been hammered by the closure of the Canadian National Railway shops, a loss of more than two thousand high-paying jobs. CP Express was looking for a way to reduce its costs, and "it wasn't like the phone was ringing off the hook," Harling recalls. It was a win-win situation, as he likes to say; he decided to focus his energy on closing the deal with CP Express.

The company was planning to centralize its office administration and accounting services, so Harling decided maybe it would help to bring the telephone company into the negotiations. Lino Celeste, the chief executive officer of NBTel, came to one of the meetings to sell CP Express on its technology. For years, the phone company had been spending millions of dollars running fibre optic cable, which could carry large volumes of data at high speed, throughout the province. Without really knowing what benefits it might bring, NBTel became the first telephone company in Canada to complete a fibre optic network, fully digitize its switches and offer combined voice and data lines to its customers.

McGuire says he knew that CP Express would likely last only a few years before it would disappear in corporate restructuring. However, if CP Express survived four years and then closed, it would leave behind trained workers. As far as the New Brunswick team was concerned, the province had to start somewhere. "We were that deliberate," McGuire says. "We knew CP Express wasn't going to survive, and we made the decision strategically: 'We've got to build on it and we'll take our lumps when it

Frank McKenna, 1993.

goes down.'" In August, 1990, Harling closed the deal with CP Express & Transport to create fifty jobs in Moncton, with the province providing $150,000 to the company to help train workers. This company was used as a marketing tool, as a lever to go after other companies.

The next target was Camco Inc., a subsidiary of General Electric Canada, the country's largest manufacturer and servicer of electronic appliances. Camco had decided to centralize its customer inquiry centres and was leaning toward a site in Waterloo, Ontario. When McKenna heard about Camco's plans in December, 1990, he met with company president Stephen Snyder and sold him on Moncton's bilingual work force — the largest and best trained outside of Quebec; the low labour costs — $21,000 to $25,000 a year, $5,000 less than workers demanded in larger Canadian cities; and NBTel's technology. To help Camco make the decision, New Brunswick put $1.5 million on the table. "We paid an arm and a leg for it," McGuire admits. "We just bought it. The decision to buy it was mine. I was saying, 'You're never going to sell anything unless you have an example.' Our negotiating position was pretty lousy, so we paid more for that, $32,000 a job, which was way out of our average." In February, 1991, Harling cut a deal for Camco's $8.8 million project, and Moncton became the home for the first McKenna call centre. Dennis Williams, former CEO of General Electric Canada Inc., the parent company of Camco, later told *Canadian Business* magazine he'd never encountered a more focused government-industry team.

The New Brunswick economic development team had adopted NBTel as its private-sector ace in the hole. "We started to realize from client reaction that they weren't used to dealing with a telephone company like this," McKenna says. "NBTel had technology that others didn't have, and the service standards were higher. NBTel sold themselves and the government sold them. We realized that we had a superior performer that gave us a competitive advantage, and we used it shamelessly."

For years, the province had been chasing everything that moved, but the McKenna team decided to face reality. The province is small. What possible advantages could there be to that? New Brunswick could move aggressively and target industries forgotten by larger players, such as call centres. Publications about New Brunswick's advantages became blatantly friendly to business and thus regularly offended the province's labour leaders. The government promoted low wages and labour legislation that was favourable to business, boasting that NBTel's clerical workers were not unionized and that there had been no concerted attempt to unionize the call centre industry. The government abolished the provincial sales tax on 1-800 numbers and amended the Workers' Compensation Act, reducing company payments into the fund and removing stress as a legitimate claim. These initiatives opened McKenna to the charges that he was reinforcing New Brunswick's image as an economic backwater, establishing low-paying electronic sweatshops instead of creating optimism or self-sufficiency. In response, McKenna argued that the people he met around the province simply wanted an opportunity to work; the end would justify the means. "We haven't created a low wage policy," McKenna told the *Globe and Mail*. "We've taken advantage of the fact that our competitive costs in New Brunswick are lower than elsewhere. Our quality of life is good, and we've always needed less to live on than in Toronto or Montreal. We're now turning that into an advantage, and I make no apology for that. It's a choice between a service sector job or nothing. We're taking every job we can get."

The sales team stripped down the bureaucratic process for approving business proposals from four months to a week. McKenna and McGuire grew increasingly frustrated by the federal Atlantic Canada Opportunities Agency and its "molasses-like" bureaucracy. "We'd try to go through them, around them, over them, anything to avoid them," McKenna says. "The process became part of the pitch. It wasn't just that we were a good place to do business. Yes, we were, better than most, but we were also a good place to conduct business."

To make up for the sluggish federal agencies, the New Brunswick cabinet gave McKenna complete freedom to close deals. "We would call the shots," McKenna says. "If we had a team in Toronto trying to make a deal, and three other provinces were competing, if they needed an extra $400,000 on the table to make it happen, they made it happen. That gave us an edge because other people would have to run around looking for authority. Everybody knew Charlie Harling had that ability to call the shots. It would be nothing for him to call me from wherever he was and say, 'Look, I had to spend another $150,000, what do you think?' And I'd say, 'Do it.' We developed an intimacy between the economic development office and the premier's office that nobody else had."

McKenna was willing to put public money on the table to attract businesses to New Brunswick, simply because in the North American corporate welfare culture this was the only way to be in the game at all. But he had his limits. In the weeks leading up to the provincial election in September, 1991, he gave up a deal proposed by Crown Life Insurance

Company to move more than twelve hundred jobs from Toronto to New Brunswick in exchange for a $250-million loan guarantee. "We didn't like the risk, we didn't like the dollar amounts, and we didn't like the principle," McKenna told the *Globe and Mail*. "We like to minimize the risk to our people in New Brunswick, and we don't like the corporations to actually benefit themselves from it." Saskatchewan premier Grant Devine, who was on the verge of going to the polls himself, happily put up the money, and Crown Life moved to Regina.

New Brunswick never had deep pockets. McKenna knew the sales pitch was as important as the dollars he could afford to put on the table, which could be matched by every province in Canada. To reinforce at the forefront of the hard sell, he launched his own toll-free telephone line. One day when doodling on his note pad, Maurice Robichaud had scribbled down 1-800-McKenna. A marketing strategy was born.

In November, 1991, Federal Express, following its policy of not accepting government assistance, decided to set up shop in New Brunswick without a subsidy, creating four hundred jobs in Moncton. "I remember winning that one, and how a good day turned into a bad day," McGuire recalls. Elsie Wayne, the outspoken mayor of Saint John, was outraged that more jobs were going to Moncton. "Elsie just went berserk. Instead of sitting and drinking champagne celebrating four hundred jobs, we spent all day fighting off the press and Elsie and the politicians from Saint John. That's when Elsie turned around on the language issue — she said, 'We have bilingual workers here, too.' The good part of that story is, it really got Elsie on side." During the next few years, they worked to attract an Air Canada reservation centre to Saint John.

Recruitment became more focused, and McGuire developed a routine that he would apply to all potential business clients. "It was so simple, and people kept falling for it," he says. The presidents of companies would generally agree to meet with the Premier of New Brunswick, even if they had no real interest in New Brunswick or, for that matter, their own lowly call centre divisions. McKenna's mission was to convince them to order some flunky to do a cost-benefit analysis of setting up shop in New Brunswick. The president would agree to it, if only to make McKenna happy. Meanwhile, McGuire knew that it would take four or five months to get the analysis done and also that most people setting up call centres don't know what their costs are. The New Brunswick team would zero in on the employee who had been assigned the analysis. "We had a whole team built, with NBTel people and ourselves, who would walk in and find out who the guy was, and say, 'Hi, do you know how to do this?' He'd say, 'No,' and they'd say, 'We have a methodology for you,'" McGuire says. "And we'd actually put analysts from NBTel in the company doing the numbers. We'd do it honestly, but that way we got to know all of their operations and all of their people. Because we were working on it, we knew when the report was done and what it said. That's when we'd re-engage Frank, who would call and say, 'I hear the report's finished, and it says you will save twenty-five per cent.'

"We learned really quickly that guys dealing with call centres were low-level kinds who had never seen a vice-president, let alone a president, so part of the thing was, we had to work with them, make them look good, give them the information, and we had to make sure the report got back to the president. Then we'd come in, and it would always be the same thing: 'Okay, it's going to save me twenty-five per cent a year, but it's going to cost me $2 million to move it.'" The New Brunswick team would know how much the company needed to be subsidized. Then McGuire would plug McKenna back into the process, and Harling would close.

In the fall of 1991, McKenna and Harling found a new big target. Purolator Courier Ltd. announced that it had decided to consolidate its fifty Canadian phone centres into four supercentres in Vancouver, Montreal, Toronto and another city. This new call centre was worth eight million dollars and had the potential to employ four hundred people, and New Brunswick and Winnipeg were being considered. For several years, McKenna had been laying the groundwork for the Purolator file, keeping in touch with his friend Gerald Schwartz, president of Onex Corp., Purolator's parent company, telling him to keep New Brunswick in mind.

As the Purolator competition became more intense, a chance telephone call to the premier's office sealed the deal. Early one evening in April, 1992, Purolator vice-president Paul Derkson called the premier's office from his office in Mississauga, Ontario, to get more information from a senior bureaucrat. The staff had gone home, so McKenna picked up the phone and answered all Derkson's questions without identifying himself. When McKenna asked Derkson to hold a moment because he had to take a call on another line from Brian Mulroney, Derkson realized he was talking to the Premier himself. At that moment, he decided the call centre should go to New Brunswick. As this story was repeated over and over again in the business press, the call from Purolator became legendary and was pushed later and later into the evening, making the story of the call more dramatic than it actually was. But one aspect of the story was completely accurate: McKenna knew the Purolator file inside and out, like every economic development file in the office. The Purolator deal was done in June, 1992.

At his home away from home, the Royal York Hotel in Toronto, McKenna was in the gym working out by six-thirty in the morning, then he grabbed a quick breakfast and read the newspapers for a half-hour. Meetings began at seven-thirty and continued into the early evening, usually with a speaking engagement squeezed in at lunch or dinner. If McKenna wasn't eating at a speaking engagement, he would order room service and keep working until winding down late in the evening with a cigar and some channel surfing.

Harling recalls one evening when a group of New Brunswick bureaucrats had gathered in McKenna's suite to report on their activities in Toronto. Eventually, someone suggested they go out to eat, and they began discussing possible restaurants, keeping in mind that Fredericton tends to be a gastronomic desert. "Frank picks up the Yellow Pages, counts the heads and says, 'We'll order Chinese and eat here. Let's keep talking business,'" Harling recalls. "So he ordered take out. The brown paper bags came in, and the boys sat there with their little containers, and that was it. That was typical. When he sat down in the evenings, he would just talk shop." The Premier could became so immersed in his job-creation program that even politics would turn into an unbearable distraction. In the year before an election, his handlers would severely limit his time in Toronto because it was important that he be seen often in the province where he was trying to get elected. The memories of Richard Hatfield being out of the province for more than a hundred and fifty days a year were still too fresh in voters' minds. "He'd get two trips to Toronto in eight or nine months before an election. It would just kill him," Maurice Robichaud says.

Two staffers, Robichaud and Steven MacKinnon, travelled with McKenna. They took turns, and the Premier still wore them out. Harling, a man who bristles with energy himself, often wondered where the Premier found his reserves. There was no down time. On the plane to and from Toronto, McKenna would scour newspaper want ads. If a company was on a hiring binge for back-office personnel, he would tear out the ad and hand it to Harling. Another opportunity. He would then pull out one of his notepads and put Harling through his paces. What happened to this one? Why didn't we get these guys? Why don't you call them again? "Nothing ever fell between the cracks with him," Harling says.

When the Royal Bank started looking for a location for a new customer service centre, every province in Canada started lobbying for the bank's business. McKenna had already made his case to bank president Allan Taylor in a canoe on the Restigouche River in northern New Brunswick. McKenna and Taylor had met at the Ristigouche Salmon Club, the most exclusive fishing club in Canada, a favourite vacation destination for the most elite business executives in North America, as well as royalty, movie stars, sports heroes and politicians. The club operates three opulent lodges deep in the New Brunswick wilderness, including Indian House, located just downstream from the Million Dollar Pool, which is arguably the greatest Atlantic salmon fishing spot in the world. "Over a period of several days, we had many long conversations about the state of the nation and the region," McKenna recalls. "I talked at length about my vision for New Brunswick and how I felt about an obligation from corporate Canada to help our region to help itself. I used the analogy of having a choice between continuing welfare and unemployment insurance or providing us with jobs. I also reminded Allan that providing jobs to us was no act of charity. We could do the work at a high level of competency and probably at lower cost. He seemed very interested in a most sincere way with our aspirations for the region."

When the Royal Bank call centre came into play, McKenna spoke regularly with Taylor, reminding him of their conversations on the river. He also spoke with Gordon Feeney, a vice-president of the bank who is originally from New Brunswick. "I always felt confident that we had strong backing at the very top level when final decisions were made," McKenna says. In May, 1994, Royal Bank built a customer service centre outside Moncton, eventually hiring a thousand people.

The McKenna job creation team continued to gain momentum. In the winter of 1995, Harling was in Florida vacationing with friends when he got a call from the Premier. "Air Canada called, they were asking for you, and they want to start negotiating right away," McKenna said. "You've got to get to Montreal." So Harling cancelled the rest of his vacation, flew off to Montreal and started negotiating. "I basically lived in Montreal for a couple of weeks under an assumed name at a hotel because Air Canada didn't want people to find out we were having this negotiation." When Air Canada called, New Brunswick hustled; the deal was made in May, 1996.

When the deals were done, Robichaud would milk the news for all it was worth. "We'd announce it four times," he says, "and then we'd repeat it a million times." The Robichaud job announcement strategy went something like this. First McKenna would hint at good news to come at a press conference on another matter. Reporters would start digging for the story, which Robichaud would pretend was a closely guarded secret. Then someone connected with the government would let details about the deal slip out, and Robichaud would reluctantly admit to the media that it appeared there had been a leak and that, yes, the premier had done another jobs deal. The media would report this news in Story One. A few days later, the details of the new jobs would be leaked, and Story Two would appear. McKenna would make the official announcement for Story Three. Then, down the road, the new business would be officially opened, McKenna would be there cutting the ribbon, and the whole story would be repeated again. If Robichaud was lucky, more enterprising news organizations would do a larger takeout on "the anatomy of the deal," and McKenna would let them in on all the intrigue, the months of hard work, the code names and the fascinating journey through the inner workings of the premier's office.

Although the local media followed these stories, McGuire and Robichaud were determined to make McKenna a national media star. The province's chief salesman needed to appear on the covers of the magazines that were read by the bankers and chief executive officers on Bay Street. "We worked it really, really hard," McGuire says. "Between the premier's office and Economic Development, we had a very tight game plan with lots of money tied into it. We started slow. Nobody would cover us. So we said, 'If you won't cover the story, we'll buy an ad to get your attention.' Some of those ads we bought, not because the advertising would be effective, but because we wanted to influence journalists. Journalists themselves were an absolute target of our advertising."

McKenna increased his public speaking schedule outside of New Brunswick, repeating again and again that his province didn't want handouts, it wanted business. Moreover, New Brunswick was getting its public finances in order, a message bankers always wanted to hear, and he systematically visited the editorial boards of magazines and newspapers across the country. "A lot of it was personal dinners," McGuire says. "If Gerry Schwartz invited Frank to dinner, we goddam well got him on the plane and got him there. All of a sudden you've got a bunch of people who want this guy, who want to hear what's happening down here." The Premier started referring to himself as the chief executive officer of New Brunswick and alluding to the people of his province and business people as clients. Doors were opening for the hustler premier, who spoke a language business could understand.

Robichaud understood how to offer the media good service. If a business magazine was planning a special issue on, for example, "the best cities for business," he invited its reporters to New Brunswick and made elaborate preparations for their visits. If reporters wanted information, the Premier's office would provide it right away. Did they need to speak to someone in the information technology sector? Well, Robichaud just happened to have a list of names and phone numbers on his desk. The New Brunswick business community, particularly in Moncton, understood this strategy and enthusiastically played their roles. In August, 1992, the *Globe and Mail's Report on Business Magazine* compiled a feature on "Canada's Best Cities for Business" and singled out Moncton: "Answering Moncton's Call: Premier McKenna's salesmanship is transforming Moncton into the back-office capital of Canada."

Every good story needs a hero, and when reporters came looking, Frank McKenna was there, often championed as a bright light shining amid the country's political woes, an antidote to the cynicism generated during the Mulroney years. Thomas Kierans, president of the C.D Howe Institute think tank in Toronto, told *Maclean's* magazine, "When people ask if there is any hope for a better and more effective political system, I say that it will come only when people in other provinces point to Frank McKenna and say, 'I want one of those.'"

Between the summer of 1992 and the spring of 1994, McKenna's face was everywhere in the national media, and the storylines were all the same: a visionary premier, a farm boy who pulled himself up by his own bootstraps, possibly a future prime minister, is transforming a have-not province with an aggressive campaign to recruit business coupled with a progressive program of fiscal and social reforms.

The cover of the *Globe and Mail's Report on Business* magazine announced: "The Win-Win World of Frank McKenna: New Brunswick's premier is the best salesman any province ever had." Inside, beneath a photograph of McKenna jogging in front of the province's Legislative Building, was the headline: "The energizer premier: In a relentless search for jobs, industry and self respect for his province, New Brunswick's Frank

McKenna just keeps going and going and going . . ." The *Financial Times* broadcast on its cover: "Overhauling New Brunswick: How Frank McKenna's wrenching economic program is getting his province off the government dole." The *Toronto Star* focused more on McKenna's politics: "The face of liberalism in the '90s: Like Bill Clinton, Frank McKenna has been putting pragmatism over ideology." *Canadian Business* concentrated on economic and social reform: "Faith, Hope and Hold the Charity: New Brunswick is plagued with illiteracy and joblessness. But Frank McKenna is sending people back to school — and out to work." *Canadian Business Review* promoted a policy-oriented interview with McKenna on its cover: "Getting Down to Business in New Brunswick." *Maclean's* first published a story inside the magazine, "Chairman Frank: New Brunswick is Run Like a Business," then followed up with a cover photograph of McKenna jogging in his business suit, briefcase in hand, and a second story, "Fast Frank: How Frank McKenna is setting the pace for Canada." *Reader's Digest* focused on personality: "Frank McKenna, Hands-on Premier: He governs New Brunswick with the same fiercely competitive drive he displayed as a sports-loving youth and honours student." *L'Actualité* brought the story to Quebec: "1-800-McKenna: Frank McKenna a une ligne directe avec le monde des affaires." In February 1994, a *Globe and Mail* columnist suggested that McKenna's counterparts were suffering from "premier envy." For McKenna's critics, the adulation was almost too much to bear. "It's gotten to the point where you head for the Gravol bottle before even opening a newspaper," Elizabeth Weir quipped. By the time the national media finally took the bait and began stumbling all over each other to write "the New Brunswick story," McGuire had already turned his attention to other issues; that mission had been accomplished.

Meanwhile, the call centre campaign continued. After the Purolator deal was done, Harling called United Parcel Service Canada Ltd. executives and arranged for McKenna to meet with them in Toronto. As a result of this meeting, in October, 1994, UPS hired two hundred people in Moncton out of 3,000 applicants; the company was impressed by the size and quality of the work force. UPS had call centres scattered throughout Canada, including one in British Columbia, but in January, 1995, the company decided to consolidate its Canadian operations in New Brunswick, creating five hundred jobs in Moncton and four hundred in Fredericton. Each job was subsidized by a ten-thousand-dollar government grant. UPS president Ronald Wallace told the *Globe and Mail*, "People here have learned very fast, they are very motivated. In the worst snowstorm so far we had only two employees show up late for work. It was the performance of the people at our call centre that helped us to make the decision."

Glen Clark, who was then British Columbia's Investment and Trade Minister, erupted, accusing McKenna of cravenly giving away money to big business. "It's not a question of sour grapes," he said, "it's a question about how the country is going to be governed if we have provincial premiers or provincial governments going out of their way, not to create jobs in their province, but to steal wealth from other parts of the country, to steal jobs."

McKenna insisted that he was giving his usual incentive of ten thousand dollars a job for training and relocation expenses. He had no problem with being labelled a job stealer. "We're not envious of British Columbia and their extraordinary wealth, the billions of dollars in Asian money they receive every year or the record-breaking growth they are experiencing. We're not envious of the oil wells in Alberta or the auto-motive plants in Ontario and Quebec. We just want others to respect the fact that we in New Brunswick want to stand on our own two feet."

McKenna asked McGuire to defend the politically sensitive UPS deal in the media. "I understood exactly what he meant," McGuire says. "If I got myself in trouble, I'd have to go. Frank's pretty hard. I knew Frank well enough. If I have to be cut for him to survive, I'll be cut." In this case, however, McGuire knew he was on safe political ground. Clark's outrage and McGuire's defence were both playing well in their home provinces.

Several years later, Manitoba Premier Gary Filmon complained that McKenna and his cohorts were putting the hard sell on some business people from across Canada during a Team Canada trade mission to Asia. As before, McKenna made no apologies. "We have a province that is poor and people are looking for work. We want work and we go after it very, very aggressively," McKenna countered. "We're here to draw business from outside, not from each other," Filmon grumbled. Filmon was in fact complaining about what had become standard McKenna operating procedure on trade missions. He and Harling would study seating plans, locate business people they wanted to speak to and develop a schedule to speak with all of them. They also would identify participants who had already had dealings with New Brunswick so that, on an airplane, an endorsement was just a few seats away.

New Brunswick's call centres became stepping stones to building an information technology economy, although this would prove to be a more difficult mission than attracting back-office operations. Before delivering his State of the Province address in January, 1994, McKenna telephoned McGuire to tell him the government needed to promote the information technology industry more heavily.

"We're really going to go after the IT industry," McKenna said. "We need a focus, we need to create a secretariat to run that." McGuire agreed and then waited for what he knew was coming.

"Okay, you're running the secretariat tomorrow," McKenna said.

"What?" McGuire replied.

"Yeah, you're in charge of it."

"Do I have a budget?"

"I'll give you $250,000."

"I have to set up a department with an annual budget of only $250,000? That will just pay for the minister's salary, his executive assistant, his car and his secretary."

"That's your problem," McKenna said. That night he announced the new Information Highway Secretariat, the first of its kind in Canada, and appointed MLA Georges Corriveau as its minister. Donald Savoie notes that the information technology sector in New Brunswick grew from three small companies in 1992 to more than two hundred by the time McKenna resigned. One of the companies, Scholars.com, would become the world's largest online trainer. McKenna recruited COM DEV International Ltd., a manufacturer of satellite and communications technology, to Moncton after meeting with the company's president and chief executive officer and agreeing to purchase $1.45 million of the company's preferred shares through Provincial Holdings Ltd. In his last year in office, McKenna's team recruited six hundred information technology jobs to the province.

No economic development project was too small for McKenna the detail man. When he discovered that the province had an opportunity to attract more conventions and national meetings, he set up a convention promotion division in his own office. "The whole idea was to spawn it and then move it out," McKenna recalls. "People couldn't believe that the Premier of New Brunswick would call the International Boy Scouts and try to convince them they should move their convention to New Brunswick. I would go right to the head office of some national organization and tell them we wanted their next convention. Again, it was just all about selling."

The McKenna team was creating jobs, but most of them were in the Fredericton-Moncton-Saint John triangle. What about the economically depressed northern regions of the province? One of the strategies was to create a high-tech textile industry on the Quebec border, a program that has met with, at best, mixed results. By 1997, there were sixty-four textile companies in New Brunswick, employing more than 2,000 people; however, a number of these were short-lived, and a series of failures brought with them a heavy price for taxpayers. In fact, the textile initiative began three years before McKenna took office with a proposal from rags-to-riches Montreal businessman Edwin Kenny to create a bed sheet manufacturing plant in Caraquet. Kenny grew up in northern New Brunswick, then moved to Montreal, where he founded Wink Industries in 1970, making oven mitts in his basement. Halifax-based business reporter Michael Tutton chronicled Wink's relationship with the New Brunswick government through documents obtained under the Right to Information Act. Tutton says the New Brunswick government's attitude toward the uncertain venture changed when McKenna began to champion the file. McKenna was anxious to bring jobs to the north, and he didn't mind taking risks to attract them. Despite the reservations of provincial bureaucrats, in 1988 his government provided Kenny with a $3-million interest-free loan to get his project off the ground. The Atlantic Canada Opportunities Agency followed with $10 million in subsidies.

If McKenna's strategy was to create some momentum with Wink, it worked. A series of new textile firms were attracted to New Brunswick in the wake of the Wink deal, including Adeem Sportswear Inc. and Calicloth International, two clothing manufacturers that set up in Bathurst with the support of more than $4 million in provincial and federal grants. However, both Adeem and Calicloth declared bankruptcy in 1998. When Wink Industries filed for bankruptcy in the fall of 1999, it had received $27 million in federal and provincial money and had consumed half the province's incentive budget for textiles. Tutton points out that Wink alone took down with it a sum of public money approaching Hatfield's Bricklin fiasco, and he calls the textile factories in the north "one of the major boondoggles of the Liberal era."

"When I took over, we were still negotiating Wink," Francis McGuire recalls. "Wink was the biggest, best deal that had hit the province of New Brunswick in fifteen years, although by today's standards it stinks. I remember the Premier getting so excited, it was wonderful, it was great. It wasn't a great deal. It was the best they had."

By the time he left office, McKenna's team had attracted more than fifty call centres and six thousand jobs to the province. However, Paul Martin's 1995 federal budget, with its $30 billion in spending cuts, hit Atlantic Canadians hard, eliminating thousands of federal jobs in New Brunswick, reducing transfer payments, hammering seasonal workers with changes to the unemployment insurance program, and slashing transportation, agricultural and industrial subsidies. Between 1987 and 1997, Ottawa eliminated more than 8,500 stable, high-paying government jobs in the province. "Every time he takes two steps ahead, the transfer payments thing comes and knocks him back one," John Bryden noted. After all McKenna's hustling to drag New Brunswick to its feet, Ottawa could knock it down again with the stroke of a pen.

On November 23, 1995, McKenna wrote to Prime Minister Jean Chrétien, pleading with him to consider the impact of unemployment insurance changes in New Brunswick, both politically and economically. McKenna noted that twenty-three per cent of all new social assistance cases in New Brunswick were people whose unemployment insurance had run out. Already, changes to the program were reverberating among the thousands of seasonal workers in the province who faced the prospect of living without income for fourteen weeks in the winter and spring of each year. "As you are undoubtedly aware, it is absolutely impossible to obtain replacement employment at this period of time," he wrote. "The end result has been disastrous and has created an enormous amount of sensitivity here." McKenna warned that the reforms would create a political backlash east of Ontario "the like of which has never been seen before in this country." (In fact, in 1997, the Liberals managed to win only three of ten seats in New Brunswick.)

"It does not make sense to penalize seasonal workers who have absolutely no chance at other employment but who are, otherwise, valuable contributors to the economy. For the province of New Brunswick alone, the impact of these changes will remove approximately $175 million per year from our economy. This is little short of devastating.

"Prime Minister, I beg of you to take the time to examine the ramifications of this legislation. We have been the strongest advocates in Canada of activist programming, deficit reduction and social innovation. We know what will work and we know what will not work. We are prepared to support that which is reasonable and that which is workable. We are not prepared to support changes such as those made last year that are poorly thought out and counterproductive."

Bernard Richard says that this letter to Chrétien reflected the Premier's deep concern about francophones in northern New Brunswick, who would suffer the most when the system was changed. "On principle, he was such a fighter for jobs and self-sufficiency, he must have had a bad taste in his mouth to send that letter, but he knew the devastation the cuts would wreak in the northern part of the province because of their dependence," Richard notes. "Obviously he was always a strong believer in independence and progress based on economic development, but he knew it couldn't be done overnight, and it had to be nurtured. That wasn't a popular message."

In his many private letters to Ottawa, and in his diary entries, McKenna expressed a desperation he would never reveal publicly. On September 11, 1996, the anniversary of his vindication at the polls in 1995, when he won a third overwhelming majority, his diary entry reveals that, despite his public optimism, privately he often fought an overwhelming sense of hopelessness. "Anniversary of election win. Everybody seems happy. I feel no real sense of joy or complacency. We still haven't made a lot of progress on the job issue." He had announced a new call centre, and then a mill or a mine had closed, cancelling any gains he had made. So much remained outside the control of one man's political will. Many mornings he would wake up to ask himself, have I done enough?

Workers protest the government wage freeze as Frank McKenna enters the Liberal nominating convention in Saint John, May, 1993.

8

PREMIER FRANK

Roadblocks appear in every effort to move.
— *Frank McKenna, diary entry, January 6, 1988*

By the time the Premier reached the concrete steps in front of the Lady Beaverbrook Arena on the morning of April 17, 1991, Steven MacKinnon was starting to panic. The parking lot beside the old arena at the foot of the University of New Brunswick campus was the staging area for a march on the Legislature organized by the Canadian Union of Public Employees to protest the Liberal government's public service wage freeze. The crowd would soon be more than three thousand strong, the largest public demonstration in Fredericton's history. Buses were arriving and protesters were spilling out onto the sidewalks of the old establishment neighbourhood along University Avenue, wearing blue baseball caps with "No Wage Freeze" printed across the front in white letters and singing "Solidarity Forever." The air crackled with anger.

The premier's office had been advised that the union planned a rally that morning inside the hockey rink, and Frank McKenna felt obliged to meet them face to face. MacKinnon had thought that the Premier would speak inside the arena in a controlled setting. He had predicted that McKenna might take some verbal abuse, but he had also assumed that, before things got out of hand, the Premier could slip away to meetings in Saint John. However, that scenario was now fading fast.

McKenna, MacKinnon and Maurice Robichaud parked a block from the arena on University Avenue and walked up the street. McKenna moved swiftly, suit jacket open, hands in his pants pockets, smiling and nodding at demonstrators he recognized. He jogged up the steps two at a time to the main entrance of the arena and pulled on the glass doors. They were locked. He walked around to a side door. Also locked. The crowd closed in, a chorus of boos growing louder.

"Two or three rambunctious types decided they'd take up their issues with him, up close, real close," MacKinnon recalls. "Of course, just like in the schoolyard, the others formed a tight little circle to watch the scrap. My instinct was, Let's get the fuck out of here." MacKinnon lunged toward McKenna. They had a simple code; when he tapped his boss on the elbow it meant, "Let's get out of here, Frank, right away." MacKinnon tapped him on the elbow, hard.

McKenna turned to face his young assistant, moving deliberately because the television cameras had also arrived and were recording his every move, and spoke to him in a tone he never heard before and has never heard since: "Steven, just stay back, fuck off," McKenna said softly. "I'm handling this."

In order to balance the province's books, McKenna had asked union members to carry a heavy burden. Just months before he went to the polls to seek a second mandate, he had abandoned New Brunswick's traditional roller-coaster fiscal policy. The ride usually began in the first years of a government's mandate as a journey of restraint, a slow, cautious, winding ascent; then, in the months before an election, the spending brakes were released, and the province would speed toward the polls in a rush of steaming asphalt trucks, government construction projects and temporary jobs. After the election, the illusion of prosperity would dissipate, and the slow, cautious ascent would begin again. McKenna flattened this fiscal midway track and pointed it straight ahead.

Although this new course may have been more prudent, it certainly wasn't as much fun. In the fourth year of his first mandate, McKenna delivered his toughest budget to date, reducing government spending by $185 million. The spending cut was financed in part by legislation that imposed a one-year wage freeze on ten thousand public servants. Finance Minister Allan Maher said he had two options — impose the wage freeze or fire two thousand people.

The Canadian Union of Public Employees said that the budget was an assault on workers whose wage increases had been negotiated in good faith and that it undermined the principle of collective bargaining itself. CUPE began soliciting donations to finance a campaign to oust McKenna in the next election. "Frank McKenna's dreams are our nightmares," union leaders proclaimed, and a "Day of Democracy" march in Fredericton would show McKenna just how formidable an opposition he faced.

Now, before the march on the Legislature even began, the union had the Premier right where it wanted him, surrounded by angry demonstrators and television cameras and with no choice but to push his way through the crowd back to his car. While it may have felt like a set-up, in fact Steven MacKinnon had failed to do advance scouting for his boss on the worst possible day. He had led him straight into the fire.

The best politicians are fine actors who are able to play whatever role the occasion demands. Francis McGuire says Frank McKenna is the best actor he has ever seen. Standing outside the arena, McKenna slipped into character, stemming the anger rising in his throat, reminding himself that, no matter what happened, he had to appear composed and project leadership. The drama on University Avenue was being recorded for the six o'clock television news. He had to deliver his lines and get them right on the first take. So he started walking casually down the street as if he had all the time in the world. When a strip of pavement opened in front of him, the crowd swarmed back around him. They shouted "No wage freeze" and "Dictator" and waved placards, one with a rough drawing of an extended middle finger that stated bluntly, "Up yours, Frank." McKenna knew he had to level the playing field. If he addressed the crowd as a whole, he was outnumbered. He would be shouted down, humiliated. However, if he began to engage the demonstrators one at a time, he could hold his own.

"I voted for you, I supported you one hundred per cent," shouted a city worker from Bathurst, shaking his finger inches from the Premier's face.

"And I hope you will again," McKenna replied, stopping and making eye contact with the man.

"How can we support this? I have to go home and tell my wife and kids that I just lost six point five per cent."

"You can tell your wife and kids I've made a decision that's in the best long-term interest of New Brunswick."

The worker began shouting at McKenna. The crowd joined in. McKenna was losing his advantage.

"Just a second." McKenna interrupted, raising his voice, speaking directly to the man from Bathurst. "You can tell your wife and children that I saved your job, that I've also made this province more financially secure, that I've avoided raising taxes for the people of New Brunswick."

McKenna was sending a message that he knew would sell to a wider audience. The demonstrators had secure jobs, and he knew there were a lot of people out there who would love to have them, wage freeze or not. "If we were to lose an election on this issue after the way we've managed the province for four years, we would leave it in an awful lot better shape than when we found it," McKenna told another demonstrator.

"We've made the decision to try and save jobs," he repeated as he tried to push his way around a woman who was shouting so close to his face he could feel her breath. "People in the public service have security, they have good paying jobs. Thousands of people would like to have those jobs. We value the work that those people do, but we want to save those jobs, not to fire people like others are doing, but to save those jobs."

As McKenna continued to move steadily back to his car, he saw a familiar face, an elderly woman wearing a blue coat and white knitted hat.

"Ah, Dorothy," McKenna said. "I've seen you at every rally that's ever taken place in New Brunswick."

"Exactly, and you made a mistake this time, dear," she said.

"But it's one that I'm prepared to live with, Dorothy."

As he slid into the front seat of the car, he turned to the reporters who had followed him in his procession down University Avenue to his car. "Okay, well, have fun, all. I'm off," he said.

The demonstration spread onto the lawns and streets around the Legislature. There, union workers raised the arms of their new champion, NDP leader Elizabeth Weir, a tough labour lawyer who was emerging as the most effective voice of opposition to the McKenna government.

The next day, McKenna told reporters that the demonstration was more orderly than some children's birthday parties he had attended. "I don't want to make these people out to be hooligans," he said. "I know working people and I like them. They've got a leadership who are trying to whip them up. I believe when you talk to most of them individually, most of them are quite reasonable and realistic."

He never let on just how angry he had been that morning. MacKinnon drove him to Saint John after the fiasco on University Avenue, knowing that he and Robichaud had engineered a potential public relations disaster. During the two-hour round trip to the port city, McKenna didn't say a single word to MacKinnon. "I knew he was just boiling, burning inside, not only at the demonstration but at the fact that we had failed," MacKinnon recalls. "He explained later that it was important for him to appear calm, to let his body language convey confidence and not to look like he was being handled or hustled along. He was right, but so was I. It could have been a very bad scene — few police, no union leadership, TV cameras. He never should have been there. We all learned a very hard lesson that day. We didn't want that to become the defining clip that overturned the government and destroyed his credibility."

In fact, the television images of McKenna standing face to face with demonstrators during the great CUPE march did become a defining moment for the Premier among his own people in New Brunswick, in the same way that images of the political and business hustler defined him for his national audience. For ten years, the people of New Brunswick lived with McKenna's restless activism. His reforms of public finances and social policy, tasty morsels for the central Canadian media, were more difficult to swallow at home. Until the day he resigned, his foot was firmly planted on the public policy accelerator. His critics would say he was often driving recklessly. However, when he faced off with union protesters on that spring morning in 1991, McKenna sent a clear message: that he was plotting a course for a collective journey; that on some days the journey would be rough; that he had the intellectual and physical courage to see it through to the end.

This hard edge, like so many parts of the Premier's persona, was something he had to acquire. If McKenna was going to attempt to transform a province, he was going to make people angry. Leadership is about making choices. Georgio Gaudet, the deputy minister in the premier's office in the final years of McKenna's tenure, remembers the Premier asking him, 'Georgio, what's right here? If we can't come to an agreement on what is the best option, what is right for New Brunswick? What's right for the people? What's right for the fiscal framework? What is right?"

McKenna may have made what he believed were the right policy decisions, but they were not always the best political decisions. Steven MacKinnon says he always knew two Frank McKennas: Premier Frank and Campaign Frank. Premier Frank was obsessed with making the right policy decisions; Campaign Frank was in touch with the mood of the public and had sharp political instincts.

Premier Frank reported for work on October 28, 1987, the morning after the Liberal government was sworn into office, and immediately dispelled any fears that he was too young, too soft and too green to bring order to the unruly political atmosphere in Fredericton. John Bryden, who had resigned as Deputy Minister of Justice when Hatfield came to power, advised McKenna to clear out any public servants who might be hostile to the Liberal agenda. Win Hackett, the long-time deputy minister in

Hatfield's office, had already resigned. While McKenna and his staff moved into the Premier's office, he dispatched Fernand Landry and John Bryden to fire three deputy ministers — Gordon Gregory, the Deputy Minister of Justice, Frederick Arseneault, the Deputy Minister of Supply and Services, and Denis Haché, the Deputy Minister of Fisheries.

"We wanted loyal people who would work with us, and we wanted to send a signal to the system and to the province that things were different," McKenna says. "I didn't expect that we would have to fire any civil servants, but I thought that we would get some resignations from some obvious ones." The Liberals considered Fred Arseneault the alter ego of Richard Hatfield; it would be impossible to coexist with him in government. There was a perception that Gordon Gregory had an agenda that was closely associated with the Conservative Party. Denis Haché had publicly clashed with his Tory minister and had been the subject of much criticism from the Liberal opposition in the Legislature. His dismissal saw these criticisms through to their logical conclusion.

Gordon Gregory had no intention of resigning. The forty-nine-year-old Harvard-educated lawyer had been appointed deputy minister of justice in 1970 to replace John Bryden. He had intended to work in the public service just four years but ended up staying seventeen, and the Justice Department had become his life. After the McKenna sweep, Gregory decided to keep his head down and stay busy in his office across the hall from the premier's office. "I liked what I was doing," he says. "I recognized that there might be some knives sharpened. But the only premier I knew was Richard Hatfield, and he was not the type of man to exact a pound of flesh."

Gregory considered himself a professional civil servant who should not serve the unrestrained wishes of the premier and his cabinet. "Civil servants are there to provide a brake and a restraint upon the sometimes emotional indulgences of those who are in the cabinet," he argues. "The public is not well served when you put an irrational fear of God into the minds of public servants. Dismissal of civil servants serves a political interest. It does not serve the interest of the public or of good government."

Gregory was working at his desk when Landry and Bryden arrived. He knew Fern Landry, whom he had hired along with Aldéa Landry to work in the Justice Department during the Hatfield administration, and he expected to discuss McKenna's plan to separate the justice and policing branches of the Department of Justice and transfer responsibilities to a new Department of the Solicitor General. He soon realized the meeting was not about his contribution to the transition. Bryden read from a prepared text: "We are meeting with you at the direction of and with the authorization of Premier McKenna and the members of his executive council. Premier McKenna has asked us to inform you that he wishes to terminate your employment with the government of New Brunswick. He asked us particularly to stress that he wishes the severance to take place as amicably and as fairly as possible. He prefers that you resign immediately. Your resignation will be considered without prejudice to any right you may have to claim compensation."

Bryden told Gregory to leave his office at once; he would arrange for his personal effects to be delivered to him. If Gregory decided not to resign within a reasonable time, he would be fired. He was welcome to discuss severance with either Landry or Saint John lawyer Ronald Lister, who had been retained to handle the file.

Gregory staggered numbly out of his office, leaving behind everything, including his overcoat. Grieving over the loss of his job, the anchor of his life, and angry at the harshness of his dismissal, he telephoned lawyer David Norman and began the process of taking Frank McKenna's government to court. Five days later, he wrote an eight-page letter to McKenna, copied to Landry and members of the executive council, informing them that he would not resign and asking for his job back. "I thought this a rather brutal manner to treat a senior government employee who, at age forty-nine and within eight years of pension, has devoted the last seventeen years to the administration of justice in this province," he wrote. "Please also bear in mind that no Deputy Minister in this Province has been dismissed because of a change of government since before the Second World War. This refusal to dismiss Deputy Ministers has spanned the depression-era administration of Premier Dysart in 1935, and the succeeding governments of premiers McNair, Flemming, Robichaud and Hatfield."

Gregory defended himself against allegations that he mixed politics with the administration of justice. "This paranoid view of contemporary justice administration was a surprise to me and the cause of constant anguish over the past ten years." He said his only comfort was that, while Liberals criticized him for not prosecuting more government members and supporters during the Hatfield kickbacks scandal, at the same time Tories were outraged that he had prosecuted too many of their own.

"No Deputy Attorney General in living memory has ever been removed from office anywhere in Canada under circumstances such as prevail now in New Brunswick," he wrote. "Regardless of your motivations, your actions will be perceived as an act of revenge by a political party. If a Deputy Attorney General is removed from office without cause, no prosecutor will believe he is safe. He will know this in every decision he makes — to prosecute or not to prosecute."

McKenna replied to his letter, saying simply, "I am appreciative of the courteous way in which you have presented your case. However, I am not persuaded to change my decision." He always maintained that Gregory's firing was driven by the perception that he was too close to the Hatfield administration. Whether that perception was true didn't matter; the change had to be made. On the other hand, Gregory believes history had finally caught up with him. New Brunswick Liberals had not forgiven him for his involvement in the public inquiry that had resulted in the resignation of Robert Higgins a decade earlier. Higgins had been on the threshold of election as premier, and they remained convinced that he had helped steal the big prize from them.

"Someone had to pay the price," Gregory says. "When Higgins fell on his own sword, no one could believe he wasn't pushed. The problem was, Higgins was dealing with a guy a lot smarter than himself in Richard Hatfield." After Hatfield had been vindicated by a public inquiry and Higgins had resigned, the Liberal leader complained that the inquiry's terms of reference weren't fair. "The urban myth grew up that I was the one who cooked the terms of reference," Gregory says. "What happened to Higgins became a sin that could never be forgiven. I don't think McKenna gave a damn about Bobby Higgins, but there are certain imperatives of political life."

After the three deputies were dismissed, McKenna met with the remaining deputy ministers and told them there would be no more firings. He outlined his agenda for change and asked for their help. Georgio Gaudet was in the room to hear McKenna's speech. Gaudet had served the governments of both Louis Robichaud and Richard Hatfield, most recently as Deputy Minister of Social Services. Whereas he always admired the disgraced Tory Premier as a man who would offer thoughtful and balanced decisions when he turned his attention to an issue, he realized that with McKenna he was dealing with a different kind of politician. "If you could get Richard's attention, he had good judgment," Gaudet maintains. "But in the last two or three years, the ship started to waver and started going in different directions. Perhaps he felt he had done the steering long enough."

By the time McKenna met with the deputies, the public service had been badly adrift for many months. Ministers and their deputies were feuding. Bureaucrats were protecting and expanding their own empires, and policy directors no longer guided those delivering services. McKenna told the deputies to brief their new ministers and get ready for change. "There was some insecurity for a period of time," Gaudet recalls. "It was an unusual move. Was it a shock to the system? Yes, it was a shock to the system. Obviously McKenna was a manager who wanted to take charge."

The wrongful dismissal suit went to trial a year and a half later. McKenna testified for the government. The judge sided with Gregory, said he was wrongfully dismissed without notice, and awarded him eighteen months pay, which amounted to about $150,000, a third of which was used to cover his legal fees. "I was not fighting for a principle on behalf of all members of the civil service," Gregory says. "I was fighting for myself. I'd been treated badly. A wrong had been done, and I wasn't going to take it. Everybody afterwards was the beneficiary of the establishment of the principle of the case, that the government, the Crown, no longer has that prerogative."

Despite the court judgment, McKenna has never regretted his decision to fire the three deputies. In fact, in retrospect, he wished he had removed more of them. "I wanted to change the leadership," he says. "What I wish I had done is sat down with more deputies and said, 'We have fundamentally different views on things; why don't we negotiate a package and let you leave.' Instead, what we did was do work-arounds." In some departments McKenna dealt directly with his minister, in others with the deputies. In departments where he wasn't seeing enough action, he ignored protocol and dealt directly with junior public servants, searching the bureaucracy for someone who could get the job done. "We gradually weeded people out," McKenna says. "There were a number of departments where I could have made progress much more quickly if I had not been a softy and left people in place. The private sector never, ever would have put up with it. If you've got the right leadership, you can move mountains. If you've got the wrong people, the mountains will fall in on you." By the time he resigned, he felt New Brunswick had a first-rate professional public service, and he was promoting career bureaucrats to senior posts instead of bringing in help from the private sector.

McKenna's public service purge didn't go nearly as far as some Liberal partisans expected. For example, hundreds of casual jobs in the Department of Transportation traditionally changed hands immediately after an election. All the wing men on snowplows had always been let go and replaced with members of the winning party. The day after the election, Liberal party supporters who had survived seventeen long years out in the cold started showing up at government transportation offices, astounded to find Tories still working in jobs they felt were theirs by partisan entitlement. Andy Scott, who was working in the Liberal Party office in 1987, was deluged with requests from Liberals for patronage appointments. Scott understood better than most the intensity of such feelings in the province; his father, Liberal stalwart Keith Scott, a diabetic, worked so hard during each election campaign that he often ended up in hospital. Nevertheless, Andy Scott realized that he was dealing with a group of Liberals whose expectations were too high. It was true that petty politics were part of New Brunswick life: in the 1960s, government snowplow operators scooped out the Scott driveway in Fredericton after every storm. On the other hand, when Hatfield came to power in 1970, Andy Scott learned how to shovel snow. Even so, the current deluge of requests for patronage was unrealistic. Furthermore, McKenna refused to play the game.

"What really drove most of this pressure was an honest belief that for seventeen years they were deliberately excluded," Scott says. "If you applied for a job, if you tried to get work for your truck, the assumption is, if you are a Liberal and you're not working when the Tories are in power, it's because you are a Liberal. Some of the people would say, 'It's my turn, fire them, I want the job.' Most simply had the sense that their partisan affiliation had hurt them for seventeen years, and surely to God it wasn't going to hurt them now."

McKenna refused to fire casual employees because of their politics. He sent a memo to Bryden and Landry a week before he was sworn in, ordering that Tory casuals be kept on at least until they had worked the ten weeks they needed to draw unemployment insurance through the winter. "This represents an excellent gesture of goodwill, a good way of addressing the whole patronage question," he wrote.

Although McKenna's government didn't fire Progressive Conservatives and in many cases allowed them to keep their positions on boards and commissions, when jobs opened up they hired Liberals. But this compromise wasn't good enough. Howls of righteous indignation reached the premier's office from all corners of the province: the Tories are driving down the road thumbing their noses at us. McKenna formed a mental picture of snowplows driving down main streets in small-town New

Brunswick with Tory wing men hanging off the sides, thumbing their noses at bedraggled, unemployed Liberals standing on the street corners. Over the years, the Liberals made their share of patronage appointments, but McKenna had more important things on his mind than responding to the demands for political payback. "Some people would tell you that, if you were a friend of mine and of the party, your chances of getting screwed were pretty good," McKenna says.

Through his first term in office, McKenna's reforms received little scrutiny from the opposition or the media. The national media were obsessed with Meech Lake, whereas the provincial press, radio and television tended to be parochial and uninspired. Mark Pedersen, the executive producer of the CBC supper-hour television news, demanded that his reporters provide systematic opposition to the one-party democracy; he approved almost any story that critiqued McKenna's policies. However, even good television journalism couldn't replace an effective opposition in the Legislature.

The sweep had left McKenna in a position with few precedents in Canadian history: the only comparable victory was a Liberal thirty-to-nothing win in Prince Edward Island in 1935. In a one-party democracy, the perception of a measure of goodwill towards the vanquished was essential. Therefore, the Liberals made some basic procedural changes in Fredericton to allow the opposition to get its message out. There was no sitting of the Legislature after a major government announcement in order to allow for opposition media day. Although no opposition party was provided with public funding for researchers, they did have office space and the use of the legislative library. An extra $200,000 was allotted to upgrade the library and hire more staff. Members of the un-elected opposition could take notes in the Legislature's public gallery and submit written questions to the Public Accounts Committee. All significant legislation was referred to the Law Amendments Committee, where opposition politicians could appear at public hearings. The Premier promised to meet with the media at least every two weeks, and he opened the Legislature to television coverage.

Question Period was like a Sunday afternoon game of slow-pitch softball. Liberal backbenchers lobbed easy questions across the ornate chamber at their cabinet colleagues, who fielded them with a smile. When the Question Period love-ins became too much for the public to bear and suffered regular ridicule by the national media, opposition politicians were given the right to ask questions from the press gallery. No matter how McKenna handled the one-party Legislature, the Tories faced a long road back. A year after Hatfield resigned, the Progressive Conservatives chose Fredericton lawyer Barbara Baird as leader. She was a promising, energetic politician who accepted an unenviable job with enthusiasm and the best of intentions, but she soon found herself under assault from the old boys' network within her party. The Liberals realized that she would never be a threat because her own party wouldn't allow her to be. Therefore McKenna laid down the law: Barbara Baird was not to be attacked politically.

Steven MacKinnon recalls the day he engineered a media assault on Baird at the Public Accounts Committee hearings. She was requesting details of Liberal expense accounts, so he retaliated by asking for her expenses during the time when she worked as a government prosecutor. When he saw reporters crowding around her demanding an explanation for some of her travel expenses, he realized immediately that in a hot-headed moment he had broken the "don't be hard on Barbara" rule. Afterwards, in the premier's office, he found McKenna conferring with Fern Landry. "Well, Barbara just got grilled in public accounts," he said, downplaying his role in the debacle.

"He looked at me. Fern must have been telling him some other bad news. He banged his desk. The blood drained out of his face. 'Yeah, you're pretty smart, MacKinnon,'" McKenna shouted. "'You think you've got it all figured out. We'd be better off without Barbara Baird, is that it?'"

Before the 1991 election, Baird resigned and Moncton school administrator Dennis Cochrane was elected leader, running a campaign just strong enough to return three members to the Legislature. The turmoil within the party continued. Cochrane, an intelligent and articulate leader, seemed too much of a gentleman for the dirty world of politics. He resigned before the next election, to be replaced by Bernard Valcourt, a francophone with roots in Madawaska who had served in Brian Mulroney's cabinet. When Valcourt was chosen leader, Maurice Robichaud and Steven MacKinnon purchased a rubber Brian Mulroney mask and recruited a tall friend to wear it at the convention and try to get his picture taken by the press. When Valcourt's photograph appeared in the newspaper after his victory, Brian Mulroney's rubber face appeared in the background.

With the former Prime Minister's popularity in the gutter, McKenna's henchmen helped make a connection that would stick.

When Elizabeth Weir was elected NDP leader in 1988, she became the unofficial leader of the opposition. Born in Belfast, Ireland, Weir moved to Toronto with her parents when she was two years old, part of the wave of immigrants who fled the bleak prospects in Northern Ireland after the Second World War; her father was a steelworker. She came east to New Brunswick to teach law at the University of New Brunswick, and she ran unsuccessfully for the NDP in the 1982 election. She became the party's executive director and was elected leader after the resignation of George Little, a veteran of political wars against both Hatfield and McKenna.

Weir was an imposing figure, both politically and personally. Standing six feet tall, she towered over McKenna physically and was his intellectual equal. Flashing her trademark gap-toothed smile, she stormed into the hallways of the Legislature before she had a seat, establishing herself as McKenna's most persistent and effective critic. In 1991, she won a seat and created a political stronghold for herself in a blue-collar Saint John neighbourhood. When Ray Frenette approached Weir to suggest she cross the floor and join the Liberals, she told him she'd rather gnaw off her right arm. In the final years of his life, Richard Hatfield befriended Weir. She found him to be a compelling man, generous of spirit and a fine conversationalist. At one of their last meetings at a Fredericton house party, Hatfield turned to Weir and said, "You're the only person who can save the province now."

Weir believed that McKenna had deliberately destroyed the legitimacy of Hatfield's government. She never bought the image of McKenna's government as lean and hard-working; as far as she was concerned, the 7-11 government was a myth. "I always thought this was such a crock because Frank McKenna would be there for Question Period and then he would be gone," she says. "He never stayed in the Legislature. We'd be debating issues on a Wednesday night, and he'd be at the hockey game. Not that I expect the premier to be in the House all the time, but he had an absolute disdain for the Legislature."

She found Liberal claims about remaking the province's image and their suggestions that nothing had happened in the province before Frank McKenna arrived offensive to New Brunswick business people and artists, who had been competing on the international stage for decades. "I don't know whether Richard Hatfield ever listened to a political strategist in his life," she remarks. "McKenna, on the other hand, was a combination of image, message and communications strategy."

When Weir and members of the Confederation of Regions Party arrived in the Legislature after the 1991 election, the Liberals who had arrived in politics with the McKenna sweep were shaken by the normal cut and thrust of parliamentary debate. "They couldn't adjust to any kind of criticism," Weir says. "They were very sensitive. It was a difficult adjustment for them." She had heated exchanges with Liberal veterans like Allan Graham or Ray Frenette in the Legislature and then afterwards bumped into them in the corridors with a "Hi, Allan. Hi, Ray." "The Liberal MLAs would be standing there in absolute shock," she recalls.

Weir believes that McKenna's activist agenda stalled during his first mandate because of the lack of an opposition. "That's why we saw the huge restructuring after the 1991 election, when we had a strong but small opposition in the Legislature that enabled them to do the things I think they wanted to do in the first term," she says. "One of the advantages of the Legislature is that it provides an outlet for airing controversial issues in some kind of public debate and then provides the legitimacy of saying you won the vote. In the absence of that, to make significant changes, especially in areas like the health care system, I think his advice from Landry and Bryden was clearly not to do that without the legitimacy of the Legislature."

McKenna believed that reform of the province's finances couldn't wait for a second term and that he had little choice but to act quickly. The Tories had left him with a $350-million current account deficit after their final, desperate pre-election spending spree. A 1987 audit revealed that the province's debt had been growing an average of $177 million a year for a decade. Government pension plans had multi-million-dollar unfunded liabilities. Donald Savoie notes that New Brunswick was on the verge of hitting a "debt wall" at the worst possible time: the federal government, facing a fiscal crisis of its own, was finding transfer payments to the provinces an "inviting target."

As McKenna told a *Globe and Mail* reporter, staring death in the face tends to focus the mind. He came to the office with job creation plans and a more typical liberal agenda; necessity turned him into a budget cutter and fiscal conservative.

If McKenna was going to sell the need for budget cutting to the public at large, members of his caucus and the public service would be allowed no indulgences. The Premier laid down the law – he would be unforgiving of mistakes involving their personal behaviour. There would be no more conducting business at the favourite political watering hole, the River Room at the Lord Beaverbrook Hotel. No alcohol and tobacco were to be charged on expense accounts. All government members and staff would fly economy class. Three meals a day on the road would cost the government no more than $24.25. No item should be claimed on an expense account that couldn't be publicly defended as reasonable.

While such guidelines would have been a joke in Hatfield's day, the parsimonious Premier followed his own rules to the letter. When the battered Crown Victoria he inherited from Hatfield needed to be replaced, he purchased a Ford Taurus as the official Premier's car and then drove it into the ground. When he and a New Brunswick delegation travelled from the Ottawa airport to 24 Sussex Drive for a First Ministers lunch with the Prime Minister, they hailed a taxi. "We got the worst-looking rusty taxi," Francis McGuire recalls. "And Frank says, 'Fine, let's pile into it.' And here we are going to 24 Sussex, laughing, saying this will be great for the media. It wasn't planned, but we all understand the symbolism. As we're driving in, five of us with briefcases all over the place piled into this shabby old taxi, I still remember the Mountie looking in the car when we got there and saying, 'Who are you?' We answered, 'We're from New Brunswick.'"

When the federal government organized trade missions abroad, McKenna would ask how many seats Ottawa was paying for and then demand that each ticket the province paid for be justified to him. "There'd be twenty bureaucrats from Ontario, Quebec and Alberta, and there'd be two from New Brunswick," McGuire recalls. "It made no difference to the outcome. In fact, it made New Brunswick more accessible."

Whereas McKenna saved money wherever he could, no matter how trivial the amount, the broad themes of his government, creating jobs and controlling spending, ran deeper than symbolic gestures. All of McKenna's reforms would fall under these two broad policy objectives. He established a cabinet Policy and Priorities Committee, chaired by himself, and a companion committee, chaired by the Minister of Finance, which was responsible for the budget. Policy and fiscal concerns were given equal status. When McKenna didn't receive enough suggestions for cuts through the normal channels of the bureaucracy, he asked Georgio Gaudet to chair a special budget committee to find ways to reduce spending. "I was really a hated guy there for a while," Gaudet recalls. "The Premier wanted to try to bring new ideas into budgeting, new alternatives. We brought in the unions and said, 'If you were going to do it, how would you do it? This is the budget we have; what would you do?' We got some really creative ideas. Some departments felt we were undermining them. Some of the ideas came from the grassroots." Gaudet met with health care and education officials to ask the blunt questions: "Here's the money. What would you do? Where would you cut?"

The Canadian Union of Public Employees continued to protest McKenna's campaign of restraint. Throughout the run-up to the 1991 election, the union staged demonstrations at Liberal meetings across the province. As he did on the Day of Democracy march in Fredericton, McKenna met them head on. Thomas O'Neil recalls an incident that occurred at his summer home in the seaside town of St. Andrews when McKenna dropped by for a short visit on his way to a nominating meeting in the town. As he prepared to leave, an RCMP officer stopped by and told the Premier there was a large crowd of union members in front of the meeting hall; the police had made arrangements to escort him in the back way. McKenna would have no of part of the plan, O'Neil recalls. "I'm going to go in the front door, and I'm going to talk to them," McKenna told the officer.

The union leaders could see that McKenna's budget-cutting program would become a template for public policy across the country. They were determined to fight him every step of the way. In June, 1992, when the government extended its wage freeze across all public sector unions, CUPE workers took to the picket lines in an illegal general strike. For four agonizing days, hospitals, schools and government offices were surrounded by angry strikers who clashed with police as they tried to escort essential workers through the picket lines. The strikers returned to work only when both sides agreed to work through a new mediator.

Union members had already been telephoning Fernand Landry, the one man they trusted to resolve the dispute, pleading with him to become involved. Landry had left the Premier's office before the 1991 election to return to teaching, his first love, at Atlantic Canada's first law school for French-speaking students at the Université de Moncton. Landry hadn't planned to stay in the Premier's office for the long term, and once he helped McKenna through his transition to power and the Meech Lake crisis, he knew it was time to allow the aggressive young

Premier to strike out on his own. Landry had worked as a labour mediator before he joined McKenna's team; his cool-headed and respectful approach to labour relations was the antithesis of McKenna's combative stance. In the end, both the government and the union asked Landry to find a way to end the fight. Having removed himself from McKenna's high-pressure world, Landry was reluctant to become involved. However, he was deeply disturbed by the shattered relationship between the government and its public service unions. He decided he would try to mediate an end to the dispute. "You don't get a second chance to resolve this matter," he told his wife.

For more than a week, Landry shuttled back and forth between the two camps, rarely taking time to sleep or eat. "He had major meetings at our house in Fredericton with national labour leaders," recalls Aldéa Landry, who was worried that her husband would collapse from fatigue. "It was like a roller coaster. He came home in the middle of the night and said, 'It's going better.' He came home and said, 'I don't think it's going to work.' I remember him calling Frank one morning when things weren't looking good. He was very firm with his former boss and close friend. 'This is the job I'm doing, and if you people don't move on this, it's not going to work, and I will call it quits,' he told him."

After a forty-eight-hour negotiating session, a deal was close, and Landry arranged for a meeting at his home on a Sunday between Frank McKenna and CUPE president Judy Darcy. "In my view, the decisive issues were very simple," McKenna says. "The union fought the battle on the grounds that the contract itself was inviolate and could not be reopened under any circumstances. The government's position was that the financial situation in New Brunswick and the rest of the country was deteriorating so rapidly that an immediate response was required. In the end, both parties were somewhat successful." The contracts were honoured, which allowed the union leaders to sell a final deal to their members, but the contracts were also extended, which allowed the government to save the money it needed to save over time.

Veteran New Brunswick political columnist Don Richardson recalls the weariness in Landry's voice when he met with reporters to announce the deal. "Fatigue seemed to drip from every pore of the man's body. His clothes hung loosely from his shoulders, suggesting he had gone without food as well as sleep in his determination to find consensus and derail conflict." Landry negotiated a labour peace for McKenna that lasted until he left office.

This peace allowed the public service to work with the McKenna government as a team. Nowhere was this more evident than in the creation of Service New Brunswick, a one-stop shopping centre for government services in which, in a single modern, efficient, computerized office, a citizen could register a car and buy a fishing license at the same time. The creation of Service New Brunswick demanded that government departments that had traditionally operated independently break down barriers and work together. Thomas O'Neil, the chairman of the crown corporation that created Service New Brunswick, notes that the model has since been copied by governments throughout North America. Citizens had become clients for the public servants to serve. "That will be one of our real legacies," O'Neil says. "New Brunswick is leading the world in electronic delivery of government services."

Following the settlement with CUPE, McKenna's government passed balanced budget legislation, and Standard & Poor's revised the province's credit rating from negative to stable. By his third term in office, the government was posting surpluses on its current account books and making payments on the debt. Nevertheless, the province's financial problems were not solved during McKenna's time in office. Donald Savoie points out that the net debt nearly doubled during the McKenna years, from $2.9 billion in 1987 to $5.6 billion in 1997. However, Savoie also points out that the Liberals added the province's unfunded public pension liability of $1.6 billion to the debt, and when he compared New Brunswick's financial performance during that period to that of other Canadian provinces, he concluded that McKenna's government "did better than other provinces of similar size in repairing its balance sheet."

As he worked to negotiate a new peace accord with public service unions, McKenna realized he would never balance the province's books until he addressed health care spending, which was escalating out of control at a rate of more than ten per cent a year. Any attempt to restructure the system, which inevitably meant eliminating duplication of services, closing beds in small hospitals and downgrading the role of small-town institutions, created political nightmares. The first step was to wrest control of health care from the communities. The government eliminated fifty-one local hospital boards and created eight health care corporations, which forced regions of the province to rationalize services, and a Physician

Resource Advisory Committee took control of the recruitment of physicians and created a program that would spread doctors more evenly around the province. These reforms were announced in the monotone of Health Minister Russell King, a cerebral Fredericton family doctor who, as far as news reporters were concerned, never uttered a sound-bite worth repeating. King was all business. In the course of this restructuring, chairpersons became chief executive officers, and McKenna even referred to his own position as Chief Executive Officer of New Brunswick. Elizabeth Weir pointed out that he was not a chief executive officer but a premier, and that there was a clear distinction between the two. Chief executives are appointed and responsible for the bottom line, not the public well being, whereas premiers are elected and accountable to the people, she argued. "It always seems to me he would have been much happier as the CEO of a corporation, but that's not what government does," she said. "Government deals in human lives. It deals in delivering services to people. It has always been a source of confusion for McKenna that New Brunswickers simply wouldn't be widgets."

The greatest test of McKenna's determination to control health care costs came when he was presented with a plan to downgrade St. Joseph's Hospital, a small but well-loved Roman Catholic hospital in downtown Saint John. St. Joseph's was a full-service hospital, fiercely independent and run by the Sisters of Charity. Native Saint Johners always believed St. Joseph's was offering a higher quality of patient care than the larger, more impersonal Regional Hospital across town. The government's plan — to turn St. Joseph's into a long-term care facility, emergency room and community health centre — put McKenna in conflict with both his church and some of his strongest Irish Catholic supporters. When King rose at a cabinet meeting and outlined plans to change the role of St. Joseph's, McKenna lowered his head and drew a deep breath. Not the Sisters of Charity, he thought. His first cousin, Sister Elaine Alexander, was a member of the order. Two of his sisters were nurses trained at St. Joseph's. The Diocese of Saint John had given him his first scholarship to start his university career at St. Francis Xavier. "It was one of those occasions when my heart went right through my stomach," he recalls. "God, do we have to do this? It was a series of days and weeks and months that I wished I could have been anywhere but in the Premier's office. It was horrible. It was excruciatingly difficult."

However, McKenna believed that if he didn't touch St. Joseph's, his government couldn't reform any other institution in the province. The

Regional Hospital had entire wings empty. When King announced that St. Joseph's would no longer be a full-service hospital, the people of Saint John took to the streets. Doctors resigned from the staff of the hospital. During the height of the uproar, McKenna attended Mass at the Cathedral in Saint John. As he was receiving the Eucharist, a priest leaned forward and whispered, "Stick to your guns, Frank." That's exactly what he did. Despite his misgivings about making changes at St. Joseph's, McKenna vigorously defended the plan. In a May 4, 1993, letter to Saint John resident Bertha Lindsay, who had written him a passionate missive in support of St. Joseph's, McKenna said that governments all across Canada had no choice but to stop the financial bleeding. He said he had eliminated a system in which New Brunswick had fifty hospital boards and administrators "all clamouring to do more," and asked the seven corporations to be as efficient as possible. The St. Joseph's plan emerged from that process. However, he noted, the hospital wouldn't be closing, just changing its role. "I don't blame you for your views," he wrote. "There were many people who were prepared to declare a disaster if they did not hear exactly what they wanted. Some doctors resigned from St. Joseph's Hospital before Dr. King even completed his announcement. One doctor suggested that people should not go to St. Joseph's because their lives would be in danger. It was a very clever tactic for gaining support for their arguments but unduly alarmed the public.

"One person I spoke with suggested that I was anything but a Liberal. She thought that Liberals should be more concerned with services and less with the bottom line. She is obviously very disappointed with me personally and with the government. But I believe a Liberal policy must be a lasting policy. We care as much about the future as we do today. Only by keeping an eye on the unattractive bottom line will we preserve our services for tomorrow. Regardless of your views on me personally or how you intend to vote in the future, I would make one request. Please step back and give these changes a chance to work. Rather than simply condemn them, work to make them work. That way they have a chance."

McKenna's longest-running and most controversial health care battle began just five months after he entered the premier's office. In January, 1988, Dr. Henry Morgentaler, a Montreal physician and abortion reform crusader, had won a landmark Supreme Court decision that struck down

Canada's abortion law. On February 8, 1988, Morgentaler wrote to Ray Frenette, then Minister of Health, to offer his services as a consultant to help the province to expand its ability to provide abortions. In 1985, Richard Hatfield's government had established a policy of allowing abortions only in hospitals and only after two doctors had approved the procedure as medically necessary. Morgentaler pointed out that every year, hundreds of New Brunswick women rejected this cumbersome and restrictive process and sought abortions outside the province; many of them travelled to the doctor's own Montreal clinic.

Frenette brusquely refused Morgentaler's offer in a letter dated February 17, 1988. The next day, in an interview published in the *Globe and Mail*, McKenna promised to give Morgentaler "the fight of his life" if he tried to establish an abortion clinic in New Brunswick. Surely McKenna was speaking with the hubris of a young politician, underestimating his adversary's iron will. Morgenthaler, a Polish Jew, had survived the Dachau concentration camp during World War II and served time in prison in Canada for performing abortions in his clinics. He had just been completely vindicated by the country's highest court. Morgentaler was already in the final rounds of the fight of his life, and he was winning them all.

The next year, Morgentaler won a court decision ordering McKenna's government to pay for three abortions he performed for New Brunswick women in his Montreal clinic. At every opportunity, he taunted his new opponent. On July 26, 1990, he wrote in a letter to McKenna, "I happened to watch your speech to the New Brunswick Legislature in which you criticized Meech Lake and proposed amendments which would guarantee the rights of women. Frankly, I was surprised that a premier who vowed never to allow an abortion clinic in New Brunswick was suddenly a protector of women's rights. Change of heart?"

In the summer of 1991, Morgentaler announced that he intended to open a Fredericton clinic. Morgentaler and McKenna continued their war of words in a series of letters that Morgentaler eventually released to the *Telegraph-Journal*, which published them under the headline, "Personal and Confrontational." In a typically nasty exchange, Morgentaler wrote, "I understand that your opposition to free-standing clinics has to do with your Catholic upbringing and your religious outlook. As Premier of a province, your sectarian religious views should not influence public policy. It strikes me that you represent yourself as a defender of women's rights and do not see the contradiction in opposing a medical facility which would alleviate the pain, the stress and the suffering to which so many women in New Brunswick are exposed."

McKenna replied, "Stripped of the offensive allegations relating to my Catholic upbringing, that I have misogynistic inclinations and that I desire to inflict unnecessary suffering on hundreds of New Brunswick women, the purpose of your letter appears to be an attempt to persuade me to invite you to establish your clinic or clinics in New Brunswick. I must say I personally find advocacy based on insult, threat and abuse quite unpersuasive."

On June 28, 1994, the seventy-one-year-old doctor arrived in Fredericton to open his clinic. His biographer, Catherine Dunphy, notes that Morgentaler was recovering from a stroke and battling depression, but still he managed to perform five abortions that day, and he also met the press, telling reporters, "Here in New Brunswick, it's as if we're in the Middle Ages again."

McKenna continued to fight. Health Minister Russell King asked the College of Physicians and Surgeons to restrict Morgentaler's license. The clinic was temporarily closed. Undaunted, Morgentaler turned to the courts, and in September, 1994, he won a decision from the New Brunswick Court of Appeal stating that the province's 1985 abortion law had nothing to do with ensuring quality health care. The province appealed to the Supreme Court of Canada and lost. Morgentaler reopened his clinic, eventually moving it from a house that had once been a restaurant on the city's north side into a new building in the heart of Fredericton's downtown. This clinic, which, Dunphy notes, cost him $450,000 and would never break even, was just a two-minute walk from the Premier's office. All McKenna could do was refuse to pay for abortions performed at the clinic, a policy Morgentaler has continued to challenge with McKenna's successors.

McKenna maintains that his reasons for confronting Morgentaler were "more pragmatic than dogmatic." He says health officials were making the medical case that abortions performed in hospitals were safer than those performed in clinics, and the cabinet believed this policy reflected the preference of the majority of New Brunswickers. "We always found it ironic that the same people who were totally opposed to two-tier health care were so dogmatically supportive of a for-profit abortion clinic," McKenna says. "As a matter of principle, I do not support the notion that legislators should put their personal views ahead of overall societal objectives. Because of our belief that we had adopted a solution that was medically supportable and representative of public opinion, I was satisfied that I had not contravened this belief. I recognize that others would argue to the contrary."

McKenna won't be remembered as a visionary health care reformer, but he did bring a measure of control and order to a system that was spinning out of control. He regularly angered health care workers by pushing ahead with reforms without seeking their counsel on the best course for a system they knew more intimately than any politician ever could; doctors and nurses tended to feel as if they were part of the problem. Yet he still commanded their respect. Thomas Barry, a family doctor in Fredericton and former president of the New Brunswick Medical Society, says that whereas he disagreed with some of McKenna's health care policies, the Premier was the first politician he had ever encountered who was respected enough by doctors and health care workers for them to buy into a decade of austerity almost without complaint. "It was purely a dollars-and-cents agenda," says Barry. "We knew it was a tough time, and he did know the system and understood it. We were a health care backwater. People laughed at us, our economics were so out of control." By the late 1990s, McKenna was travelling across the country speaking to doctors and health care managers about health care reform. "He did give us pride," Barry says. "We became a leader, and in that sense the health care system was better when Frank left than when he got there."

Although Frank McKenna spent time and energy managing health care spending, he was most interested in creating jobs and building an educated and literate work force. Only education, he believed, could transform the economy in the long term. According to Francis McGuire, "If you look at health care versus literacy, Frank had to manage health care, but he became an incredible advocate of literacy."

When McKenna was elected, New Brunswick had the third-worst literacy rate in Canada, followed only by Newfoundland and the Northwest Territories. More than twenty per cent of New Brunswickers couldn't read at a grade-nine level. He believed young people who couldn't read would be trapped in a cycle of unemployment, especially when so many of the new jobs that were emerging were information technology positions.

Literacy teachers were asked to become literacy advocates. Andy Scott, who was appointed to organize a provincial campaign to fight illiteracy, put a map on his office wall and stuck pins into the fifteen communities where there were literacy classrooms. His goal was to increase the number of pins. In January, 1990, he invited literacy co-ordinators from all over the province to meet with the Premier. As they sat around the cabinet table, McKenna spoke to them about their vocation, telling them that what they were doing for society went far beyond simply teaching people how to read.

The government launched the Community Access Service Program, a plan whose principles were borrowed from a successful literacy program in Thailand. Communities would raise two-thirds of the $18,000 needed to create each literacy classroom. Teachers would be recruited from the welfare rolls, where there were surprising numbers of qualified people who had fallen into a trap from which they couldn't escape. Literacy New Brunswick Inc. was launched to raise money for the program, and the funds poured in. At revival-like fundraisers, adults spoke about how the program had changed their lives; audiences were moved to tears. One hundred literacy centres were created in nine months, and eventually more than three hundred literacy classrooms were established across the province. In 1995, the United Nations Educational, Scientific and Cultural Organization awarded the New Brunswick program its International Reading Association Prize in recognition of its work in French and English communities — in particular for its work teaching Acadian women to read French.

McKenna was outraged that the school system was turning out illiterate graduates. To accompany his literacy program for adults, McKenna began to champion other educational initiatives that he hoped would benefit the province long after he left office. The first was kindergarten. Francis McGuire remembers trying to convince McKenna that although the kindergarten program was a good idea, it wasn't the right time to start it. "I was one of those who said, 'Frank, we can't afford it.' We had a deficit. It was during the recession. And he said, 'We're going to do it, we're going to have to negotiate with the unions, find a way to make it affordable, because if kids don't have a chance in kindergarten, then we've lost them, and they'll never get into the economy.'" In 1994, the government began to turn its attention to children before they reached kindergarten age through an Early Childhood Initiative, which was designed to help children from birth to age five who were at risk of slow development because of physical or emotional problems, neglect or abuse.

McKenna decided the control of education had to be centralized. The Minister of Education would be responsible for the system, and school principals would have to answer for the quality of education in their schools and meet provincial standards. Just as he had angered health care workers by pushing ahead with reforms despite their strong objections, he also angered educators by imposing a reform agenda from Fredericton. In 1991, his government reduced the number of school boards from forty-two to eighteen and moved all funding and curriculum decisions to Fredericton. Five years later, the government eliminated elected school boards altogether, replacing them with a system of parent advisory councils; New Brunswick was the first province in Canada to abolish school boards, but others soon followed its lead. However, school boards were so symbolic of community involvement in education that Bernard Lord's promise to restore elected school boards helped propel his Conservatives back to power in 1999. Even so, because he centralized educational planning for as long as he did, New Brunswick's schools took on a distinctly Frank McKenna flavour.

High school students were required to take twice as many science and math courses and to become computer literate before graduation. The school year was lengthened. Students were urged to stay in school, and when they were at risk of dropping out, educators were required to reach out to them through a series of intervention programs to keep them in school. Consequently, New Brunswick went from having one of the highest dropout rates in Canada to having the lowest.

The Department of Education spent millions of dollars installing computers in classrooms, and by 1996, all schools in New Brunswick were connected to the Internet. The wiring of New Brunswick schools also helped adults become computer literate. In 1994, when McKenna was campaigning in the Miramichi River town of Blackville, he stumbled on a little known Industry Canada initiative called the Community Access Program, which allowed parents to come into the school in the evening and work on computers, often with their children at their sides. After the 1995 election, in typical McKenna damn-the-process fashion, without clearance from Industry Canada's mandarins, he went directly to the bureaucrat in Ottawa who was leading the federal program. He said New Brunswick would take as many Community Access Centres as Ottawa could offer and would put money and organizational help on the table. As a result, community computer centres began opening by the dozens in schools throughout the province. Community colleges changed drastically, too, shifting their focus from trades to information technology. From top to bottom, education reform was designed with the vision of creating an educated workforce for the province's emerging information technology economy.

———

A more immediate problem faced the government, however: the chronically unemployed. What about the people who were already trapped in a cycle of dependency? As far as McKenna was concerned, welfare was never meant to be a way of life. He understood the nature of poverty better than most, but he also remembered how he and his siblings had made better lives for themselves through education and hard work. In his view, welfare programs encouraged dependency instead of helping people find a more productive way to live.

In the spring of 1992, the government launched NB Works, a six-year $177-million project that guaranteed people on welfare twenty weeks of summer work if they agreed to complete their high school education and take part in a managed job search while receiving a training allowance. The program got off to a rocky start. Elizabeth Weir ridiculed the image of welfare mothers cutting brush along the province's highways. Half of the first two thousand participants dropped out. And it was expensive, costing taxpayers about $100,000 for each person in the program. However, McKenna took heart from each story of how the program changed the course of someone caught in the welfare trap.

In the wake of the mixed results of NB Works, McKenna ensured that the province became a partner with a federal government initiative called the Self-Sufficiency Project, which attempted to move hundreds of welfare recipients in New Brunswick and British Columbia, mostly single mothers, off welfare. The project, managed by the Social Research and Demonstration Corporation, a non-profit research organization based in Ottawa, addressed the most pressing question of welfare reform: how does a government both encourage work and alleviate poverty? Most welfare recipients who re-enter the job market must accept low wages. Therefore, they often face the untenable prospect of earning less when they take a job than they did on welfare and are caught in the classic welfare trap — governments pay people to remain dependent.

The Self-Sufficiency Project was launched in November, 1992, and eventually enrolled 9,000 participants in New Brunswick and British Columbia. The participants were offered income supplements if, within one year of signing on, they left welfare to work at least thirty hours a week. They could receive the supplement for as long as three years. About one in three of the participants in the group that received the supplement left welfare to take a full-time job in the first year. By the fifth quarter, twenty-nine per cent of these project members were working full time, compared to fourteen per cent in the control group. Full-time employment had doubled; there were increases in earnings and reductions in welfare payments. As the participants in the study continued to be tracked by researchers, the project showed great promise as an escape route from the welfare trap.

Despite these innovative social experiments, there continued to be a hard edge to McKenna's welfare policies. New Brunswick had the lowest welfare rates in the country. Eight thousand welfare recipients were forced to line up outside one winter morning to receive their cheques during an investigation to eliminate fraud. Single mothers on welfare were required to name the fathers of their children so the government could go after the fathers for child support. (Elizabeth Weir responded with a campaign asking single mothers to name Frank McKenna as the father.) Worst of all in the eyes of his critics, McKenna himself had referred to welfare and social assistance as "programs which foster dependency, which make it comfortable for people to do nothing and learn nothing."

In 1994, Robert Mullaly, a professor of social work at St. Thomas University, and Joan Weinman, executive assistant to Elizabeth Weir, published a scathing attack of McKenna's welfare policies in the *Canadian Review of Social Policy*. "Such cynical, moralistic and punitive views would probably be considered as inciting hatred toward an identifiable group of people if it were any other group in society but poor people," they wrote. "And, as with most acts of discrimination, they are based entirely on myth and stereotype, and fly in the face of all evidence. People do not choose poverty and income assistance as a career goal. There are many thousands of New Brunswickers working at poverty wages who do not leave their jobs. There are thousands of unemployed New Brunswickers who beat the pavement every day in search of a job. People are unemployed by circumstance, not by choice." Referring to McKenna as the "Billy Graham of self-sufficiency," they said he continued to pursue policies "based on an ideal that the state should do less and that people should do more to assist themselves."

When Fern Landry left the Premier's office before the 1991 election, McKenna recruited Paul Lordon, his old law partner from Chatham, to fill the position until 1993, when Georgio Gaudet took over. The Gaudet-McKenna team was an odd marriage between a veteran bureaucrat who had worked primarily in social policy and a fiscally conservative premier. However, like McKenna, Gaudet was enterprising and had no time for process. Now there were two men in the premier's office fighting for the public policy accelerator. "People say Frank was a slave driver; Georgio was his own slave driver," Gaudet admits. "We had the same work ethic. He started working earlier than I did, and I ended up closing the office at eight, nine, ten o'clock. There's no question that I bought into Frank's agenda. But I believed in that agenda as well."

With Gaudet's encouragement, McKenna forged ahead with some of his most politically dangerous initiatives, public-private partnerships. "We didn't set out to enrich the private sector," McKenna insists, "we set out to transform government. We had this very ambitious set of things that we wanted to do, and we really didn't have the money. This was the only leverage we had."

The most notorious partnership arose out of a public scandal that dated back to the administrations of Louis Robichaud and Richard Hatfield. Delinquent and homeless boys, wards of the state, had been sexually and physically abused in provincial institutions, primarily at the New Brunswick Training School at Kingsclear, just north of Fredericton. McKenna ordered a public inquiry after former Kingsclear guard Karl Toft was charged with multiple counts of sexually abusing boys in his care. The inquiry revealed that some members of the corrections staff had reason to believe Toft was a child abuser, but that they failed to take steps to protect the children.

In 1991, McKenna appointed Edmond Blanchard, a Campbellton lawyer, Attorney General, and asked him to deal with the Kingsclear file. "It was a hellish time for the reputation of the province and the departments and the senior people involved," Blanchard recalls. "It was the whole issue of the administration of justice coming under fire. When wards of the state are treated in such a fashion, it really speaks volumes about the unfairness and absolute trauma that you are imposing on the most vulnerable people in our society. It was our department of corrections that had dealt with these people. We still had some of the same people in place who had caused much of this pain. I believed I was obligated to find out exactly what happened and put a system in place to ensure, as much as humanly possible, that it would not happen again."

Blanchard recalls McKenna expressing outrage at cabinet meetings when they would review the evidence emerging at the inquiry. He bluntly ordered Blanchard to fix the problem. The solution that cabinet settled on was to close the youth prison at Kingsclear and create a new facility on the Miramichi that would be built and operated by a private company. They called for tenders, and the contract was won by the Florida-based Wackenhut Corporation, founded in the 1950s by former FBI agent George Wackenhut.

"They walked in and said, the winner of this competition is Wackenhut," McKenna recalls. "I looked at it politically and said, 'This is just awful. We have Canadian and even New Brunswick solutions, and you're giving me this?' And they said, 'That's the solution.' You always felt obliged to follow the recommendation that you got, even when it hurt. We knew we were going to get it in spades. My relationships with the private sector tended to be pragmatic, not doctrinaire. I was horrified every time they would come in with a big American firm as one of our partners, but unfortunately, when you go through a competitive process, sometimes you get what you get."

The Wackenhut story dominated the New Brunswick media in the months leading up to the 1995 election. Elizabeth Weir seized the issue, uncovering horror story after horror story about Wackenhut-operated prisons around the world. "She had the media eating out of her hand on this issue," Gaudet says. "Nobody wanted Wackenhut, nobody. But you have a tendering process, and government needs to be transparent. If we had had the capital money and the development money to do all of this, I don't think the government would necessarily have gone that route."

During the 1995 campaign debates, Weir hammered McKenna over public-private partnerships, especially over the contentious Wackenhut plan. By the third week of the campaign, the only lingering issue for McKenna was Wackenhut. But now Campaign Frank was in charge. He asked Bryden and McGuire to find a way to pull out of the operating side of the contract. Wackenhut could build the facility, but it would be operated by New Brunswickers. After a Friday night meeting in the premier's office, Robichaud leaked the news to the *Telegraph-Journal*. The official announcement about the new Wackenhut plan was made on a

Saturday morning outside an Irving gas station on the outskirts of Saint John.

"The Wackenhut decision was a Premier Frank decision; the decision to pull the operating side of that contract was a Campaign Frank decision," MacKinnon says. "If Campaign Frank had made the original decision, they would have leased it, built it, mopped the floors, operated it, but not administered the corrections programs. Let's call a spade a spade. Wackenhut is eminently qualified to run prisons, in New Brunswick or anywhere else. We lost the communications fight on that. Elizabeth had this daily barrage of just bullshit stuff, but she was getting fed by some unions in the US who felt similarly aggrieved. It was the only issue. We had killed Valcourt. He was dead, writhing on the ground. It was just Wackenhut, Wackenhut, Wackenhut every day. We could have survived it, no problem, but we just wanted the noise to stop."

Wackenhut wasn't the only political nightmare to emerge from the public-private partnership initiative. The government had called for proposals to overhaul the Human Resources Development department, New Brunswick's welfare bureaucracy. Again, a large American firm won the contract, Andersen Consulting. In 1995, after Andersen had successfully completed the welfare project, the government called for proposals to create an integrated computerized justice system, an ambitious project to break down barriers between all branches of the system: courts, jails, police and probation officers. Andersen Consulting won this contract as well, and the company promised to create a centre of excellence in New Brunswick to sell the technology once the job was completed.

However, by early 1996, the integrated justice system project was collapsing, and Justice Minister Bernard Richard had to convince McKenna to change course. "The first briefing I got on it when I was justice minister, I felt very uncomfortable," Richard recalls. "The costs were going up, and they were proposing changes that would increase our costs but decrease our benefits. I got together with my deputy minister and asked to see the Premier and made the strongest argument I could come up with that we had to get out of the deal. I felt we were better off walking away from it now and making some kind of settlement with them. This was a big one for him because it was new technology, and it looked so good at first, and it was something he felt very strongly about."

Richard discussed various options with McKenna. Then the Premier stopped his justice minister and said, "You're the minister, if you feel that strongly about it then bring it to cabinet." The province ended up paying

$2.9 million to get out of the Andersen deal, claiming weakly that it had gained some intellectual property out of the ruins of the ambitious plan.

Elizabeth Weir called the Andersen failure McKenna's Bricklin, saying the big American firm did a good job of "scouting around for some gullible hick from the Maritimes." She wondered aloud why Richard was taking the heat for the failure of the deal. "It's not good enough, in the dead of summer, while the Premier is conveniently away on vacation, for the minister of justice and the solicitor general to sneak out one afternoon and say, 'Guess what, they've gone away, and we've paid them almost $3 million to do it.' This desire to transform the province using American corporations was really part of his future national agenda, when he was going to be running for the prime ministership of the country."

When Auditor General Darryl Wilson examined the Andersen contracts, he found that the Human Resources Development project was saving money in excess of the amount paid to Andersen. In the case of the justice contract, the province put more than $4 million into the project and paid Andersen $2.9 million for benefits that were "intangible" at best.

The private partnerships continued. Working in partnership with Canada Post and Andersen Consulting, NBTel successfully computerized New Brunswick's antiquated 911 system. Private firms were even allowed into the sacred public domain of education. Private contractors were recruited to design and build Leo Hayes High School in Fredericton and Evergreen Park Elementary School in Moncton and then lease them to the province. In the end, the government had the new schools it needed and kept construction costs off its books. However, there were also failures. By the time McKenna left office, the government had cancelled a contract with Blue Cross to develop a multi-million-dollar Medicare billing and administrative system. It also cancelled its deal with IBM to improve its tax collection system when the decision to harmonize its sales tax with the federal goods and services tax made the project obsolete.

"Overall I think it's fair to say that we had mixed results from our efforts at public-private partnerships," McKenna says. "We learned a lot of lessons. I'm not sure that we had the sophistication of project management needed for those relationships. We took the political hit, but we didn't take the economic hit. We refused to capitulate to those guys. Once they get inside your doors, I think they just feel they can pry open the safe. In the end we had to pull the plug. It was painful as hell. I felt let down. The idea was really innovative and I think it was right. When we made it work, it worked well. When it didn't, it was just a big clinker."

The Premier was leaving behind some nasty political problems for his successor. The government negotiated a deal to create a four-lane toll highway between Fredericton and Moncton, a decision that created a storm of political controversy, particularly near Moncton, where drivers would start paying tolls almost immediately on sections of highway that had already been completed. "He didn't feel we should wait for twenty years to build the Trans-Canada Highway," Gaudet says. "And he was right. That was the option. No one liked tolls, but do you prefer to slaughter people on the highway by the hundreds?" The deal also came under attack because the contract to build the road was landed by the Maritime Road Development Corporation, of which Doug Young, former Liberal leader and Chrétien cabinet minister, was chairman.

To add to the political problems in Moncton, the government announced as part of a municipal amalgamation plan that local police forces in Moncton and its suburbs would be replaced by the RCMP, whether or not Moncton city councillors agreed to the change. Cabinet members from the Moncton region were all asking the same question: why do we need to fix the Moncton policing problem right now? Meanwhile, the Tories elected Bernard Lord, a young bilingual lawyer from Moncton as party leader; Lord exploited both the toll road and policing issues to build his political base.

———

In Steven MacKinnon's view, Premier Frank took over entirely from Campaign Frank in his final two years. "Frank in premier mode was so concentrated, so motivated to get things done, that political considerations became one of only a subset of considerations that had to be taken into account," MacKinnon says. "Sometimes politics got shunted aside in favour of getting things done. The more time he spent in premier mode, the worse his political judgment became. He was a guy who consistently needed to renew with people. I think you saw this in the last year: his political instincts were diminished because we spent a lot less time getting out and about."

Premier Frank found himself in the kind of political trouble he had rarely experienced in his first two terms in office. On July 29, 1996, McKenna was confronted by reporters who asked him whether it was appropriate that IBM had paid the airfare, hotel and ticket expenses for a three-day trip to the Olympic Games in Atlanta. McKenna had returned home from Atlanta on a high after three days of job hunting. He had been cheering in the stands when Fredericton swimmer Marianne Limpert turned in a gutsy performance in the pool to win a silver medal, one of the high points of the games for Canada. Now he was being asked about conflict of interest, a suggestion of scandal he had never encountered during his first two terms in office. The media scrum about the IBM Olympic trip was a disaster, one of the worst moments of Maurice Robichaud's career as a political handler. McKenna told reporters that he had been working for the province in Atlanta and argued that taking the IBM gift was better than having taxpayers pick up the tab. "You seem to be implying that I accepted it as Frank McKenna," he said. "I just don't understand what you're saying. It wasn't a perk for me. I don't see any conflict of interest in that. In what possible way could this benefit me?"

New Brunswick's conflict of interest legislation forbids ministers from taking gifts that could be seen as substantial enough to influence policy decisions. IBM, one of the Olympic sponsors, flew more than one hundred corporate and government leaders to the games. McKenna's government was doing business with IBM. Quite apart from any conflict of interest questions, many New Brunswickers believed that the IBM trip was unseemly. The province wasn't a corporate charity case.

Within days, McKenna reversed his position and announced he would ask for a bill from IBM and pay for the trip himself. "In order to dispel any doubts as to the appropriateness of payment of the expenses during my trip, I will be reimbursing in full the province of New Brunswick and IBM for costs related to the trip," he told reporters. "This ensures the trip becomes strictly a private one, paid for in its entirety by my wife Julie and myself. I would never do anything that would reflect on the integrity of this office. I don't want a single person to think I let them down."

In the fall of 1996, McKenna started writing in his diary regularly, often expressing his ambivalence about the progress of his government. On Wednesday, September 11, 1996, the anniversary of his triumphant election victory, McKenna wrote, "I feel no real sense of joy or complacency. We still haven't made a lot of progress on the jobs issue." His moods swung up and down. On September 23, he noted in his diary that he had met a stranger on his morning walk to work who had given him a moral boost. "A nice talk on the way to work," he wrote. "Positive feeling from an outsider." He recorded on October 9, 1996, that his assistant Nat Richard told him that Tory member Dale Graham was overheard saying McKenna might lose his own seat in the next election. "This kind of talk really hurts."

Two days later, he wrote, "End of a somewhat horrible week." On the positive side, he noted that the province would record a surplus on its current account budget and could start making payments on the province's debt; however, McKenna did not see this achievement as an end in itself. Also on the positive side, *Elm Street* magazine had called him "Mr. Perfect" in a story about premier makeovers, a title that might have made his groomers Francis McGuire and Arthur Doyle proud. On the negative side, consumer watchdog Energy Probe was calling debt-ridden NB Power "a basket case." Furthermore, new employment numbers showed that the province had lost nine thousand jobs and that the unemployment rate had risen a percentage point to twelve and a half per cent. "What is going on?" McKenna asked. "I continue to believe we are doing the right things. Why are things going bad?"

On Monday, October 13, the final countdown began. "Today is the day," he wrote. "One year to go. Feel like Gretzky. He is starting to get some hard press and bad results. He's still a star, though, and will leave good memories. I want to finish strong. Need to deal with NB Power and jobs issue. Everything else is going in the right direction." The next day he was planning another series of health cuts, including closing a number of surgical units around the province. On October 18, he returned from Toronto having sealed a deal to build a new hotel and resort on Chatham's waterfront, a project he had been pursuing for more than a decade. In December, his government handed down a budget that projected a $25 million surplus and announced the first significant tax cuts in more than a decade.

Meanwhile, there was open speculation that McKenna would keep his promise and leave office after ten years. On December 16, 1996, the *Globe and Mail* published an article about McKenna written by Atlantic bureau chief Kevin Cox. Cox had asked McKenna if he was planning to get out of politics. He quoted McKenna's response: "I'm not running on a clock, I'm running on an agenda." The clock had, in fact, been ticking for nine years and two months.

Frank McKenna and Quebec Premier Lucien Bouchard shake hands after the Premiers' Conference at St. Andrews, New Brunswick, August 8, 1997. Looking on are Ontario Premier Mike Harris and Saskatchewan Premier Roy Romanow.

TRIUMVIRATE

We must fight our own battles.
— *Frank McKenna, diary entry, August 8, 1997*

The August sun burned off a morning mist as news reporters and pundits assembled in a Great Gatsby party atmosphere on the grounds of the elegant Algonquin Hotel in St. Andrews, on the southwest coast of New Brunswick. They ambled across manicured lawns in their tennis whites and settled into Adirondack chairs on the sprawling veranda of the eighty-five-year-old railway hotel, waiting for the premiers to arrive. They were keeping an eye out for a news story, but on this perfect, blue summer day, a game of tennis, a dip in the pool or a tall cold drink was all they really needed to keep them busy. On August 6, 1997, St. Andrews, Canada's oldest seaside resort town, was putting on its best face for the event of the summer, the annual Premiers' Conference.

As the reporters prepared for a week of light lifting and heavy partying, word that a real news story was emerging before the conference even officially began forced them out of their deck chairs, scrambling for their tape recorders and cameras. Quebec Premier Lucien Bouchard was arriving in a foul mood, infuriated that his host, Premier Frank McKenna, had sent a letter of support to a group that supported the partition of Quebec should the province separate from Canada.

At first blush, the story didn't make sense. What was the usually shrewd Frank McKenna thinking, wading into this hornet's nest just as he was preparing to host the premiers and their families for a quiet week of low-level political manoeuvering? Youthful as he was, after ten years McKenna had become a grizzled veteran of national unity battles. He of all people should know better. However, it appeared that he had waded into the controversy with both feet. In a letter dated July 23, 1997, to the Quebec

Committee for Canada, an association advocating partition, McKenna had written, "I not only give my unequivocal support, but I applaud your effort and your initiative in the formation and continuation of this group. It is indeed a worthy accomplishment to obtain the commitment of forty Quebec municipalities to 'Staying Canadian.' I am in full agreement with the resolutions that you have put forward to the municipalities of Quebec, and I am optimistic that even more will embrace them."

Bouchard was incensed. "Your intervention in this file constitutes not only an unprecedented interference by a provincial premier in Quebec affairs, but comes in support of a fundamentally antidemocratic position that international law and history of peoples have rejected many times," he wrote in a letter to McKenna, which he strategically released to the media on the eve of the conference.

When he arrived in St. Andrews, Bouchard told reporters that McKenna's letter was "improper and incorrect," that he had considered staying home, but that he had decided at the last minute to travel to New Brunswick only because the meetings involved premiers other than McKenna. Surrounded by reporters in the lobby of the Algonquin, McKenna insisted he was only supporting federalists in Quebec, not partition in particular, a dubious argument indeed considering the wording of the letter. Dramatically covering his eyes with his hands, he told reporters, "I am not a Canadian who is prepared to put my hands over my eyes and sleepwalk through the whole situation and pretend it doesn't exist." As is so often the case, the media, through no fault of its own, reported only this fragment of the story.

"Meeting started on a bad note with the letter to Quebec municipalities supporting their cause," McKenna noted in his diary. "I defended the letter all the way, saying if that was interference, it was also interference to cut us off from the rest of Canada without a say. What isn't known is that the letter went out under the signature machine." McKenna hadn't seen the letter before it reached Bouchard's hands and set off the political fireworks. His correspondence staff had decided that the letter to the Quebec Committee for Canada required just the standard federalist response and wasn't significant enough for the Premier's attention. After dealing with the media scrum in the lobby of the hotel, McKenna met with Bouchard alone, told him about his office slip-up and shut the story down. "I told Bouchard privately," McKenna later wrote. "He told me that he felt better, that he didn't believe I would do that to him, that he had too much respect for me."

Oddly enough, the clerical error played well politically. "We actually received a huge amount of support for our position," McKenna recorded. "The general assessment was that the conference turned around quickly and became a superb success. The other premiers were very supportive of me, told me not to back down." McKenna also noted that Newfoundland Premier Brian Tobin said he would support him for the national leadership. This wasn't the first time that McKenna's name had been mentioned as Jean Chrétien's successor, and McKenna gave him what had become his standard reply — he wasn't interested in the job.

On the final day of the conference, at a private lunch for first ministers only, the premiers held a remarkable conversation, speculating about where the aftershocks would strike if Quebec decided to separate from Canada, the very subject of the contentious letter to the Quebec Committee for Canada. Bouchard had agreed to attend, even though constitutional matters would be discussed. He "said Meech would have worked," McKenna wrote in his diary. "Now he's very pessimistic. Wants rest of Canada to stay united." Other premiers told Bouchard that, in their view, it would be difficult for the rest of the country to remain united should Quebec secede. British Columbia Premier Glen Clark said his province might also separate if Quebec left the country. Brian Tobin suggested there would be pressure for Newfoundland to "call the U.S. within minutes." Nova Scotia Premier Russell MacLellan contended that some people in his province would also be interested in talking to the United States. "Bouchard seemed surprised and disappointed," McKenna wrote. "I asked, if Quebec separated, would the rest of Canada still support Atlantic Canada?" There was dead silence in the room. "We must fight our own battles," McKenna reminded himself at the end of his diary entry that day.

In fact, McKenna had been fighting his own battles since the collapse of the Meech Lake Accord. Although he continued to play a role as a national unity mediator, McKenna had become more pragmatic about Canada's need for a strong central government, which had been an article of faith among Trudeau Liberals. Ottawa was cutting transfer payments and appeared to be less and less interested in helping the regions. As McKenna faced a constant struggle to keep his province's books in the black, he witnessed a wasteful duplication of services among the two levels of government every day. Moreover, far too great a proportion of Ottawa's bureaucrats remained isolated from the people they served. McKenna had come to believe that the best hope for a renewed federation would be found in a more practical sharing of power. Every national constitutional initiative since he had become Premier had ended in failure. He knew that in New Brunswick, his dogged pragmatism had helped to close a cultural divide between English and French communities, and that in many ways they represented a microcosm of Canada's two solitudes.

Because of his role as a constitutional fixer during Meech Lake's dying days, McKenna had been intimately involved in the drafting of the Charlottetown Accord. "Ever since his days as Meech Lake foe-turned-supporter in 1990, McKenna had tried to carve out a reputation for himself as an agent of compromise in the country," writes Susan Delacourt in *United We Fall*, her study of the Charlottetown Accord. "He liked to be seen as the great moderate, the conciliator. All his efforts during the final days of Meech had been aimed at placating and soothing both sides." McKenna and his new friend, Saskatchewan Premier Roy Romanow, joined forces "to bridge the chasm between the individual rights craze of English Canada and the collective rights demand of Quebec," Delacourt observed. In August, 1992, after two agonizing years of commissions, conferences and constitutional wrangling, Constitutional Affairs Minister Joe Clark had cobbled together a deal, and Prime Minister Brian Mulroney and the premiers agreed to a compromise constitutional package that included an equal Senate and a guarantee for Quebec of twenty-five per cent of the seats in the House of Commons.

On August 28, the Charlottetown Accord was released to Canadians. When Mulroney promised to wage war against the "enemies of Canada" in two referendums to be held simultaneously in Quebec and across the country, the Yes campaign stumbled out of the starting block. Instead of selling the accord as a bold new vision for the country, it would be promoted as a compromise, a deal Canadians must accept if only to avoid the unthinkable consequences of another failure.

For McKenna and New Brunswick Acadians, the Charlottetown Accord carried with it the constitutional amendment he had been seeking since 1987, when he stepped forward as an opponent of the Meech Lake Accord. If Charlottetown carried the day in the referendums, there would be a special New Brunswick amendment to Canada's Constitution requiring only the consent of Parliament and the New Brunswick legislature. The New Brunswick clause of the Charlottetown Accord stated: "The amendment would entrench the equality of status of the English and French linguistic communities in New Brunswick, including the right to distinct educational institutions and such distinct cultural institutions as are necessary for the preservation and promotion of these communities. The amendment would also affirm the role of the legislature and government of New Brunswick to preserve and promote this equality of status." The words *preserve* and *promote*, which had played so central a role in derailing Meech Lake and had caused so much consternation in Quebec when applied to minority languages rights outside that province, were front and centre in the new accord.

McKenna pulled Francis McGuire from his job in Economic Development and Tourism to prepare a strategy to sell the deal in New Brunswick. In McGuire's view, the Yes campaign was failing to articulate a vision of what Canada would look like after the Charlottetown Accord was approved. "We said, despite all this shit that's in here, this is essentially a debate about one primary issue, 'Do we agree that in a modern society there has to be a devolution from the centre to the regions?' If we cast the question along those lines we will find that the response is positive," McGuire recalls. While conventional wisdom suggested that the people of a have-not province would continue to support a Canada with a strong central government, McGuire's polling was suggesting that New Brunswickers supported a devolution of powers from Ottawa. Frank McKenna's message of self-sufficiency, of being small but standing tall, was truly changing the way New Brunswickers viewed their future in the federation.

"I said, 'That's what Charlottetown is about, so say it,'" McGuire recalls. "The feds were saying no. Mulroney was saying, 'That will get everybody upset, let's not do that.' You can't run campaigns on all the clauses in there. Public policy is decided on trends or positions of principle, not on detail. In my view they blew it, because people sensed that they were dishonest about the process, and they had the problem of every interest group picking on them." McKenna realized that the Charlottetown Accord was dying a death of a thousand clauses when he telephoned Stompin' Tom Connors, hoping that the legendary folk singer and fervent nationalist might join the Yes campaign and help turn the referendum into a celebration of Canadian patriotism. Instead, Connors began expressing concerns about various clauses; it seemed everyone had become an arm-chair constitutional lawyer.

On October 26, 1992, Canadians across the country emphatically rejected the Charlottetown Accord. However, New Brunswickers voted sixty-one per cent in favour of the accord, including a majority of both anglophone and francophone voters, compared to thirty-eight per cent who voted No. The New Brunswick campaign was non-partisan, featuring the unusual sight of Elizabeth Weir and Frank McKenna standing side-by-side on podiums throughout the province.

In Delacourt's view, the massive rejection of the Charlottetown Accord expressed a profound loss of confidence in Canada's political leaders and institutions. While this may have been true in many areas of the country, such as British Columbia, where sixty-eight per cent of voters had said No, it certainly wasn't the case in New Brunswick. The victory of the Yes campaign in New Brunswick suggested that McKenna had restored some measure of the faith in political leaders that had all but vanished during the final troubled years of Richard Hatfield's hold on power.

McKenna considered the Charlottetown vote a mandate to entrench French language rights in New Brunswick in the Canadian Constitution as soon as possible. Whereas his advisors, including Paul Lordon, Francis McGuire and Maurice Robichaud, were unanimously urging him to move slowly and cautiously in the wake of the failures of both Meech Lake and Charlottetown, McKenna's instincts told him to entrench right away. The Yes side had won big in New Brunswick, and French language rights had been a central issue the campaign. Morally, it was the right thing to do for the Acadian people; politically, it would extinguish the one issue — anti-bilingualism — of New Brunswick's Official Opposition, the Confederation of Regions party.

On December 4, 1992, the New Brunswick Legislature adopted a resolution calling for an amendment to the Constitution that would forever protect the principle of equality of the English and French linguistic communities in the province. During the winter of 1993, the necessary resolutions were adopted in the Senate and the House of Commons. Before Brian Mulroney resigned in late February, he had assured the ratification of the amendment. For Acadians in New Brunswick, Mulroney was a man of his word, keeping his end of a bargain he had made with McKenna three years earlier when the former opponents had launched their Meech Lake rescue mission together.

On March 12, 1993, the Governor General issued the Constitution Amendment Proclamation, 1993 (New Brunswick Act), amending section 16 of the Charter of Rights and Freedoms. This amendment recognizes the equality of the anglophone and francophone communities of New Brunswick and provides for the New Brunswick Legislature and government to "preserve and promote the status, rights and privileges" of both linguistic groups.

———

Steven MacKinnon recalls sitting in the Legislature gallery, listening to the CoR members speak in opposition to the equality amendment. As the Premier closed the debate, MacKinnon turned to a friend and said, "That's the end of the CoR Party."

Throughout the period leading to the 1995 election, the McKenna team was determined to wipe the CoR party off the map. Aldéa Landry had lost her own seat in the 1991 election, but her loss paled in comparison to the fact that CoR had become the Official Opposition. "We just couldn't believe it," she recalls. "We had this sinking feeling that we were going backward again. It was a gloomy time."

McKenna promised himself that he would eliminate CoR the next time he went to the polls, and the Premier's aides made it their mission as well. "These were the guys who couldn't have their way under Richard Hatfield," MacKinnon says. "They were determined to bring New Brunswick back to the old days. This was the anti-Equal Opportunity campaign all over again. This was bad stuff, it was base stuff, but it had struck a chord and we hated these guys with every fibre of our being. We hated everything they stood for. As far as we were concerned, they were evil. We were idealistic, bilingual people who had a vision of New Brunswick that was much broader than theirs."

In the Legislature, McKenna was delivering the most passionate speeches of his political career. "It's a question of principle, *principle*," he said one day, responding to a CoR member during Question Period. "It's a word you should get used to. In this province of ours, this very precious province of ours, francophones and anglophones are equal and are entitled to equal treatment under the law and equal protection under the law and equal access to the services of government. The direct answer to your question is that we will, in my view, eliminate and wipe out the CoR Party in the province of New Brunswick by standing on our principles, by facing the public in another general election and by proving to them that we are right on this question of principle and the CoR Party is wrong."

Acadians couldn't have found a stronger advocate in the struggle against CoR. At the same time, they recognized that McKenna's fight for equality in the province was a continuation of the pioneering work of Louis

Robichaud and Richard Hatfield. On April 23, 1994, five hundred of the most prominent Acadian leaders in the province gathered to fête their three champions in a banquet room at the Hotel Beauséjour in Moncton, the city that had seen some of the most strident anti-French bigotry in the province. Robichaud, Hatfield and McKenna were to receive the Société nationale de l'Acadie's Médaille Léger Comeau, its highest honour, which recognizes those who have contributed to the development of Acadie and the Acadian people.

Steven MacKinnon recalls meeting in a suite at the hotel with Fern Landry and McKenna to prepare for his speech that evening. The draft of the speech MacKinnon had prepared stated unequivocally that the Liberal Party planned to "wipe out CoR" in the next election. The cautious Landry, who had long since departed the Premier's office, thought the words were unduly provocative and unneccessary.

"I argued for keeping it, thinking that if we were ever going to throw down the gauntlet, this was the time," MacKinnon says. CoR was already in trouble. In the midst of divisive leadership struggles, it was seeking a new direction after its reason for being had been undermined by the passage of the constitutional amendment the year before. McKenna shrugged off Landry's concerns; he'd wake up the crowd when he spoke.

Louis Robichaud, always unpredictable, delivered a remarkably un-emotional and terse speech, concluding by thanking the society and promising to put the award in a drawer with all of his other medals. One of Hatfield's nieces spoke on behalf of her late uncle. McKenna spoke last and laid down his challenge to CoR. "The passage stuck," MacKinnon recalls. "When Frank said the words, the place exploded. In retrospect, it was a pretty nationalist-Acadian type of speech. But the audience was comprised of nationalists, who were always a little suspicious of Frank as opposed to mainstream and business-minded Acadians. I think Frank looked good in appearing determined to eradicate CoR. I was glad, even proud, that he said it. That's the second time it hit me that they were done."

In the summer of 1994, New Brunswick hosted the first Acadian World Congress, a landmark event that welcomed a hundred thousand Acadians from all over the world to the province for a giant celebration of culture and history and some of the largest family reunions imaginable. The province's provincial newspaper, the traditionally staid and conservative *Telegraph-Journal*, which had come under the innovative leadership of editor-in-chief Neil Reynolds, dispatched reporters to Louisiana to write about the Acadian (Cajun) culture which had developed there after the Expulsion. The newspaper told the story of the struggles of the Acadian people and published genealogies of individual families. For this work, it was nominated for the Roland Michener Award for Public Service Journalism, the most prestigious award a media organization can receive in Canada. Never before had Acadian culture been so widely celebrated, in New Brunswick or anywhere else.

In the end, CoR went a long way toward destroying itself. After party founder Arch Pafford had lost his bid for a seat in the 1991 election, millionaire Danny Cameron, a former Hatfield Tory, had won the leadership over Miramichi native Brent Taylor, a more youthful grassroots candidate, at a bitterly contested convention held in Campbellton, the English heartland of northern New Brunswick. The party never united under Cameron's leadership. As the 1995 election approached, the party had reluctantly turned to thirty-six-year-old Greg Hargrove, its fourth leader in four years. "I disagreed with them on language, and they disagreed with themselves on language, too," McKenna says. "I finally realized that their demonstrable incompetence would ultimately destroy them more than anything else."

At the end of August, 1995, McKenna announced he was going to the polls; the campaign would be twenty-eight days long, the shortest in New Brunswick history. The pre-election polls were devastating for the opposition, despite the contentious nature of McKenna's aggressive reforms to the health care, education and social welfare systems. A Corporate Research Associates survey suggested that forty-four per cent of voters supported the Liberals, fourteen per cent the Progressive Conservatives, three per cent CoR, and two per cent the NDP.

Bernard Valcourt charged that the Liberals were all spin and no substance. "For eight years, New Brunswick has been subjected to slogans not solutions, sales instead of real jobs," he told reporters. McKenna responded by pointing to the Royal Bank of Canada's prediction that New Brunswick would have the second best growth of any province in 1995-1996. He campaigned using the New Brunswick motto *spem reduxit*, hope restored. "Hope has been restored, but we are not vain enough to think that hope has been restored for everyone or that the job is done yet," he told reporters. "We have a long, long way to go. We have too much poverty and too much unemployment and too many roads in bad condition, too many needs in education and health care. We have too many things that have to be done."

On September 11, 1995, when McKenna won his third overwhelming majority, he not only wiped CoR off the map, but also won back all of the CoR seats the Liberals had lost in 1991. Valcourt's Tories won six seats. Weir won only her own seat in Saint John.

"That was total and complete vindication," MacKinnon says. "A party founded on hate died on hate. They're a footnote now. They contributed nothing, accomplished nothing, except to rid us of this evil, insidious psychographic forever."

The rise and fall of CoR sent a message to New Brunswickers that they had to be vigilant and stand strongly for the equality of the two linguistic communities in the province, says Aldéa Landry. "It was probably, in hindsight, a good thing that they elected members. We saw their true colours, and people were able to focus on that and say, 'We don't want this for our province.'

"New Brunswick has evolved in recognizing the equality of the two linguistic communities," she says. "It's a combination of leadership and understanding and generosity. It started with Louis Robichaud and continued with Hatfield, and Frank put his stamp on it, and stomped his foot sometimes in the case of CoR. You can do all of that, but if you're not able to convince people that this is the right way to go, it's going nowhere."

For a time during the mid-1990s, New Brunswick seemed to come alive and turn its back on the entrenched divisions that had so hindered its economic and social progress. More than anything, McKenna's economic development program was bridging the divide. "The thing that broke its back, strangely enough, was the call centres," says Francis McGuire. "It took enough people to say, 'Hey, my son or daughter is over there as an anglophone working for Purolator, but that's only because there's forty people over there who are bilingual, and that's why we have the work here.' For the first time, it was taken on a very personal level, how this bilingualism stuff is an economic asset. All of a sudden you have cities like Saint John clamouring that they have a bilingual population, and it's really important."

As bilingualism started to be seen as one of the most attractive economic development features of New Brunswick, suddenly the two communities didn't seem so far apart, says Ray Frenette. Anglophones were proud to see their children learning a second language in school, and more students began enrolling in French immersion programs. "Frank saw this revolution that was taking place into the information age, and he saw the linguistic capacity of New Brunswickers as being an asset. All of a sudden, New Brunswickers were proud. All of a sudden we found ourselves using the very thing that was a problem not very many years before as an asset."

During these years, McKenna was seeing the results of what he calls the doctrine of the inevitability of change. If he preached the gospel of self-sufficiency long enough, if he spread the word that New Brunswick was changing widely enough, the wheels of change that had been mired in history would begin to work their way loose. McKenna was accused of running a government that was all smoke and mirrors, of masterminding a communications campaign that exaggerated the progress of his province, and while he would dispute his critics who claimed that nothing concrete was happening, he would freely admit that he deliberately created a buzz. "Change can sometimes be introduced by doing things that create an inevitable sense of change," he told Don Cayo, the editorial page editor of the *Telegraph-Journal*.

From the day he entered the Premier's office, McKenna realized that the success or failure of the province would be determined by the thousands of decisions made every day by hundreds of people in dozens of departments. If those decisions were being made in one frame of mind and with one sense of purpose, then he could transform the nature of the province. "This was going to be the mission: self-sufficiency, feeling better about ourselves," says Andy Scott. "We were no longer going to run from the fact that we had a bilingual province. That was a strength, not a liability, that was something to be proud of, not simply to be tolerated."

At a tribute to McKenna held at the Hotel Beauséjour in Moncton after his resignation, Antonine Maillet spoke of how Louis Robichaud had introduced the concept of equality to New Brunswick, how Richard Hatfield had embraced equality and made francophone aspirations a legitimate cause for anglophones, and how McKenna had allowed both communities to dream a common dream. In the audience, Fernand Landry and Francis McGuire were moved to tears as they listened to Maillet's words. "That was the goal, to get both communities to share the same vision, the same dream," McGuire recalls. "None of us who had lived this could stop crying."

While McKenna was moving New Brunswick closer to linguistic and cultural peace, the country's divisions were as deep and wide as they had ever been. In the fall of 1995, as the approaching Quebec sovereignty referendum remained too close to call, McKenna telephoned Donald Savoie. The country is in trouble, he said. We need to do something. They decided to co-author a paper about the changing nature of federalism, which they planned to publish in *Queen's Quarterly*, hoping to stimulate a debate about the possibilities of a renewed vision of federalism. Before it was published, Savoie advised McKenna to send a copy to Prime Minister Jean Chrétien to warn him about what was coming. McKenna dispatched Savoie and Georgio Gaudet to meet with Chrétien's long-time advisor Eddie Goldenberg in Ottawa to discuss the paper. Goldenberg said the Prime Minister didn't want the paper published before the referendum. McKenna reluctantly assented.

In November, 1995, after the country had marched to the edge of the precipice of separation and back again, the paper was released, arguing that in many respects Quebeckers had it right. The Savoie-McKenna paper concluded that the best hope for a united Canada will come from reforms outside the Constitution. Change was coming whether Ottawa wanted it or not. "The very nature of government is changing, and Canada's written Constitution will not be able to stop it," they wrote. Quebeckers had correctly identified the problem: there was too much federal presence in too many policy areas. A blurring of constitutional responsibilities had alienated citizens from governments. Citizens were receiving services from inaccessible federal bureaucrats, many of whom spent their days managing intergovernmental processes. The paper suggested a national expansion of McKenna's vision for his province: a federation of self-sufficient and independent provinces as a unifying principle for the country.

"There are signs everywhere that the old order has run its course," Savoie and McKenna wrote. "Historians will likely look back to the period between 1945 and 1995 and conclude that in the later part of the fifty year cycle, governments learned the limits of their interventions, discovered that there are only certain things that they do well, and understand that interventions to soften the sting of economic misfortune can in fact play havoc with the long-term ability of people, communities and regions to become self-sufficient and to secure a sense of independence and control over their own future.

"It has become clear that the rise of the welfare state has many negative side effects — apart from the fact that it is turning out to be much more costly than it was first envisaged, it has also disrupted the ties between effort and reward and has established disincentives on various fronts, notably on work, savings and entrepreneurship."

New Brunswickers were recognizing the need to question things they had been taking for granted, Savoie and McKenna wrote. They wanted to become self-sufficient, and they were prepared for change. "It would be a sad day indeed for Canada and for Quebec if we were to tear our nation apart on the basis of yesterday's battles. A new order is emerging. We need to focus our energy to exploit new opportunities it presents, and we can best do this by remaining united and working hand in hand to meet the challenge."

———

Five days before Christmas in 1996, McKenna had a long private lunch with Jean Chrétien at 24 Sussex Drive. "He had a bad week re GST, but it was obvious that wasn't what was on his mind," McKenna wrote in his diary. "He wanted to know, 'What are you going to do, Frank?' Said I would have a very good chance of succeeding him although he couldn't guarantee it. Thought I would be wise to run federally this time to get positioned. He said I could go in the private sector and make a lot of money, stay on as Premier of New Brunswick or run federally. He said 'You don't look like the kind of guy who wants to make a lot of money.' I told him I would consider national office for two reasons. A fiscal disaster. A constitutional disaster." McKenna recognized that his strength is as a politician with a cause rather than as a statesmen who would act as a caretaker for a country in a time of prosperity.

Meanwhile, McKenna had his own small crisis at home to address, one which would threaten to erode the goodwill that had been established between French and English communities. In December, 1996, the government announced plans to close several schools with declining enrollment, including schools in the francophone communities of Saint-Simon and Saint-Sauveur on the Acadian Peninsula. Residents of both communities formed a committee to try to convince the government to reverse its decision. In May, 1997, the government announced its final word on the matter: the schools would be closed. The residents took to the streets, setting up roadblocks and lighting fires along the highways. RCMP tactical units set upon the protesters with police dogs and tear gas. The television footage of small-town Acadians being gassed and attacked by dogs for standing up for their community schools was horrifying; the police response appeared heavy-handed in the extreme. Twelve protesters were arrested in Saint-Simon and seven in Saint-Sauveur. Four years later, after a critical report about police response to the protests was released by the RCMP Public Complaints Commission, the RCMP held a public meeting in the communities and apologized.

However, at the time, community outrage was directed at Frank McKenna's government. At no time during his decade in power had there been such a display of violence as a result of his fiscal reforms. Bernard Richard, the Justice Minister, felt physically ill as he watched the protests and the response. The soft-spoken Acadian lawyer, who would later become interim leader of the party, believed cabinet had made a legal and moral error in deciding to close the schools without consulting with the communities. He believed the province was on shaky legal ground. The Charter of Rights and Freedoms obligates governments to consult communities when making decisions about minority language education, and the communities were planning to take their case to the courts.

"I felt that we would just be shot out of the water on this one," Richard recalls. "I thought we would be embarrassed in front of the courts." Richard had just returned from a trip to France, Haiti and Romania, lobbying for the next Francophone Summit to be held in New Brunswick, the only officially bilingual province in Canada where linguistic minority rights were respected and protected by law. "I thought we were such a strong model for countries where that doesn't happen," Richard says. "We didn't need that kind of embarrassment."

In the late spring and early summer of 1997, Richard met McKenna at Friel Beach in Cap-Pelé where he owns a summer cottage adjacent to Julie McKenna's family's property. During a series of informal meetings in their backyards and on the beach, Richard convinced McKenna to reverse his decision on the school closures. It was a tough sell. McKenna believed the government had a financial responsibility to close any school that didn't have enough students to justify its existence. In his view, it wasn't a question of minority language rights; he didn't think the Acadian Peninsula should be exempted from decisions that were nothing more than good fiscal management.

"I told him that I felt we were going down the wrong path, that we would lose in court, and that we would be found to be the only bilingual province in Canada that didn't respect its minority," Richard recalls. "We had a weak case." When he returned from his vacation, McKenna shuffled his cabinet, appointed Richard as the new Education Minister, and told him to reverse the school closure decision on the Acadian Peninsula. On July 24, 1997, McKenna travelled with Richard to Saint-Sauveur and Saint-Simon to make the announcement.

———

After putting out this political fire at home, McKenna turned his attention to one final national unity assignment before he left office. Following the Premiers Conference in St. Andrews in August 1997, Chrétien asked McKenna to lead a mission, with the help of his friend Roy Romanow, to persuade the first ministers to agree on a plan to reform the Constitution. And so McKenna launched a final national unity crusade, despite having already expressed grave concerns about the benefits of attempting constitutional reform.

As always, McKenna turned to Francis McGuire for help. He needed some numbers; he needed to understand the politics. What was the mood in the country? Was there any common ground among the premiers in the wake of Meech Lake and Charlottetown? "We've got to look at the politics here," he told McGuire. "It's a political dilemma, so we have to find a political solution." In McGuire's view, McKenna had matured as a politician since the days when he was struggling with his position on the Meech Lake Accord. "This was Frank McKenna saying, 'I need to understand this, and then I will execute for you. I'm not going to operate just on instinct. I need the facts and I need the information.'"

McKenna asked Chrétien's office to share its extensive polling data, and McGuire travelled to Ottawa with Georgio Gaudet to retrieve data from those files. To fill in the gaps, McGuire started calling his friends in the polling industry to ask them to release figures that would ordinarily be highly confidential. "I'm going to ask you to do something illegitimate and unethical," he told his friends. "Here's the problem. We have to go into Calgary, and we have to talk to the premiers, and we have to understand things, and we have to create a package that meets the political imperatives of everybody, including Quebec. Here's the stuff we need to know. We haven't paid for it. Will you help us?"

As far as McGuire was concerned, this was a political campaign just like every other campaign he had helped to organize for his boss. "We learned from Meech and Charlottetown that if you start going down the issues, you're dead, you're cooked," McGuire says. "What you have to do is understand what Quebeckers want and what Albertans want, and go through that and say, 'There's got to be some common ground here.' And yes, there is. So, armed with that, we went to that two-day meeting."

On September 14, 1997, McKenna chaired the meeting of premiers in Calgary with Georgio Gaudet at his side. McGuire remained in Fredericton, watching the television for progress reports. Several hours later, McKenna adjourned the meeting and announced they had an agreement. "Jeez, it worked," McGuire said to himself. The premiers headed for the golf course.

The Calgary Declaration endorsed "the unique character" of Quebec society, including language, culture and civil law, as fundamental to the well-being of Canada. However, unlike the Meech Lake Accord, the declaration clearly affirmed the equality of all Canadians and provinces and respect for aboriginal peoples and multiculturalism. Moreover, future constitutional amendments that granted powers to one province would have to grant the same powers to all provinces. The first ministers outlined a plan for public consultation on future constitutional amendments. The Calgary Declaration was only the first small step in a larger plan McGuire outlined for McKenna. He recommended that the first ministers sell the broad vision for renewing the federation in a deliberate, choreographed public relations campaign, then draft the details when the deal had already been sealed with the public.

Lucien Bouchard, who declined the invitation to the Calgary meeting, denounced the McKenna initiative. "What a discovery. Quebeckers are unique," Bouchard scoffed when he met with reporters. "Like everyone. Unique like the Regina choir or the Escoumins River; unique like the SkyDome, Cape Breton, Labatt Blue and Wayne Gretzky. The premiers have demonstrated without a shadow of a doubt that if Quebeckers want to be recognized as a people, if they want to be masters of their destiny, there's only one way to get there, that's for a majority to vote for sovereignty the next time."

"What did we expect from Mr. Bouchard? He was invited, he chose not to attend," McKenna responded as he arrived in Ottawa to meet with Chrétien. "We knew that he would resent it. We knew that there's nothing short of the separation of Quebec from Canada that would be acceptable to him." In the end, Chrétien chose to turn away from the process that the first ministers began in Calgary. Constitutional reform of any kind was too painful and politically dangerous.

Regardless of what happened after Calgary, McKenna knew he wasn't going to be around to see it through. Six months earlier, McKenna had invited Ray Frenette to his Fredericton home for dinner. Frenette was planning to get out of politics, but McKenna had one last favour to ask of his loyal lieutenant. McKenna told him he would be leaving in October and asked Frenette to stay on to act as interim premier after his resignation. Frenette had accepted the offer. It would be a fitting ending to a distinguished political career for the man who had realized he was not suited for the job he had fought so hard to win in 1985. "After I saw him in operation, I said to myself how glad I was that I had not won the leadership because I don't think I could have done the kind of job that needed to be done."

McKenna was carefully scripting his exit, but life after politics was unthinkable for a man whose every move had been part of a progression to this place. "Life after politics for me is just a big black void," he told John Demont of *Maclean's* magazine. "I see no images. I see nothing."

However, for Julie McKenna, real life would begin again after resignation day. From her perspective, the McKenna family had already paid a high price for politics.

Julie and Frank McKenna boarding the 1995 campaign bus.

Olive McKenna and Frank McKenna after McKenna's swearing-in as Premier, October, 1987.

Jamie, Toby, Frank, Julie, and Christine McKenna, 1986.

Jamie McKenna at the 1985 Liberal leadership convention.

Frank and Toby McKenna.

Frank and Jamie McKenna, February, 1993.

10

JULIE

Must change my work habits. Julie is very upset about me
being a workaholic. She's right. I am trying, but I feel so
strongly about doing the job well for the people.
— *Frank McKenna, diary entry, March 28, 1988*

The applause, that's all for you, not for you and your
wife, and you stand up and say, "I want to thank my wife
for putting up with all this," but that's not the same as
sharing in a real relationship. It's like saying, "Well, thank
you very much, wife. You've been working for me for twenty-
five years, and I want to give you this watch."
— *Richard Hatfield*

Frank McKenna pulled up the collar of his navy trench coat as he jogged
across the tarmac, bracing himself against the raw breeze gusting across
the dirty spring snowbanks that lined the runways at the Fredericton
airport. He settled into his seat at about two-thirty on the afternoon of
April 13, 1992. As was his custom on trips to Chatham, he was travelling
only with pilot Rob Derrah and co-pilot Alan Cooper of Diamond Aviation
Services, the company contracted to fly the Premier's plane. The leased
1981 four-seater Beech 60 Duke had been the backup plane to Richard
Hatfield's more lavish government-owned Beech King Air, which McKenna
had sold in 1988. He didn't save any money by leasing from Diamond
Aviation, but jettisoning Hatfield's favourite toy was a symbolic gesture
to usher in a new era of frugality.

He struggled to calm the familiar knot of anxiety in his gut. He would
touch down in his riding in about thirty minutes, and his executive
assistant, Maura McClusky, had warned him that a group of disgruntled
teachers awaited him. He had learned to control his emotions during
these public encounters, but he still found them disturbing. Had it not

been for the teachers, McKenna would have looked forward to a Monday afternoon in Chatham, a twice-monthly occurrence. He knew that McClusky would be waiting for him when he arrived.

With white hair and gentle manners, McClusky seems more like a doting grandmother than a political operative, but for a decade she had been the Premier's right hand at base camp. She helped him win his first election, and after the 1987 sweep she became his executive assistant in Chatham. She had leased two vacant rooms in the back of his law firm's building, furnished a waiting room and office with a desk and chairs from her basement, and hung a shingle outside the door: "Frank McKenna, Chatham, MLA."

After meeting McKenna at the airstrip with his agenda, she usually joined him in a bit of mainstreeting downtown before they retreated to the office. There he sat in McClusky's chair and made phone calls. When the phone rang, he picked it up, answering either "Frank McKenna's MLA office" or "Frank here." More often than not, he handed the phone to his assistant, saying, "Maura, it's for you."

McKenna roused himself from a catnap as they approached Chatham that April afternoon. Derrah flicked a switch to lower the landing gear and heard an odd clunking sound. He checked his control panel. The wheel under the right wing hadn't come down. He tried to raise the left and centre wheels but found they were stuck in the down position. The pilot turned back to McKenna. Something was wrong with the landing gear. They would have to return to Fredericton. Waiting in her car beside the airstrip, McClusky watched the plane approach, then bank away and disappear. The Premier's first reaction was relief. Now he had a good excuse for not facing the teachers. At least they couldn't say he didn't try to get there. Surely they would fix the problem, and in no time he would be safely back in the office. The affairs of Chatham could wait another week.

Back at the Premier's office, Maurice Robichaud took a call from CBC Radio reporter Rick Leguerrier. He had heard there was a plane in distress. Where was the Premier? He was on his way to Miramichi and should have landed already, but for some reason he hadn't arrived. Robichaud's heart skipped a beat, but he wasn't about to fuel a media frenzy before he knew what was going on. "I can't imagine there's a problem," he said in his calmest voice. "I'm sure if there was a problem I'd be aware of it." Robichaud hung up the phone and raced down the hall to Ruth McCrea's office.

"Where's the Premier?"

She glanced at her watch. "He's probably landed by now."

"Leguerrier called and said there's a plane in distress."

"Oh my God." She reached for the phone and called McClusky in Chatham, who told her the plane had turned back. McCrea found Diamond Aviation's chief pilot Glyn Morgan at home. She told him the Premier's plane had not landed at Miramichi and was on its way back to Fredericton, and she didn't know why. "I had a call right after that from the flight service station here in Fredericton to say the aircraft was coming here with mechanical problems," recalls Morgan, a veteran pilot who for more than a decade had shepherded the high-flying Hatfield across the continent. He snatched up his portable aircraft radio and ran to his car, listening to the conversations between the flight crew and the air traffic controllers as he drove to the airport.

When Robichaud returned to his office, his phone was ringing. It was Leguerrier again, this time with hard information. "They're saying it's the Premier's plane," he said. Robichaud hung up the phone and headed for the parking lot. There was no point in trying to control the media now.

By the time Morgan arrived at the airport, the plane was circling overhead. He spoke to Derrah by radio. We're not in a hurry, Morgan assured the pilot. You have lots of fuel and the weather is fine. Relax and we'll sort it out. Morgan asked the pilot to make a low pass over the hangar so he could see for himself what was happening. The left and front wheels were down; the right one was fully retracted. Morgan and the maintenance crew spread out the airplane's blueprints while Derrah bounced the plane up and down, trying to jar the wheel loose. The pilots tore up the floor of the plane to try to free the wheel from above.

"They did another two or three low passes, and it didn't change anything at all," Morgan recalls. "They tried the emergency extension system, and it had no effect. So then we decided to land without all three wheels." Only one question remained — what was the best way to crash-land the plane?

As the Premier's staff, politicians and every news reporter in town converged on the airport, Julie, Toby, Christine and Jamie McKenna found themselves in familiar territory for a political family — in the dark and alone. The events of that afternoon only confirmed what Julie McKenna already knew about her place in the provincial hierarchy, but nonetheless she was wounded as she had never been wounded before as a political wife.

She was teaching at an adult education centre in downtown Fredericton when she received a message that her husband's plane was in trouble. By this time the plane had already been in the air for more than an hour. Terrified, tears streaming down her face, she drove to Woodstock Road to pick up Jamie, who had arrived home from junior high school. They turned on the radio and television and listened to updates from the airport, none of them reassuring. The Premier's plane was burning off fuel, preparing for a crash landing. Julie telephoned Fredericton High School, where Christine was working out with the girls' rugby team. Christine's coach told her she had a phone call. When she arrived at the school office, Jamie was on the other end of the line, telling her that her father was in trouble. She could hear her mother crying in the background.

As Julie and Jamie rushed out the door, Julie thought about Toby, who was then a student at St. Francis Xavier in Antigonish. Somehow she would have to send word to him. "I drove, hysterical, from our house to Fredericton High and picked up Christine," Julie recalls. "She had to drive because I couldn't at that point. Jamie was the only one who was calm. He kept saying, 'This is going to be fine.' So we went out to the airport, the three of us alone."

In Antigonish, Toby was making his way to the cafeteria when one of his friends said, "Hey, your dad's having a rough time up the air." Toby didn't understand, figured it was just another crack about his father in the news and responded with a casual, "Yeah, whatever." When he returned to his dormitory, a message was waiting saying that his dad's plane was in distress and his mom would be calling soon. He ran to the TV room and turned on the news broadcasts. Moments later, he was called to the phone. It was Jamie calling from the car phone. "We're on the way to the airport," he said matter-of-factly. "There's a lot of concern, and it doesn't look good." Toby could hear his mother sobbing. "Keep me posted," Toby said, then returned to the television and wept silently as he sat alone, listening to reporters speculate about the fate of the plane and the Premier.

When Julie, Christine and Jamie arrived at the airport, cars were lined up along the road watching the spectacle. It seemed that everyone in New Brunswick had heard about the drama in the sky before word had reached the Premier's family. When they walked into the hangar, Glyn Morgan looked up from the blueprints long enough to assure Julie he was doing everything he could, then turned his attention back to the stricken plane. "We watched this, the plane circling, and it was horrible," she recalls. "I've never forgiven the staff for the way this was handled. I think nobody knew what to do, nobody knew how to handle it, but we just felt we had been left totally out there, that nobody considered the family at all."

Years later, Ruth McCrea can't explain why Julie and the children were forgotten that afternoon. "Maybe we tried to find her but she had left school to collect the kids," she says. "More likely, we were shaken badly, to the point that we didn't handle things very well, although one would think calling her should have been obvious. Our first concern was Frank, he was always our first concern, and sometimes, Julie would say lots of times, we neglected her. Only looking back do I see this."

As the plane passed low over the airport, McKenna realized he was at the centre of a public spectacle. "I didn't think this was even a public issue. It was just us trying to get this thing worked out. And all of a sudden you see a car pulled up beside the road and then another one, and then all of a sudden you see police cars starting to come in, and fire trucks and ambulances." What he didn't know was that the emergency team had brought a vascular surgeon with a blood supply to the runway, preparing for the worst when the plane came down.

"I thought I was going to get hurt, but I didn't think I was going to die," he recalls. "I thought I might die. I didn't feel terror or anything like that. I didn't feel the kind of anxiety I felt over some of the things we did in government. We were working on a lot of things. We opened up the floor, and we were trying to jerk the aircraft. We were doing a lot of things like that."

At one point, the pilots were preparing to land the plane on two wheels, but they pulled back up and started circling again. "Before we actually got into our final approach, there was a call, and then we pulled up and started going around. I said, 'What's going on?' and they said the factory had just called, and we can't go in on two wheels or we'll somersault. That didn't sound to me like a very good thing to do, to somersault down the runway. That was kind of nerve-racking."

Inside the hangar, Christine and Jamie had been ushered into a back room. Christine was furious that the Premier's office staff weren't allowing her to see what was happening, and she found herself feeling angry about the reporters gathered at the airport. She wrongly assumed they were hoping for a tragic end to the story, when in fact they were rooting for the Premier and the pilots. "In my heart I knew they all wanted the plane to explode. They wanted the headline, 'Frank McKenna dies in plane crash.' The whole situation was awful."

Morgan decided that the pilots had no choice but to bring the plane in on its belly. "It gives you more control over the aircraft. What happens if you try to land on two of the three wheels is that, as soon as the side that doesn't have any landing gear contacts the ground, you end up spinning in circles out of control. At that point, you're simply along for the ride. So it was preferable, if we could, to retract the other two landing gears and land on the belly. Our concern at that point was getting the other two landing gears up."

The normal retraction system had failed. The only system left was an emergency extension system designed to open the landing gear. Morgan telephoned the plane's manufacturer in Wichita, Kansas, to see whether the emergency system would somehow pull wheels back into the belly of the plane. The mechanics said they thought it would work. Morgan told Derrah to try. Finally, the left and front wheels slowly retracted back into the plane. About five-thirty, Derrah turned to McKenna. It was time to put the plane on the ground. "They told me how they wanted me to sit, and I was to try to get the door open quickly," McKenna recalls. "I thought they were capable of landing that aircraft one way or the other. Even though we might end up getting beaten up pretty good, this was going to be a survivable crash."

A belly landing is something pilots learn in school but hope they never have to use. Technically, it is a normal landing, except for the last few feet. Derrah brought the plane in over the runway the same way he would have had the wheels been down. Then, just before it touched, he shut down the engines as well as the fuel and electrical systems to reduce the risk of fire.

Morgan had driven out onto the runway with the emergency crew — three fire trucks, an ambulance and two RCMP cruisers. "I was holding my breath, but I wasn't even aware of it. There was constant chatter on the radio, then seconds before the aircraft contacted the ground, everything went silent. It was almost like everybody just took a collective breath in and held it and waited for the plane to land."

The plane skimmed the runway, then dug in nose first, snapping off its propellers, skidding for more than five hundred feet. The moment the plane stopped, the emergency exit on the left side of the plane opened. McKenna emerged and jogged across the runway, turning back to find Derrah and Cooper on his heels. The fire trucks moved in and sprayed the plane and runway with foam. "It was probably when we got on the ground that I realized it was even more serious than I thought," McKenna recalls. "I was trying to get the door open, and the pilots went right over top of me, got the door opened, grabbed me and pushed me out and ran. That's when I saw the foam trucks spraying us." As the police drove McKenna and Morgan back across the runway to the airport, the Premier glanced at his chief pilot and smiled. "I knew you were there, and I knew everything was fine."

McKenna entered the hangar, embraced Julie and his children, then asked for a telephone. Moments after Toby watched his father running from the plane on television, the phone rang in his dormitory. It was his father. "He was very emotional," Toby recalls. "He said, 'Look, that was an awful experience.' He said he and the pilots talked about the possibility that they weren't going to make it, and that he had written us a letter. He wanted us to know how much he cared about us. He was going to rip it up now that everything was fine."

As the crowd in the hangar gathered around her husband, Julie took a deep breath, shuddered and said simply, "Okay, this is over." She gathered her children and left the airport, still pale and shaking as she mumbled an obligatory but unconvincing "I knew everything was going to be fine" for the reporters who followed her. Julie drove home with Jamie in her own car. Christine drove herself in her father's car, tears of relief and anger streaming down her cheeks.

McKenna had a job to do before he could go home. He scanned the crowd for Maurice Robichaud. "I shook his hand, and he had a big smile on his face," Robichaud recalls. "He was like a kid on Christmas morning. And he didn't seem to be the worse for wear. We ended up doing a scrum, and all the reporters were more worked up than he was, which is a pretty good situation because you want your premier to be calm, cool and collected. He likes the situation where the impression people are left with is, here's somebody who's got his act together and who's got the things that he's responsible for under control. That was important to him."

As he waded into the agitated flock of reporters, McKenna called Derrah and Cooper to his side, praising them for remaining calm under pressure. He said Glyn Morgan and the emergency crew had been towers of strength. "I was afraid, but I had faith in them," he said. Was it a rough landing? "There was a lot of screeching and banging, and we decelerated quickly. Other than that, it was as good as some of their other landings," McKenna said, turning to Derrah and laughing.

Robichaud drove McKenna home. "It was like a second chance, and his mind was just riveted on what had happened, but he was real light about it," he recalls. "It wasn't like, 'Am I ever lucky,' but 'Wow, it was interesting.' He was animated. He was laughing and telling jokes and kind of making fun of it." When they arrived at Woodstock Road, McKenna invited Robichaud in for a beer. When Robichaud left, the family returned to its coping mechanism of choice — denial.

"We just kind of did it, got through it, I cooked dinner, and the next morning everybody went off to work and school," Julie McKenna says. "It was like, 'We don't have time to deal with this.'" A political family doesn't have time to experience any crisis fully. "It's very rare that we all get together and engage in whimsy or nostalgia," McKenna says. "For the most part, all we do is look ahead. I just do not rewind tape."

Morgan and the maintenance crew did an autopsy on the plane and quickly found the source of the problem. When the landing gear was washed that morning, moisture had seeped into the plastic-covered cable that served to unlock the landing gear. Although the temperature on the ground was above freezing, the cable had frozen in the air. Therefore, when the landing gear began to descend, it crushed against the closed lock, and nothing the pilots could have done would have fixed it. Whereas Ruth McCrea later hung the defective cable along with a photograph of the crash-landing on the wall of her office, Julie McKenna just tried to forget that the whole thing ever happened.

For eight years, the McKennas didn't rewind the tape of that April afternoon. Only when prompted by a reporter's questions did they discuss what had happened. "It was harder for Julie than it was for me," McKenna said. Julie interjected, "That's not true, Frank. You wrote a letter. So you must have thought you were going to die." In the end, he didn't destroy the letter he had mentioned to Toby.

When it became clear that the plane was going to crash-land, McKenna steadied himself in his seat and wrote a letter that he hoped would be found with his body if the landing went poorly.

Dear Julie, Toby, Tina and Jamie,

I am writing this letter just in case things don't work out well on landing. We have two gears down but the third won't retract. The pilots are terrific and I am sure we will be OK.

I confess to being a little afraid. We have gone over exit procedures and should be OK if there's no explosion.

I really wanted to say how much I loved you all. I am sorry for all the hardship I have caused you through my ambition. I really did believe I could do a good job and make New Brunswick a better place to live. I hope people realize in time how right my agenda was for our future. I regret the pain that I am causing our employees and others in New Brunswick. I really do care for them.

Toby, keep up your hard work. You're a great kid. Tina — you can be whatever you want to be. Do it for me. Jamie, you're a wonderful son and friend. I think you even have politics in your blood.

All of you — look after your mother. Julie, I love you dearly. Please enjoy the good things in life — you deserve it.

Love you all,
Dad

P.S. Sorry about the writing. It's very rough up here.

"It wasn't even well written," he says sheepishly years later. "It's kind of a dumb letter. If I wanted to make a grand closing statement, this is not the one." Perhaps there is more honesty in the simple than in the grand. If nothing else, his words define the life of a political family. A family is always wounded by political ambition, whether it is simple ambition for power or a more noble ambition to improve society. At various times, McKenna was possessed by both, but in the end, the political agenda doesn't matter to the victims. For Julie McKenna, the cost of ambition has always been too high. She had learned this as a child growing up in Moncton, where politics divided her family. She learned this again as a wife who lost her husband to politics.

In an interview with the *Toronto Star*, Richard Hatfield reflected on the life of a political family, reaffirming his belief that his bachelorhood was well suited to his profession. Hatfield sketched the life story of a woman like Julie McKenna. "The situation is one of a woman marrying the hometown boy — the manager of the bank, or the minister of the church, or the lawyer — and they share this ambition," Hatfield said. "Then all of a sudden, bang, he becomes a Member of Parliament, and then super-bang, he becomes Prime Minister or Premier, and all of a sudden he is alone, and you are not part of his life, you are not his wife, you are just his spouse."

When McKenna ran against Hatfield in 1987, his campaign literature made much of the fact that he was a family man, suggesting that his morals were more pure than those of the flamboyant bachelor Premier. In response, Hatfield always maintained that, while family photographs look nice on Christmas cards, we should never forget that the smiles mask the awful price political families pay.

Julie Wetmore Friel McKenna was born in Moncton on January 13, 1950, one of six children. Her mother, Marion Aileen Creaghan, was raised in an affluent Tory establishment family. Marion's cousin, Paul Creaghan, was a minister in the Hatfield government and later became a judge, and her uncle, William Creaghan, a federal Tory MP in the Diefenbaker government, was also eventually appointed to the bench. When Marion married Moncton lawyer Donal James Friel, an ardent Liberal, she found herself caught in a nasty political crossfire. Friel had served his political apprenticeship campaigning for Louis Robichaud.

Julie grew up in Moncton but spent her summers at the family cottage on the beach in Cap-Pelé, where her great-grandfather Friel, a pre-famine Irish immigrant, had settled and taught school. Julie's mother was university educated, but she never worked outside the home. Donal Friel eventually became a Crown prosecutor in Moncton, and he worked the Liberal back rooms. When Marion's parents moved out of their home in downtown Moncton, Marion and Donal converted it into a duplex. Uncle Bill Creaghan moved into one side, and Marion and Donal and their family lived on the other side.

"Very early on, politics was something that wasn't very pleasant for me, serious stuff that created a lot of family arguments," Julie recalls. Her mother grew to hate politics, the ugly phone calls and yelling from one side of the duplex to the other. "My mother saw politics as being something dirty that took time away from the family," says John Friel, Julie's older brother. "I can remember storing little bottles, little half-pints of liquor, and we'd have cases and cases and cases of them in the basement of the house. My father would have them for election day. They'd go and drive people to the polls and give them a drink. We as kids knew that this was going on. One thing I remember is that somebody came to the door of the house. The kids were alone, and my parents were out. They said my father had sent them over to get the liquor. So I showed them where the liquor was, and they carted out all these bottles of liquor. When my father came home I got shit because the Tories had come in and stolen the liquor."

As far as Julie's mother was concerned, politics encouraged her husband to drink to excess, an affliction he battled throughout his life. "Politics was drinking," John Friel recalls. "That's all I can picture. It is everybody drinking. That's my childhood memory."

When Julie left for St. Francis Xavier University and started dating Frank McKenna, her mother told her that whatever course she chose for her life, her ambitious boyfriend shouldn't be part of it. From the moment Marion laid eyes on Frank McKenna, she saw politician written all over him. "Early on, when he would have a meal at our house, my mother wouldn't even talk to him," Julie recalls. "She would say, 'Julie, does Frank want something else to eat?' She told me, 'You shouldn't marry him. He's going to be a politician, and you're not going to have a good life.'" For her part, Julie was in love. While she, too, saw his political ambition, in the foolhardy fashion of young lovers, she believed she could change him, or thought perhaps it wouldn't be as bad as her mother predicted. Marion Friel would grow to love her son-in-law. But when Frank began his political journey, Julie could hear her mother's voice ringing in her ears.

After McKenna was elected MLA for Chatham, he started living part-time in Fredericton, and in the midst of his leadership bid, he only found the time to come home on Sundays. Julie stopped teaching at the Community College to become a full-time mother. For awhile, he and Julie reserved Sundays for the family. They attended Mass in the morning and watched *Disney* on television in the evening. Frank lounged around the house eating popcorn and wearing sweatpants. But over time, even these moments felt staged, like another event on a long list that had to be attended to.

During election campaigns, Julie stayed home with the children unless Fern Landry telephoned to say that they needed her on the road for a few days to settle her husband, who was refusing to rest. Landry would call her if McKenna hadn't slept in several days because Julie was the only person who could calm him down. "He would come to bed if I was there," Julie says. "He would feel he had to spend some time with me. He has a tendency to drive himself to the point of physical exhaustion. It's a McKenna tendency. It's that way with everything Frank does. There's no calmness there."

Other than occasionally dropping into campaigns to keep her husband from breaking down, Julie never participated in her husband's political life. There were always lots of willing volunteers who were stronger campaigners than she was. She deferred to them and put all her energy into the children. "That was my job," she says. "They were the ones who needed me."

During the months leading up to the 1987 election, CBC Radio reporter Roger Bill travelled with McKenna. One Sunday in the winter of 1986, he visited the family home in Chatham to prepare an intimate radio documentary that would be broadcast on CBC's *Sunday Morning* a week after the sweep. As a rule, Julie McKenna avoids the media, but when she does grant rare interviews, she tends to speak with disarming honesty. She is unpretentious and direct, qualities that have been confused with naïveté and bitterness in political circles, which tend to celebrate superficiality. She doesn't put on a show for anybody, especially reporters. If she's going to take the time to allow an invasion of her privacy, she's going to retain her integrity by speaking plainly. On this occasion, Julie spoke softly and deliberately into Bill's tape recorder. "I see myself as a single parent, in that I have three children to raise on my own, totally on my own, I mean twenty-four hours," she said. "I see my husband one day a week. Everything is scheduled. I know I'm certainly not number one, ever. Look at his lists. It's all the things that have to be done, and maybe number twelve is call home. There's no question I'm not number one. But he has so many other things to do, and really, really important things, although I'd like to be the most important thing."

Her husband had fallen out of the family orbit. Now, all family plans involving McKenna went through Ruth McCrea in Fredericton. "If we want him home for a confirmation or something like that, I have to phone in and book him for it," she said. "It's very definitely scheduled. We don't do anything on the spur of the moment because there are no moments. As for a personal social life, we don't have one." As far as the routine activities of the children's daily lives were concerned — drives to hockey and figure skating, teacher interviews, homework, discipline — Julie did all of that, and she and the children learned to keep most minor family crises to themselves. McKenna had become too busy and stressed with other matters to concern himself with the minutiae of family life.

Eventually, work started intruding on the family Sundays because McKenna felt guilty about taking even one day a week off. He campaigned constantly, driven by his insecurity. He would overcome his shortcomings by outworking everyone else, by wanting the prize more. In the meantime, there was no doubt that Julie was strong enough to take care of herself and the children.

As the 1987 election approached, Julie braced herself for more changes to their lives, and on election night she began preparing the children for the rocky road ahead. She tucked Christine and Jamie in bed after the returns came in, and on the drive to the Miramichi Exhibition Centre she told Toby to brace himself: his Dad was going to be the Premier. There were going to be big crowds that night and lots of people taking his picture and asking him questions.

Toby McKenna recalls that people in the crowd first reached out to touch his father, and then they starting to touch him as well. "I remember thinking, what an odd feeling, people wanting to shake my hand," he says. "I had nothing to do with it."

Frank and Julie had decided that after he won the election they would all move to Fredericton so they could live in the same city. The deal was simple. In Fredericton, McKenna had to come home for dinner when he was in town. If Julie was going to uproot the children, she told her husband, she needed a reason to do it. Just having him home for dinner, even if he was often distracted, would be an improvement over his almost complete absence from their lives in Chatham. "The children saw more of their dad on the six o'clock news than they did at home," Julie told *Chatelaine* magazine in an interview shortly after the election. "I didn't want to leave Chatham," Christine recalls. "Fredericton to us was the biggest city in the world."

In January, 1988, the McKennas paid $230,000 for a white clapboard extended Cape Cod on Woodstock Road near the Sheraton Hotel and close to the walking trails along the St. John River. The 4,800-square-foot home, which was a step up from their modest bungalow in Chatham, would give them space for entertaining. It had a large dining room and drawing room downstairs overlooking a fenced-in back yard, and a garden. This garden became the site for an annual spring strawberries and ice-cream party. Julie furnished the house with items she bought at auctions and some of her family heirlooms, including her grandmother's antique chandelier, which she converted from gas to electricity and hung in the dining room.

Julie was determined to live the way other ordinary Fredericton families did. The children attended public schools, played sports and worked in the summers at Tingley's ice cream stand. She politely excused herself from the social circle of Fredericton's establishment. If some of the city's better citizens considered her a social misfit and a political liability, she couldn't have cared less. When she first moved to Fredericton, she was aware of the gossip about herself, everything from criticism of her decision to let the children hold summer jobs to stories about how she resented the amount of attention being paid to her husband and wanted more of it for herself.

"I knew I couldn't make everybody happy," she says. "I wasn't good at the tea-party circuit. I couldn't listen to that. I had to do what was right for us, and I couldn't get caught up in what other people thought. It was a question of survival. I had to say, okay, I accept my priorities, and they were the children, they had to be kept safe. I had to make sure they had what they needed. The province was last, as far as I was concerned. Frank was devoted full-time to the province. We couldn't both do that."

There were public events that required Julie's presence, and when protocol demanded it, she would be at the Premier's side. Neither of them learned to enjoy these ceremonial events. For McKenna, they were distractions. Whereas Hatfield delighted in the details of the Throne Speech and the opening of the Legislature, lingering over guest lists and seating arrangements, McKenna left all the arrangements to his staff and asked for a briefing moments before the ceremonies began. Although Julie enjoyed meeting many of the people who would move through receiving lines, she remembers how her hands would swell and how she had to stop wearing rings to public events. When Frank and Julie finished shaking hands, they would leave these events at the earliest possible opportunity. Often they retreated to a pizza joint somewhere in Fredericton, overdressed but unwinding before heading home to the children.

Apart from these obligatory public appearances, Julie studiously avoided the media. After granting a handful of interviews after the 1987 election at the request of the Liberal Party, she made it clear that she and her children were off limits. Soon after they moved to Fredericton, Julie answered a knock on her door and found a CBC-TV reporter and camera-man asking to interview the Premier. "This is a private home," she said firmly. "If you want to interview my husband, you'll have to do it at his office." When word of this encounter spread through the press gallery, reporters made an informal pact to respect the family's privacy. Whereas photographers and reporters were often waiting outside on the sidewalk for the Premier, they never again knocked on the door. "I always felt that if I became a public person, it was just opening the children up, it was opening all of us," Julie says. "They had Frank. He made lots of news. They didn't need more than that." Reporters were welcomed into the Premier's home once a year for a pizza party, an event which Maurice Robichaud encouraged but which was always scheduled when Julie was out of town. "She would just say, 'I don't want them in my house,'" McKenna recalls. "She made no effort to court them, no effort to find favour."

Julie steered clear of government controversy with one exception, a case she was drawn into more by suspicion and innuendo than hard facts. When former deputy ministers Gordon Gregory and Denis Haché launched wrongful dismissal lawsuits against the province, McKenna was questioned during pre-trial discovery hearings. On July 29, 1988, Gregory's lawyer, David Norman, attempted to draw Julie McKenna into the case, alleging that the infamous firing had been personal, not political. A persistent rumour had circulated through Fredericton that McKenna had fired his deputy minister of justice at his wife's request, as payback for Gregory's involvement in forcing the early retirement of Donal Friel as a Crown prosecutor several years before the election. Friel is a brilliant lawyer, but he has been plagued throughout his life by manic depression and alcoholism. When his drinking and depression began to interfere seriously with his work in the courtroom and cases weren't coming to trial on time, the Justice Department quietly stepped in and allowed him to take early retirement. Norman pointed out that at the time McKenna had spoken to Justice Minister John Baxter about his father-in law's situation.

"For what purpose?" Norman asked.

"Simply to ensure that he received a fair deal," McKenna replied, easily falling into the legalese of his interrogator. "As I recall it, simply to apprise him of what was going on."

"There has been a persistent story that has been circulating that the fact of Mr. Friel's termination has had something to do with Mr. Gregory's termination. Can you comment on that?"

"It's ridiculous," McKenna replied. "I never associated Mr. Gregory with Mr. Friel's termination, number one. Number two, I've never really questioned the reasons for his termination, in the sense that I was aware of the problems, and I had some sympathy for the position the department was in."

"You have never discussed with your wife the termination of Mr. Gregory?" Norman asked.

"I've heard there were rumours to that effect. The fact of the matter is, I don't think my wife would even know who Mr. Gregory is, short of this. No, my wife has never made representations to me."

"And you have never heard her discuss with anyone else the termination of Mr. Gregory?"

"No, I haven't. Quite frankly, I'm not sure my wife has any issue to take with the way in which her father was handled."

As far as the court case was concerned, the issue ended there. But in small cities like Fredericton, rumours persist for years, and long after McKenna's resignation, the story of Julie McKenna's alleged retribution against Gordon Gregory still makes the rounds on the political cocktail circuit. When asked about it, Julie says that she didn't have any problem with the way the department dealt with her father and that, before her husband was elected Premier and fired Gordon Gregory, she had no idea who the man was. She speaks openly about her father's problems and also about her mother's struggles with alcohol before she died of cancer when she was in her fifties. Julie herself quit drinking while the family was still living in Chatham when she recognized that she, too, was experiencing symptoms of alcoholism.

Julie's reluctance to become a public person was also rooted in the lessons of her youth. Politics could hurt you. She considered her husband to be naïve on that score, and she tried to protect him from people she believed would take advantage of him and give him bad advice. She also tried to keep him grounded. She knew that politicians tend to lose a feel for the street once they take office, and she was aware that Frank was no different. "If there's a crisis, it's a major crisis for them, but people at the grocery store really don't give a damn," Julie says. "Like, nobody else would be talking about it, but it would go on and on for days. I would say, 'Shut up. People on the street don't know and don't care. They want jobs.' There was always a constant crisis in the premier's office. That was how they lived."

McKenna feels that Julie's grounding has saved his life, that without her he would have been too obsessive and compulsive about work, would have burned out and faded away. "I had a huge respect for her judgment and her discipline and her values," McKenna says. "I thought they were really strong and rooted. Those things were things that I fed on. It was important for me to have someone who was so committed to family and to faith. Julie's never had her head turned by people of influence."

Even with Julie applying the brakes, McKenna's life revolved around his work, seven days a week. On Saturday mornings, after a long week at the office, McKenna rose early and walked to the Boyce Farmer's Market, picked up some breakfast and then retreated to his office across the street, where he read the newspapers, dictated a series of letters and started putting together plans for the next week. On Sunday mornings the family went to Mass. Throughout the rest of the day, he would continue his reading and note-taking, preparing for Monday's staff meetings. He was a restless sleeper. Julie would roll over to see her husband sitting, jotting notes on the pad he kept next to the bed.

His obsession with his work continued during family outings. When they drove anywhere in the province, after a few miles Julie would ask him to pull over and let her drive. He couldn't keep his eyes on the road. He would be looking at construction work along the highways, and then he would start dialing his cell phone to speak to various cabinet ministers about problems he saw along the way. When they went on rare vacations together, Julie came to expect two things. First, her husband would get sick the moment he started to relax. Second, the vacation would invariably be cut short by a crisis in the premier's office. John Bryden tried to slow McKenna down, arguing that everyone in New Brunswick took a vacation, and no one would begrudge a short break for the premier. Bryden suggested that McKenna consider a vacation part of the job, that he could work as hard at relaxing as he did at being premier.

"That was wonderful advice," McKenna recalled during a conversation with Julie after his resignation. "It took all the guilt away and I just felt great."

"Except that you worked all the time," Julie interjected. "You would just write all the time, so you would come back from vacation and the whole civil service would think, 'Oh, he's coming back, what are we going to have to do?'"

"It wasn't so much heavy lifting as just sitting on the beach or walking through the woods and saying, 'My God, why not this?' or, reading a newspaper wherever we might be, 'Oh, look at that.' I clip incessantly. I keep idea books. There are always things to do. I just keep trotting them out all the time: 'Let's try this. We looked at that. Did you see what they are doing in Trinidad? Do you know what they are doing in Australia? What about this, why can't we do that?' Every vacation became a treasure trove of ideas."

McKenna did keep his end of his initial bargain with Julie and the children: he usually made it home for dinner when he was in Fredericton.

At home, he watched the evening newscasts and discussed the events of the day with his family. However, he was often there but not there, so distracted that when he was driving a carload of children home he sometimes drove right past his house until the children told him to stop and turn around.

"It's not just a matter of time, because we probably did as good a job of balancing time as anybody," McKenna recalls. "It's also the quality of the time when you're there. I think that's even more important. I would be really distracted. I'd come in, then I would be trying to watch three newscasts, and then I would be just trying to relax from all of the hundred different things that had happened that day. It would take hours before I was even listening to anybody. I could be in the room and they could talk about a nuclear bomb attack and I wouldn't hear them. There was an awful lot of that, just shutting everything out around me. The affairs of the province went around in my head all the time, like a noise that wouldn't stop."

There were no barriers between the McKenna family and the community; their home was often filled with friends of the children who looked upon Frank and Julie as just another set of parents. One boy came up from the basement after sleeping over on a Saturday night to find McKenna cooking breakfast in the kitchen. "Oh my God, it's the Premier," he said. "What are you doing here?" The family home had been outfitted with a security system, but they rarely locked their doors. The only times Christine remembers the emergency buzzers being pushed were when there were too many kids running around the house and someone fell into the button installed beside the front door.

There were two notable exceptions to this life without restrictions. Both occurred in the fall of 1989, one of the most tumultuous and frightening periods in New Brunswick history. In September, 1989, RCMP officers arrested a five-member Colombian hit squad heading for the York County Jail in Fredericton, armed with assault rifles, submachine guns, tear gas and more than three thousand rounds of ammunition. The squad was on its way to release two Colombian pilots who, the previous spring, had crashed their plane carrying $250,000 worth of cocaine on a remote airstrip forty kilometres outside Fredericton. One of the pilots, José Ali Galindo-Escobar, was believed to be the first cousin of Pablo Escobar, the billionaire godfather of the Medellin drug cartel. The York County Jail was a small stone building with an exercise yard surrounded by barbed wire next to the Boyce Farmer's Market in the capital city's downtown. If the squad had made it to Fredericton, they would have certainly overrun the handful of guards at the hundred-and-fifty-year-old jail.

Four of the Five Amigos, as they came to be known, were arrested in Edmundston, while an accomplice armed with two .22 calibre pistols was picked up in Saint John a couple of blocks away from where Frank McKenna was addressing a national conference about the future of VIA Rail. The Colombians instantly drew international attention. Fearing the men might have been planning to assassinate United States President George H.W. Bush at his summer home in Kennebunkport, Maine, Secret Service agents escorted Bush's daughter, Dorothy LeBlond, from her office in Portland, Maine, and began protecting her around the clock.

The pilots were moved out of the Fredericton jail. Fearing that the Five Amigos had more accomplices on the loose in New Brunswick, police transformed Fredericton into a war zone, positioning snipers on rooftops around the courthouse when the Colombians made a court appearance. The police also threw a tight blanket of security around the Premier and his family.

"I remember a police car following me as I walked to work," says McKenna, who always refused to alter his daily routine for the sake of security. He understood the job the police had to do but never liked being guarded. This time, he had no choice. "There were snipers all over the place. We got briefed, and the next thing we got security on us big time." A team of heavily armed police officers were stationed at the McKenna home on Woodstock Road. "They had the vests on and machine guns and everything," McKenna says. "The kids didn't know much about this. They came traipsing through the back yard, and this guy jumps out. That's what the kids remember."

Christine was walking from her school to her father's office to hitch a ride to figure skating practice when an army truck stopped in front of the Centennial Building and troops began pouring out the back. She lay down in the grass until they passed. Later, she had to go figure skating with an armed guard sitting in the stands. She was horribly embarrassed, and even more so when, the next day, her entire class had to stay inside during lunch hour because the police didn't want Christine on the streets.

Another situation that fall was even more terrifying than the arrival of the Five Amigos. Convicted murderer Allan Legere had escaped, remained at large and become the main suspect in a series of killings on the Miramichi. On May 3, 1989, Legere broke away from prison guards while visiting a hospital in Moncton to be treated for an ear infection. In the bathroom, he freed himself from his handcuffs with a homemade key, overpowered two guards, took a female hostage, hijacked her car and escaped. Twenty-six days later, Chatham shopkeeper Annie Flam was murdered, and her sister, Nina Flam, was badly beaten; their home was partially burned by their assailant. Legere was the prime suspect. When they lived in Chatham, the McKennas often shopped at Annie and Nina Flam's store, and McKenna had handled some legal work for them after a car accident.

"We were terrified," McKenna says. "I went up to the hospital. Nina Flam asked me to go up. She and her sister had been raped and brutalized. And it was just awful. These people were friends of ours, and here she was just beat to hell. She didn't know what had happened to her. She could hardly describe what happened, it was just so brutal. She was lucky to get out. It was a terrible nightmare."

The McKennas had heard about Legere when they lived in Chatham. When he was a child of Chatham Head's poor back roads, Legere was pelted with rocks by the other Newcastle schoolchildren. He grew up to be a bully, a perpetrator of assault and petty crimes, known and feared on the Miramichi long before he was convicted of murder. The McKenna bungalow was situated on the edge of a wooded area where the family hiked and cross-country skied, and occasionally they met Legere there when he was out on a hunting or trapping expedition. In January, 1987, he was convicted of beating elderly shopkeeper John Glendenning to death during a home invasion and robbery in Newcastle and was sentenced to life in prison.

On October 14, 1989, Newcastle sisters Linda and Donna Daughney were sexually assaulted and beaten to death in their home. On November 16, Father James Smith, a sixty-nine-year-old priest, was beaten to death in the rectory of the Nativity of the Blessed Virgin Mary Church in Chatham Head. The McKennas knew Smith well. He was a brother of the former Liberal MP for Northumberland, Percy Smith, and the family had occasionally attended Mass in Chatham Head and received communion from him. They had also regularly attended church suppers, and McKenna had worked with Father Smith on a number of Chatham Head community projects. For weeks, Miramichiers were terrified in their own homes, installing security systems and arming themselves against Legere. He had become part myth, part terrifying reality, a shadow who eluded a massive police manhunt for months, who reappeared on the Miramichi for a killing and then disappeared again.

Shortly after Smith's death, McKenna was holding a press conference in the Centennial Building in Fredericton when a reporter changed the subject to ask him if there was anything to be done about Legere's reign of terror on the Miramichi. Without consulting with his aides or the police, McKenna announced that he was going back to the Miramichi to live until Legere was captured. "Christ Almighty," muttered Maurice Robichaud. "Well, you just wiped out your headline."

"I can remember people calling and telling me that people were absolutely terrified, that it would help an awful lot if I would show I wasn't afraid, if I would go there," McKenna recalls. "I went just to show that there is a rule of law here and people have a right to protection under the law. But I was scared. The police went ballistic when they found out I was going. They really got upset, as well they should. It was a real security risk, and it was done without any advance consultation. This was probably the last thing they needed. On the other hand, we needed to show that people can expect to be protected."

As far as the RCMP were concerned, the Premier had gone from being a possible target of Legere to a probable target. They dispatched extra security to the family's Fredericton home, where Julie and the children remained, and to Chatham, where McKenna stayed with his friends Ed and Marjorie MacDermaid in the Riverside Drive subdivision about half a block from his former family home.

On the afternoon of November 24, Legere left a Saint John bar in an early winter snowstorm and headed for Chatham, straight into the police dragnet. First he hijacked a taxi with a sawed-off rifle. When the taxi went off the road near Moncton, he flagged down a passing car. The car stopped; he produced his rifle and took a second hostage, this time a woman. However, this hostage was actually an off-duty RCMP officer. When they stopped for gas, she pulled a duplicate set of keys out of her pocket and escaped with the car and the taxi driver. Legere kept going, next hijacking a transport truck. Shortly before six in the morning, the police surrounded the truck, and Legere surrendered peacefully.

The morning Legere was captured, the people of Chatham danced in the streets. The bells rang at St. Michael's Basilica in Chatham and St. Mary's Church in Newcastle. McKenna emerged from his friends' home and joined the party. "I'm overjoyed and feel an enormous sense of relief," he told *Telegraph-Journal* reporter Derwin Gowan. "Miramichiers are a resilient lot, and they've experienced hardship before, and they traditionally come together because of it."

———

During the first few years after their move to Fredericton, life as the premier's son was most difficult for the youngest McKenna, ten-year-old Jamie, not because of security concerns or his father's brutal work schedule but because of little-boy worries. He missed his home and friends in Chatham and, at times, his anonymity. Back in Chatham, Jamie liked to wear scruffy sweatpants to school, and his mother thought that was just fine. Soon after he arrived in Fredericton, a schoolmate said, "Why don't you dress like a premier's kid? You shouldn't be wearing sweatpants with holes." From that day forward, Jamie has been self-conscious about the way he dresses in public. Then there was the great hockey controversy. Jamie had been playing competitive hockey in Chatham, and so his parents registered him with a competitive team rather than in the recreational program when they moved to Fredericton. When minor hockey officials found a place for Jamie, other parents voiced their outrage, as only hockey parents can, over what they perceived to be special treatment for the Premier's son. After several weeks of agony, Jamie joined a recreational team.

Nevertheless, following a couple of difficult years adjusting to life in Fredericton, Jamie made new friends and became comfortable as the Premier's son. In many ways, he resembles his father. Aldéa Landry recalls that when she took the McKenna children across town in a taxi during the 1985 leadership convention, Jamie piped up from the back seat, "Who's paying for this? How much is this going to cost?" Like father, like son, Aldéa thought. Jamie began to enjoy being the Premier's son. He travelled with his father on the government plane whenever he could and toured the province on the campaign bus. He could recite his father's speeches and knew the names of all the members of the Legislature. As he grew older, he harboured none of his mother's cynicism about political life.

During his first year at St. Francis Xavier University, Jamie wrote a Father's Day essay that showed no trace of bitterness about life in the public eye. "People always ask me, 'What is it like to have a father as the premier?' My response is, 'What is it like not to have a father as a premier?'

Another question people always ask me is, 'Is your father home a lot?' To this I say, he makes every effort to be home for every free minute he can spare. The whole family respects him for this. The only problem with him being home is that he tries to spend every second he has with us kids. People will say, 'What's wrong with that?' I say, when you're my age all you want to do is hang out with your friends, and I always feel guilty when I have to tell him I already have plans." He reminisced about trips with his father, the most memorable being a canoe trip in the wilderness of North-ern Ontario with David Peterson and his son, who is Jamie's age. "If you had seen what my father looked like at the end of the trip, you would definitely not think he had a very prestigious job," he wrote.

Christine, the middle child, settled into Fredericton more easily than her younger brother, but she also experienced uncomfortable moments at school. "Everybody stared at me the first day," she recalls. "We didn't change. We weren't different people." When she was in junior high and the teachers' union began working to rule during contract negotiations, one of Christine's teachers invited television cameras into the classroom to conduct interviews about the negative impact her father was having on the education system. "I couldn't believe this was happening," she recalls. "I'd gotten used to people criticizing my dad, but I felt this was a direct attack on me." Christine told her mother what had happened, but Julie felt helpless to protect her children from these subtle messages without causing a public scandal. "We couldn't do anything, that was the problem," Julie says. "You can't do anything because, as soon as you do, you're a bitch. You can't say anything. If I had done anything, it would just have made it worse for her." Julie repeated her own mother's warnings to Christine: Don't marry a politician. You don't want that kind of life.

Christine, a self-reliant young woman, worried her parents very little, whereas her older brother Toby was a difficult child from the day he came into the world. As he grew older, he inherited his father's energy and looks (he is the spitting image, only taller)   but not his discipline. He was bored in school, had a short attention span and never studied. When Frank and Julie heard about Toby's exploits, from his teachers or on occasion from the police, Toby would always deny that he'd done anything wrong. "Someone is using my name," he'd say. His parents started referring to this imaginary boy as Toby's evil twin. Toby's teenage years became the most stressful time in the McKennas' marriage.

"Toby was strong-headed, and he's hugely confident, but he did not want to do his work," McKenna says. "He didn't like doing his school work and he just didn't want to accept discipline. And Julie, unfortunately, was the one who had to supply most of it. I would come in, usually after the event, and be asked to reinforce the discipline, not really having known what was taking place and hearing his version of events, which was different, and just being put in the horrible spot of trying to choose sides. I found that really difficult." Toby would say, "You're always siding with Mom, you don't even care what I say." In Julie's eyes, it would have been easier being a single parent than having a child who so easily manipulated both parents.

Toby maintains that he wasn't rebelling against his high-achieving father. Rather, he says that he had the system worked out by the time he was in junior high. He would do just enough work to get by, and then, when the time came to turn on the steam, he turned it on. "I was a rebel on my own account, and I would have been a rebel whether my father was a premier or a bum," he says. "It was in my blood to push everything to the edge, and my marks were just one of the ways in my life that I did that. I got caught for everything. I had a nine-out-of-ten chance of getting caught for everything I did. I had a cocky attitude. I didn't care. I thought I had it figured out. In my mind, I had my shit together. Looking back, I probably didn't."

Nor did he feel pressure because of being the Premier's son. He remembers entering Fredericton High School with a mixture of excitement and apprehension. "I was excited about some of the girls who might think I was a celebrity, and I was a bit nervous about the guys who might hate me." His mother warned him that people were watching him and waiting to tear him apart, but he didn't think about the consequences of drinking underage, staying out past curfew or driving before he had a license.

The McKennas were always wondering if they themselves were putting too much pressure on Toby. They wanted him to believe he could be whatever he wanted to be. They would tell him if he wanted to be a farmer, that was okay. If he wanted to be a policeman, that was okay, too. He didn't need to be a lawyer or even a university graduate to please his parents, but Frank and Julie didn't want him to end up doing something he didn't want to do, merely out of indifference. "We tried to take that kind of rational approach," McKenna says. "We have a lot of sympathy for what parents go through because we were really torn as to whether what he needed was tough love or some trust and independence."

Julie McKenna decided her son needed tough love, and her view was reinforced one Saturday evening when Toby was in his final year of high school. Frank and Julie were spending a rare quiet evening at home together when two Fredericton police officers arrived at their door and asked if they knew where Toby was. Some members of the Fredericton High School football team had gotten into a fight in the parking lot of Burger King. When the police arrived, the teenagers milling about at the scene said Toby McKenna had been in the middle of it. "To this day, I'm still innocent on that one," Toby says. He was drinking beer at a friend's house when he got word that the police and his parents were looking for him. He avoided his parents because he had been drinking, not because he had done anything wrong at Burger King. "I was legitimately innocent of whatever the hell the police were there for."

"We didn't know where he was," Julie recalls. "We knew who his friends were, so there we were, the Premier and his wife, running around town. We'd go into a teenage party, and we'd go in one door and Toby would go out the other."

"And they'd all lie," McKenna recalls. "'No, I don't think Toby was here.' Did anybody see Toby? 'No, no, no.'"

"And then we'd get to the next drunken brawl," Julie continues.

"That's just exactly what it was," McKenna adds. "We chased him all over the city. He knew we were after him."

Toby didn't come home that night. Eventually a friend called and said she was looking after him. The matter turned out not to be serious for the police; they were just trying to send Toby a warning. The matter was dropped. Toby started paying more attention to his studies, preparing for university. "He just turned in grade twelve," McKenna recalls. "He played football, and that brought a lot of discipline into his life. He decided he was going to university, he just turned on in school, and he ended up graduating with good marks. We knew that he was strong, and it infuriated us that he wanted to loaf along."

"It was a very stressful time," McKenna admitted during a conversation after he stepped down as premier. "Although we make it sound even bigger today than it was."

"No, Frank, we don't," Julie interrupted. "For me, it was hell."

When Toby left for St. Francis Xavier University, Julie decided it was time to get back into the workforce. She needed to do something for herself, and besides, the family could use the money. The Premier's salary didn't go far considering the lifestyle they had to maintain. She started out by entering her name in the pool of supply teachers for Fredericton's community college, teaching computer skills and office technology to adults, mainly women who were attempting to re-enter the job market. For Julie, teaching was a reawakening to the real world. Her students knew who Frank McKenna was because he was their teacher's husband. Most of them couldn't name a single minister in his cabinet. They didn't have time to deal with what politicians thought; they were too busy trying to finish their education.

After a couple of years of supply teaching, Julie started teaching literacy to adults, and she loved the work. She decided to go back to school and complete her Master's degree. "The university was a safe place. I always felt safe there." When she completed her degree, she began to work on course development for the Department of Education. By the time McKenna resigned, she had been fully accepted into the system.

She often told her children that she wanted all of them to be treated just like anyone else in New Brunswick. One day when she was driving home with Christine, an RCMP officer pulled her over for speeding. As the officer looked at Julie's driver's license, Christine leaned across the front seat and said, "She just wants to be treated like everybody else." Still, there were always reminders that they weren't just like anybody else. In the summer of 1997, after Christine graduated from St. Francis Xavier University with a degree in Business Administration, she was admitted to the hospital, and Julie found herself once again in an impossible situation as the wife of the Premier. Christine had been suffering from abdominal pain and vomiting, and, because she had planned a trip to Asia, her parents wanted to find out what was wrong. When doctors discovered that her appendix was scarred, they admitted her to hospital for an appendectomy. McKenna's government had been squeezing hospital budgets, and there was a general grumbling throughout the province about the falling quality of patient care. Julie booked her daughter into a double room because she had been hearing how stressed the nursing staff was, and she didn't want her to be alone. At first she was sharing a room with a quiet elderly woman, but that roommate was replaced by a patient with Alzheimer's disease who cried out constantly. Christine couldn't sleep.

"I said, 'We've got to get her out of here and get her a private room.' And we couldn't. How are we going to get her a private room without it looking like we are not happy with the health care system? We left her there. Can you believe that? Finally, the doctor couldn't handle it, and he released her. Nobody else would have left their daughter in that situation. I still feel bad about it. I think it's horrible that we did that.

But that's the kind of thing that you cannot react to because it would have been all over the province. It would have been a very significant event by the time people finished talking about it. You would get slapped in the face with that every once in a while, and you'd say, 'Okay, we are not normal people.'"

———

Meantime, Olive McKenna, who had become ill, wanted her son to leave politics before he got hurt. Richard Hatfield's mother had given her son the same advice, which in retrospect he no doubt wished he had heeded. Olive McKenna loved being the mother of the Premier, but she was worried about what politics was doing to her son and his family. "She'd been saying for the past few years, 'Look, you've done your share, it's time to get out,'" Julie McKenna recalls. "She felt we had done enough." After consulting with his mother, McKenna sat down with his family. The decision was unanimous: it was time for a change.

"I remember thinking, that's great, you're going to resign," Toby McKenna recalls. "He spent every minute of his life working. He put his whole life into being premier." At the same time, Toby found it hard to believe his father was going to leave the battle he had led for so many years. "I don't think he was one hundred per cent confident that he wanted to resign, in fact I know he wasn't. I felt he was doing something that deep in his heart he didn't want to do. He felt he had so many things he had left undone. I felt bad for him that he had to give up this fight. It was almost like his life was over. If he didn't have a family, he would still be there today, I think."

"When he told the children that he was leaving, it wasn't much of a surprise to any of us because we had always counted on ten years," Julie maintains. "If anything, you have to understand that this is a very honourable man. If he says something, it will happen. I have lived with him a long time. It always happens. So if he says, I'm going to stay here ten years, then it's going to be ten years."

When McKenna entered his tenth year in the premier's office, he knew it was time for him to keep the promise to his family. "We always looked at ten years, and when it got to the ten years, I started saying, okay, what are we going to do now?" Julie says. "We made a commitment to each other. When we decided that Frank would run as premier, we made a commitment to the province, and we would see it through."

In her own way, Julie had lived up to her side of the bargain. However, her political memories are vastly different from her husband's. One of her most vivid recollections is of watching her children at the 1985 leadership convention in the Moncton Coliseum, all of them dressed in their Sunday best, Toby the self-conscious young teenager, shy Christine clutching a Cabbage Patch doll, innocent, curious Jamie with a white McKenna visor falling down over his eyes. She remembers worrying constantly over Jamie, who was nine years old. "He was so little, and he had this big hat on, and he was teetering on the railing that was separating the seats from the arena floor," she recalls. "That's what I remember from the leadership convention."

When Toby was listening to Ray Frenette's vitriolic speech, he turned to his mother and asked, "Why would he say that about Dad?"

"It's just politics," she replied. When Frenette came over to McKenna and shook his hand after the vote, Toby told his mother he couldn't believe his dad would shake Ray Frenette's hand after the awful things he had said.

"That means your father just won," Julie told her son.

Since then, whenever Julie McKenna watches a political convention on television and sees a politician's wife and children in the fray, she starts to cry.

Nova Scotia Premier Russell MacLellan, Prime Minister Jean Chrétien, Newfoundland Premier Brian Tobin, and Frank McKenna at Highland Links, Ingonish, Nova Scotia, August 18, 1997.

11

THE HEALING GAME

Notre vie est de très courte durée.

— Fernand Landry

A man's character is often revealed in the way he plays games. Frank McKenna's sport of choice is hockey, the game he learned on the frozen flood plains and back yard rinks near the family farm in Apohaqui. He liked to play centre, the position that defines the character of the offensive play during a forward line's shift on the ice; his lines played fast and aggressively, skating with more grit than finesse. By the time he graduated from Sussex High School, he was starting to realize that the fulfillment of his hockey dreams would be limited by his size. But he never stopped playing.

During his years in the premier's office, McKenna served as captain of the Big Red Machine, a team made up of Liberal members and a scattering of talent recruited from among the bureaucrats. McKenna played centre on the first line. The Big Red Machine played exhibition games in New Brunswick and occasionally in other provinces. In March, 1990, the team played a two-game series against Quebec provincial politicians during the height of the Meech Lake crisis, the first game in Edmundston and the second at Val-Belair, north of Quebec City. McKenna scored the first goal of the game in Edmundston, which Quebec won 7-5. "Good warm feeling with MLAs," McKenna wrote in his diary. "Hockey Night for Canada." New Brunswick's team scored a 3-1 win at Val-Belair. At McKenna's request, the third game was played the following March at the Montreal Forum, and retired Canadiens Serge Savard and Jacques Lemaire joined the Quebec lineup. McKenna and his teammates, who included his son Jamie, lost to Quebec 7-6 in a shootout. "Like everyone else on our team, I was in awe," McKenna recalls. "I'm not sure my skates touched the ice through the whole game." Although he had taken a far different route than he had imagined on those cold winter nights in Apohaqui, his childhood dreams were fulfilled that night.

When Jim Lockyer, his education minister, suffered a heart attack during a charity game, McKenna decided that hockey was for younger men. He made up for this loss by throwing himself into his golf game. McKenna's a better than average golfer, but he doesn't swing like a natural. His backswing is a little short, and he doesn't follow through enough after contact. Nevertheless, what he lacks in fluidity, he tries to make up with sheer power. He's strong and he knows it. When he has a choice between a safe play with a shorter club or a risky play that will take him precariously close to trouble but, he hopes, right to the hole, he always reaches for the long stick. He likes to hit the ball as far as he can. He may end up in the woods or in the water, but when he walks off the course he knows that he pushed himself beyond his limits. He's a pleasant companion on a golf course, completely engaged with the game, unfailingly gracious. He doesn't believe in following the rule book to the letter and has never liked anyone telling him how to play; rules are for people who can't think for themselves.

Jean Chrétien loves golf and plays at about the same level as McKenna. Chrétien plays quickly and enjoys himself, although he has some help along the way. When he hits his ball into the woods, RCMP security officers walking in front of and behind him find the balls and put them on tees back in the fairway. The Prime Minister of Canada doesn't face the same hazards of the game as the average player.

On July 30, 1997, Chrétien invited McKenna to Ottawa for golf and lunch, just the two of them. He knew McKenna was planning to resign, and they needed some one-on-one time. Chrétien wanted to discuss McKenna's future in politics, whereas McKenna needed the Prime Minister's help on more immediate issues. First, he wanted Ottawa to sign a multi-million dollar federal-provincial cost-sharing agreement to continue the rebuilding of New Brunswick's highways, a cause he had pursued relentlessly in a steady stream of letters to Brian Mulroney and then to Chrétien. Every time someone died on a New Brunswick highway, the Prime Minister of the day could expect a letter from Frank McKenna, usually accompanied by a newspaper clipping. When Senator Nancy Clark Teed, a friend and shopping companion of Mila Mulroney, died in an accident on her way from Saint John to Fredericton on slippery winter roads, McKenna wrote a letter to Brian Mulroney pointing out that

Teed's death might have been avoided on better highways. Mulroney was offended. However, McKenna believed he was just doing his job. In addition to highway money, McKenna also wanted Chrétien's help in organizing and funding a conference to define an economic vision for Atlantic Canada. He wanted a last chance to create some momentum for the region's economy before he retired.

The morning at the Hunt Club in Ottawa was a golfer's dream — cool, soft summer air, no wind, dew on the grass. The two first ministers played quickly, the front nine in just an hour and fifteen minutes. Chrétien was "very, very competitive," McKenna noted in his diary. "He takes mulligans and very long gimmes" — that is, Chrétien played bad shots over again and picked up his ball when it was near the hole, assuming he would have made the putt anyway. Like many golfers, Chrétien was accustomed to bending the rules to lower scores and speed up play.

McKenna won the front nine decisively, forty strokes to Chrétien's forty-four. He was winning off the course as well; by the time they made the turn to the back nine, Chrétien had agreed to both of McKenna's requests. The competition continued. Chrétien started narrowing the gap on the back nine, and by the time they reached the final hole, the Prime Minister was only one shot back. Chrétien sank his putt for par. McKenna had a twelve-foot putt that broke sharply left to right. If he made it, he would tie the hole and win the match.

He paused before striking the ball. He thought about what he had negotiated during the round. Perhaps he should miss the putt and let Chrétien win the hole and tie the match. It was a putt that he could easily miss, and no one would suspect he had thrown the game. For a moment, he wondered whether there was too much at stake to risk upsetting the Prime Minister's mood.

"I couldn't do it," McKenna later wrote in his diary. "I sank the putt." As they walked to the clubhouse, McKenna pretended they had tied and that the score didn't matter. When they returned to 24 Sussex Drive for showers, beer and lunch, Chrétien appeared to be going along with the "we tied" story until the moment they were parting, when he said, "You beat me by a stroke. We have to do it again." Clearly, the Prime Minister had also been counting.

Donald Savoie uses this golf game between the Prime Minister and the Premier of New Brunswick to illustrate the thesis of his ground-breaking public policy book, *Governing from the Centre: The Concentration of Power in Canadian Politics*. Savoie argues that in recent years Canada has witnessed an unprecedented concentration of power in the offices of first ministers, a trend McKenna had understood and used to his advantage for years. McKenna had controlled the public policy agenda in New Brunswick by seizing every ounce of power available to him and enlarging it. He knew the federal government was run in the same fashion, just on a larger scale. Almost all his letters demanding action on highway construction and every other issue of significance were directed to the Prime Minister's Office. When he was about to retire from politics and needed immediate action on two issues important to his agenda and legacy, he made his case directly to the Prime Minister on the golf course. That's how business is done in Canadian politics. After the golf game, the federal government offered to provide funding for the Atlantic Vision conference, and several ministers, including the Prime Minister himself, promised to attend. Chrétien also instructed his staff to prepare a Treasury Board submission for the highways agreement.

"Within a few weeks, everything had been sorted out, and an announcement was made on both an Atlantic Vision conference and a new Canada/ Highways agreement," Savoie writes. "The Prime Minister did not ask Privy Council and Treasury Board Secretariat officials to prepare a submission and then to submit it for consideration in the government's decision making process. His instructions were clear — make these two initiatives happen."

During lunch, Chrétien addressed the major issue on his own agenda — Frank McKenna's political future. This wasn't the first time that Chrétien had suggested to McKenna that he was his preferred successor, rather than the front-runner, Finance Minister Paul Martin. McKenna recorded in his diary that Chrétien advised him that day in Ottawa to sit out for a time, then run federally; Charlie Hubbard, the Liberal MP from Miramichi, would be offered a patronage appointment to step aside. "He says I would be in a great position to succeed him," McKenna wrote.

However, McKenna wasn't ready to consider a second political career seriously. The problem was not that he wasn't a long-term planner. Since he was a young man in Apohaqui, he had deliberately plotted the course of his life so that he would eventually become Premier of New Brunswick. The problem was not that he hadn't often thought about the possibility of being Prime Minister someday. He couldn't help but think about it over the years when various people, including the Prime Minister himself, had urged him to establish a base camp in the federal cabinet and make a push for the summit when the conditions were right. During the times when his confidence was running high, he never doubted he could succeed. But McKenna's strategic long-term planning seemed to stop the day he entered the premier's office. He simply intended to serve ten years and step down. The date for his departure was set — October 13, 1997. Until then, he had work to do.

Early in the fall of 1997, the media began to speculate that McKenna was on the verge of stepping down. Canadian Press reporter Chris Morris, always alert to anything that moved in Fredericton, reported among other things that the always-frugal McKenna had opted for a patch when the roof of his Fredericton home leaked, instead of replacing the whole roof — suggesting he might not be living there much longer. In September, 1997, Jeffrey Simpson turned his *Globe and Mail* column into an open letter to McKenna counselling him to quit while he was winning, in the fashion of baseball legend Ted Williams. "Whenever you're tempted by all those inner and external voices urging you to stay, think of former premiers Peter Lougheed or William Davis. They quit on top, their reputations intact, their career prospects enhanced by their years of public service. They gave what they could and departed. After ten years, we all run out of gas a bit, even if we don't admit it to ourselves. The files all look the same. You've done a first-class job as premier, and it hasn't been all show biz as your critics claim. Don't tempt fate. Hang up the cleats."

On October 7, 1997, McKenna met with his office staff and then walked downstairs with Julie to meet reporters in the main press briefing room in the Centennial Building. The reporters, bureaucrats and Liberal members gave McKenna a long standing ovation as he entered the room. Julie squeezed her husband's hand under the table as he struggled to hold back tears.

"I tried to make only promises that I could keep during my public life, and I'm proud I've been able to deliver programs such as kindergarten and better highways, things we said we would do and have done," he began. "I'm here now to keep my final promise to the people of the province of New Brunswick. I'm announcing my resignation as premier of the province, as the leader of the Liberal Party of New Brunswick and as the member for Miramichi Bay du Vin, effective October 13."

He began with the customary speech of retiring politicians, thanking the people of the Miramichi, his office staff and his caucus, and he spoke fondly of the members of the public service, with whom he had often had a stormy relationship. Then, with a smile, he said he was going to ruin the day of the reporters in the room. "I actually have liked you and have enjoyed working with you. I'll miss you. I've enjoyed the jousting and the interplay." He thanked the public for supporting him through some difficult times. "I've had a public much more faithful and supportive than I deserve," he said. Finally, he thanked his family and said he hoped they would now have a chance to catch up on lost time.

"I'm surprised at just how hard getting out is," he continued. "It's much more difficult than I thought ten years ago. I thought getting out would be easy." Few politicians find a way to step down on their own terms, he said. "We get in with such fanfare and such excitement, but when we leave it's usually under difficult circumstances."

He noted that in the summer of 1999, Moncton would be hosting La Francophonie, a conference attended by heads of state and delegates from the French-speaking countries of the world. As well as being a great economic boost and an enhancement of the region's international prestige, La Francophonie would be an important symbolic event for the Acadian people and the province. "It's just a wonderful joy in my life to be able to live and work and speak in French and English."

He described the emotional drain of the last few weeks as he waited for the day to arrive. "I feel a huge sense of sadness at the relationships which will change with so many people I know and love. I can also tell you that Julie and I feel a sense of joy. We've carried a huge burden these last ten years. I don't know what it's like for other premiers or leaders. But for me this has been an intense, emotionally filled exercise. I felt every pain in New Brunswick, every joy. If the river was flooding, it affected me, if the forests were on fire. I checked the weather every day to see how our potatoes were doing. If somebody wrote to me looking for a job, I'd look after it personally. Every issue became my issue, and it's such an emotional relationship that it's almost too much to bear indefinitely. I just feel now that I've got the weight of the world off my shoulders, and I feel quite good about it."

Julie McKenna recognized that it wasn't going to be easy for her husband to make the transition to private life. When a reporter asked him, "How long will you take to decide what to do next?" Julie leaned over, clutched her husband's arm and laughed. "I said I'd only support him until Christmas. After that, he'd better get a job."

Dalton Camp, who had been a consistent critic of much of McKenna's agenda, especially of his role in derailing the Meech Lake Accord, was feeling generous when he sat down to compose a political epitaph that day. He wrote that he saw the McKenna political agenda as mainly smoke, mirrors and office hyperbole; but, he concluded, "Among all the politicians I have known in this country, Frank McKenna seemed to me one of the best and brightest. When he was wrong, he was terribly wrong; most of the time, however, he was a man of good and honourable intention, and of trust and civility. They don't come much better, or last much longer. For those who see a future for Frank in federal politics, forget it. Ten years in the business is long enough; Frank should go get a life."

On October 8, the lead editorial in the *Globe and Mail* praised McKenna for his vision, energy and salesmanship. The editorial noted that he had reformed the education system, balanced the books, pursued social welfare experiments and resolved tensions between French and English. McKenna had launched an information technology industry in the province and changed the image of the New Brunswick from "picturesque backwater to economic dynamo, where business is not merely welcome but aggressively wooed. More impressive than all these accomplishments, however, is the way Mr. McKenna has made New Brunswickers believe in themselves and the future of their province. Their optimism, enthusiasm and determination is palpable, a radical — and welcome — departure from the gloom and helplessness and dependence of the not-so-distant past."

The editorial writers argued that McKenna had bungled his handling of the Meech Lake Accord and failed to deal with NB Power's ruinous debts. "On balance, however, this is a record that can and should make the other premiers jealous, New Brunswick voters grateful and Frank McKenna proud."

After he announced his resignation, McKenna travelled to Moncton to deliver his address to the Atlantic Vision conference. Speaking without notes, he outlined an economic strategy for Atlantic Canada. He argued that, while Ottawa had been generous to Atlantic Canada, its generosity had been misdirected. It came in the form of dependency — unemployment insurance, welfare cheques and transfer payments. "There is not a person in this room who can tell you and me that we have not been influenced and affected and had our behaviour modified by being part of that culture, because it shaped everything that we are."

Atlantic Canada needs help, he said, but not more of the same. First, it needs people. Atlantic Canada's shrinking population results in fewer schools and hospitals, more nursing home beds and fewer people in the workforce to support social services. "We need thousands of immigrants coming to Atlantic Canada to bring those technical skills that are so important to building the kind of society we want, fuelling us with the richness of their entrepreneurship, with the vitality of their cultures."

He further maintained that governments need to change all the incentives and disincentives that allow people to justify not working. For example, people are often better off financially when they work seasonally and collect employment insurance or to go on welfare than when they work at a permanent job. Get rid of make-work projects, he advised, change the tax structure, and offer incentives to put people back in the workforce. At the same time, Atlantic Canada should make the information technology industry "our auto industry. Make this our oil patch. Make this our aerospace industry. Make this knowledge-rich economic base the life-blood of Atlantic Canada. We have the market of the world. We can live where we want and service clients all around the world."

How could this happen? His proposal was simple. The government of Canada would loan New Brunswick $161 million, and the province would create ten thousand good-paying jobs. If the unemployment rate dropped three per cent, the province wouldn't have to pay back the money.

Where should the province invest? In early childhood intervention programs, more technology in schools, more technology in homes, research and development, upgrading networks, and in the infrastructures at universities and community colleges.

"I despise people who whine and snivel about their lot in life within this country," he said. "We should never, no matter what, under any circumstances, even in jest, whatever our lot in life is, say we would be happier if we weren't in Canada. I've never felt a day in ten years that I didn't feel privileged to serve the people of my province and the people of Canada. So my final words are: *Vive le Canada!*"

McKenna worked until the day he cleaned out his office. The next day, he was home with time on his hands. "It was kind of like, 'I'm premier, now I'm not premier,'" Julie recalls. "It was just so quick. So we were really in limbo. He had no job, although we've never worried about that. I had a job. People say he must have known what he was going to do. He had no idea what he was going to do. We just said, 'You don't want to make a mistake, take lots of time.' But he was, like, *home*. So I go from not seeing this man for ten years to him all of a sudden being there all the time. We had to adjust completely. He had a wonderful time. He wasn't at all bored, he kept getting offers."

McKenna slowly started to build a private life. In November, he travelled to Kimberly, South Africa, to speak to political leaders about the New Brunswick experience. He and Julie spent Christmas in Jamaica.

Soon after he resigned, McKenna was more thankful than ever that he left when he did. When his mother's health declined early in 1998, he had the time to be with her when she needed him and to help his sisters and brothers with her care. On Monday, February 16, 1998, he visited her at the Moncton Hospital. He travelled to Toronto that evening and was at the Royal York Hotel on February 17 when Julie called to say she had died. On February 21, Olive McKenna was buried after a funeral at St. Francis Xavier Church in Sussex.

Two years after her husband's resignation, in the fall of 1999, the discovery that she had breast cancer changed the course of Julie McKenna's life again. She started spending more time with the people she cared about. She made a conscious effort to reduce stress. She took the time to visit art galleries. She no longer felt she had a duty to do things she didn't want to do. She and Frank travelled together on business trips and added days onto the ends of trips to go out to dinner and attend the theatre. "I visited a lot of the world when I was premier but didn't see any of it," McKenna says. "Now we stop to do those things. We are conscious of the fact that we don't have forever, and we're trying to soak up as much as we can."

In the spring of 2000, while the McKenna family was still struggling with the reality of Julie's illness and recovery, cancer struck Fernand Landry. A year earlier, while he was in the midst of his latest job as the chief organizer of the Francophone Summit, Landry was diagnosed with cancer in his bladder. After several surgeries, it appeared he had beaten the disease. In the fall of 1999, he withdrew his name from a short-list of candidates for president of the Université de Moncton, and he and Aldéa travelled to Australia and New Zealand to celebrate their new lease on life. On March 1, 2000, he joined the law firm McInnes Cooper, in Moncton as a partner, and he and McKenna were working together again. Then, during an Easter retreat with Aldéa to the Trappist Monastery in Rogersville, Fernand started experiencing back pain. On May 26, he was admitted to the Georges Dumont Hospital in Moncton. His cancer had returned and metastasized into his spine and liver. By early July, the cancer was pro-gressing too rapidly for treatment.

From the moment Landry entered the hospital, McKenna telephoned every day and visited him almost every day. During the final weeks of Fernand's life, Aldéa tried to limit the number of visitors because he was becoming fatigued, and they needed to spend as much private time together as possible. She had a hard time keeping McKenna away. He was trying to squeeze in every single moment he could with his friend. "If I went to the kitchen to prepare something or if I was out of the room, I'd come back and Frank would be there," Aldéa recalls. "He'd say, 'Well, Aldéa those rules are not really for me, are they?' He was totally unmanageable. I think Frank cried for five solid weeks. He was totally shattered at the thought that he was going to lose Fern."

Landry faced the end of his life with serenity and dignity, preparing his wife and friends for life without him. He and McKenna spent hours reliving their political journey and planning McKenna's future in politics, discussing in particular the possibility of his running in the next federal election and positioning himself to become prime minister. They called their planning "the project." Aldéa often told McKenna when he arrived at the hospital, "Fern wants to talk to you about the project." Landry recommended that he run.

"Fern thought that politics was so much in Frank's blood that we should not try to be in the way, that we should not be an obstacle for him to realize his dream of going back into politics," Aldéa says. "But I think that all that was happening was making him have second thoughts about what he wanted to do." All along, Landry had brought balance to his life, and McKenna assumed that his friend would be with him whenever he needed him. "I always thought of Fern as being far superior to me," McKenna says. "He seemed invulnerable. He could shield me from every storm." A new political journey without Fernand Landry at his side was unthinkable.

Fernand and Aldéa treated the weeks in the hospital as their own final journey together, the end of a great love story that began when they were both undergraduate students in Bathurst. In order to have a record of their conversations after he died, she kept a daily diary. On July 15, Fernand told his wife, "It's strange. These days it seems like everyone talks about the universe, which is a concept of space, but hardly anyone talks about eternity, a concept of time. When you think about it, our passage on Earth is infinitely short compared with eternity. Even compared with other species — some animals and trees live a very long time — our life is extremely short."

Fernand Landry died thirteen days later. He was fifty-two. The province's political and business elite gathered for his funeral at the stately Notre Dame de l'Assomption Cathedral in Moncton, as did Louis

Robichaud and every Liberal leader who followed him. Frank and Julie McKenna, with Toby and Christine, sat directly behind Premier Bernard Lord and his wife Diane. Aldéa Landry, dressed in black, placed a single rose on her husband's casket as it was carried down the steps of the cathedral.

McKenna wept throughout the service, making no attempt to hide his grief. Never had he appeared in public in so vulnerable a state, tears streaming down his face, dark circles under his eyes. Christine said she had seen her father cry only twice before — at his mother's funeral and on the day she left home to go to St. Francis Xavier University. McKenna left the cathedral listening to renowned Acadian soprano Rosemarie Landry sing *L'hymne d'espoir*, written by Édith Butler, the Acadian singer and composer.

Aldéa Landry says Frank McKenna was a changed man after Fernand's death. "It put him in front of the finality of life," she says. "I wasn't surprised that he was so devastated, or to see him cry out of control every time he came to our room. That side of Frank has always been there, but being the combative and ambitious person he always was, it didn't come through. It came through to people who knew him closely. But I think that what happened to Julie and Fern changed him, in that he allows himself to show more of his emotions, to show this sensitive side of himself."

For Aldéa, the presence of Frank and Julie as her "guardian angels" both before and after her husband's death clarified for her the question that clouds so many relationships born out of politics. Who are your real friends and who are merely your partners in ambition? "In the case of Frank and Julie, we really discovered the depth of their friendship with us," she says.

This genuine friendship between Fernand Landry and Frank McKenna was in many ways a reflection of the journey and growth of the province. Both men grew up poor, and through their intellect and determination escaped the limitations their backgrounds might have imposed. A Roman Catholic farm boy of Irish descent from Apohaqui and an Acadian Catholic son of a shopkeeper from Evangeline, both growing up far from the centres of traditional Loyalist power, had come together, driven by the belief that they could transform their homeland. Landry learned to speak English, McKenna learned to speak French. These men came to understand and love each other for their differences. If they could find a way to work together for a common purpose, perhaps the province did have a destiny beyond the divisions that had separated its people for so long.

The most remarkable feature of Frank McKenna's story is that during only a decade in office, he changed the deeply rooted attitudes of New Brunswickers, says George Perlin. As he continued to track public opinion, he watched the people gain self-confidence and self-reliance, leaving behind the "dependency syndrome" that was hindering the province's economic and social growth. Leadership, in Perlin's view, is about persuasion. "You could see it changing," Perlin says. "He made people feel better about what was happening in New Brunswick. He helped the people of New Brunswick see what they had the potential to be."

Steven MacKinnon says New Brunswickers will never forget what he calls the province's brief moment in the sun. "There was a period when we were everywhere, in all the national papers, all the national newscasts," he recalls. "New Brunswick was a hotbed of innovation and economic development. We were getting all this validation from the central Canadian media. Suddenly all our beaches seemed prettier. The tourists liked it here more, and they were coming here saying, 'We love your Premier.' New Brunswick was hot. I don't think people will forget that, the sense that we had this in our grasp."

David Peterson says McKenna's great accomplishment was that he showed how government can be a constructive force in people's lives. "It can educate people. It can create jobs. It can provide decent health care. It can give people a leg up. Not that it is the be-all and end-all. Not that it is an employer of last resort. Not that it is going to take care of everybody, but that it can make a difference, and Frank has proven that."

Julie isn't ruling out the possibility of her husband's returning to public life and won't stand in his way if he does, but she knows what she wants from her life. "We talked about this many times, and we all, as a family, said to Frank, 'Keep your ten-year commitment, give private life a decent chance, and if you're unhappy, then we'll support whatever decision you make.' It's not my choice for a lifestyle. I would prefer not to be in politics again."

When McKenna's business and political friends continue to urge him to position himself to make a run for the federal leadership, he finds their advocacy more tiring than flattering. "One of the things that I'm conscious of, but that the people who are doing this kind of talking don't realize, is that I'm almost an addict, but I know my addiction," he says. "And my difficulty is in taking on something and doing it reasonably. I know that about myself. I consider it a shortcoming. That's why I would be prepared to face, not only the pleasure in the sense of accomplishment, but also just the physical beating I would take, only if I thought it was really important and I had certain special gifts that would be useful. It would take that kind of motivation for me to be able once again to put on the blinders and think, No matter what indignity, no matter what criticism, no matter what anxiety or stress there is, it is worth enduring because this is so important. I'm not overly vain, and I'm deeply conscious of the fact that I'm not the only person who can do things. I'm aware there are all kinds of other high-quality people out there who can do things. It would be an act of vanity to think I'm the only one who could do it. The motivation that I might become prime minister and occupy Sussex Drive would not be the motivation that would get me into federal politics. It's as simple as that. If the Prime Minister were to say, 'Frank, I can anoint you prime minister tomorrow,' that would not influence my thinking. A lot of people in public life like the trappings of public life. We never cared about that."

Toby McKenna doesn't think his father has been entirely happy and fulfilled since he left public life. However, when Frank is spending time with his children or doting on Toby's son James, the first grandchild, he says, "Boy, did I make the right decision."

"When he's not around his family, he's thinking, 'I can't believe the Tories have control of all the hard work that I put in, and I can't believe there's so much more work that needs to be done that they're not paying attention to,'" Toby says. "He's obsessed with doing the right thing. He's not so concerned that someone else took over for him. He's more concerned that they're not doing it the way he would. I don't think he cares particularly about money or power. He cares about doing the right thing. If he has the chance to do something right, he'll do it. For him, it's about being in a place where he can make a difference. When he does it, he won't look back."

By the time the federal Liberals prepared to go to the polls again, the incentives for McKenna to return to politics were becoming stronger than ever. Jean Chrétien arrived in Cap-Pelé in August, 2000, on a mission to convince McKenna to become a candidate in the fall election. He offered him an immediate cabinet position as industry minister. Chrétien said he would be stepping down a couple of years after the election to make way for a new leader, which could very well be McKenna. McKenna was tempted, but again he declined. "Curiously, I found myself very comfortable with that," he says.

The day Chrétien arrived in New Brunswick, he played a round of golf with McKenna, Camille Thériault and Ray Frenette at the Royal Oaks

Golf Club in Moncton. Frenette had retired from provincial politics but was running the federal campaign in New Brunswick. Thériault was still leader of the Liberal Party but was looking for a way out after his election disaster the previous year. While the politicians golfed and talked business, Julie McKenna and Aline Chrétien golfed together at the picturesque Pine Needles course near Shediac. They all made plans to return to Cap-Pelé for dinner.

Jean Chrétien was filled with energy at the prospect of another election victory and handily won the match on the golf course that afternoon. Perhaps it was the frightening prospect of losing Julie that changed the way Frank McKenna played. Or perhaps it was the still-raw pain of losing Fernand Landry. At any rate, the fierce competition of the game at the Hunt Club in Ottawa three years earlier seemed a lifetime away. When he walked off the course that afternoon and drove back to Friel Beach for dinner, maybe he was thinking that just playing the game mattered more than the score. Clearly, he was no longer playing the same game. Maybe, on that day at least, the new game felt just fine.

ENDNOTES

Chapter One
BAY STREET BLUES

The definitive works on Bay Street and the Canadian establishment are Peter C. Newman's *The Canadian Establishment* (Toronto: McClelland and Stewart, 1975) and the updated *Titans* (Toronto: McClelland and Stewart, 1998). This chapter relies on Newman's descriptions of Bay Street. Donald Savoie kindly shared both his research and an early draft of the manuscript of his study of McKenna's economic policies, *Pulling Against Gravity: Economic Development During the Frank McKenna Years* (Montreal: Institute for Research on Public Policy, 2001). Savoie's fine scholarship assisted in this chapter and throughout the book. Dalton Camp's observations on the 1999 New Brunswick election were published in the *Telegraph-Journal*. Camp's more general political observations are part of his classic *Gentlemen, Players and Politicians* (Toronto: McClelland and Stewart, 1970). Roy MacGregor's column, "Something's Missing for Frank McKenna," was published in the *National Post* on June 21, 1999.

Chapter Two
ACROSS THE GREAT DIVIDE

Richard Hatfield's essay on New Brunswick was published in the *Telegraph-Journal* on August 1, 1990. A wide variety of sources offered insights into New Brunswick's history and politics. W.S. MacNutt, *New Brunswick: A History; 1784-1867* (Toronto: Macmillan, 1963); Hugh G. Thorburn, *Politics in New Brunswick* (Toronto: University of Toronto Press, 1961) are essential sources. Arthur T. Doyle, *Front Benches and Back Rooms: A Story of Political Intrigue and Corruption in New Brunswick* (Fredericton: Omega Publications, 1977), offers a fascinating account of the rise and fall of James Kidd Flemming. Doyle provides short essays on all the province's premiers in his *The Premiers of New Brunswick* (Fredericton: Brunswick Press, 1983). Scott W. See, *Riots in New Brunswick: Orange Nativism and Social Violence in the 1840s* (Toronto: University of Toronto Press, 1975), paints a revealing portrait of a dark period in New Brunswick history. Dalton Camp, *Gentlemen Players and Politicians*, recounts the fall of Andrew Blair. Della Stanley, *Louis Robichaud: A Decade of Power* (Halifax: Nimbus, 1984), captures the political atmosphere of the Robichaud years and allows the former premier to tell his story. Michel Cormier and Achille Michaud, *Richard Hatfield: Power and Disobedience*, translated by Daphne Ponder (Fredericton: Goose Lane, 1992), an excellent biography of the enigmatic Hatfield, was a valuable source throughout this work. The collection of short essays edited by Nancy Southam, *Remembering Richard* (Halifax: Formac, 1993), is a marvellous source of Hatfield anecdotes. Jeffrey Simpson, *Spoils of Power: The Politics of Patronage* (Toronto: Harper Collins, 1988), offers a splendid chapter on the Hatfield kickbacks scandal. Hugh Mellon's essay "New Brunswick: The Politics of Reform," in *The Provincial State*, edited by Keith Brownsley and Michael Howlett (Toronto: Copp Clark Pitman, 1992) examines the progressive side of the politics of Robichaud, Hatfield and McKenna. Don Hoyt's *A Brief History of the Liberal Party of New Brunswick* (Fredericton: privately printed, 2000) provides an insider's look at the Liberal Party and is especially strong in its chapters on early party history.

Chapter Three
THE CHOSEN ONE
Alden Nowlan wrote about Horatio Alger in his essay, "Horatio Alger and King Arthur's Sword," published in the *Atlantic Advocate*, October, 1976. A history of Apohaqui by Harley S. Jones was published in the *Telegraph-Journal* in March, 1928. Grace Aiton's *The Story of Sussex and Vicinity* (Kings County Historical Society, 1967) is a source for the history of the Apohaqui region. Charles Edward MacKinnon's *Out of Saddleback: The Genealogy of the McManus, Montgomery, McKenna and McIntyre Families* was helpful in tracing Frank McKenna's family history. One of the best profiles of McKenna and his family by any reporter for print or broadcast

was produced in 1987 by veteran Newfoundland journalist Roger Bill for CBC Radio's *Sunday Morning*. The collection of essays edited by New Brunswick historian Peter Toner, *New Ireland Remembered* (Fredericton: New Ireland, 1989), tells the story of Irish immigration in New Brunswick. David Adams Richards's observations of Frank McKenna are contained in Josh Beutel's collection of essays and cartoons, *True (Blue) Grit: A Frank McKenna Review* (Saint John: Lanceman Productions, 1996).

Chapter Four
THE FIGHTER
The story of Yvon Durelle's shooting of Albain Poirier and his murder trial was primarily pieced together from interviews and Frank McKenna's original trial books. The Moncton *Times* and *Transcript*'s blanket coverage of the trial was also helpful. For biographical information about Durelle, and for some details of the trial, this chapter relies on Durelle's biography, *The Fighting Fisherman* (Toronto: Doubleday, 1980), written by the fine New Brunswick poet and novelist Raymond Fraser. He covered the trial as a reporter and recorded several of the key exchanges during the trial which are repeated in this chapter, and I am indebted to Fraser's reporting. A story by former *Miramichi Leader* editor Rick Maclean, "Making McKenna," published in *The New Brunswick Reader*, October 11, 1997, tells the story of McKenna's years on the Miramichi and was helpful here.

Chapter Five
SWEEP
Again, for the Richard Hatfield story, Michel Cormier and Achille Michaud were crucial sources. Throughout the final years of Richard Hatfield's government and the early years of Frank McKenna's sojourn in Fredericton, Don Hoyt's daily *Telegraph-Journal* column was the best source of New Brunswick political news. Hoyt's work was helpful in this chapter and throughout the book.

Chapter Six
RETURN TO ACADIE
Antonine Maillet's *Pélagie-la-Charrette* was translated by Philip Stratford and published in English as *Pelagie: The Return to a Homeland* (Toronto:

Doubleday, 1992). The most detailed and even-handed source on the Meech Lake story is Andrew Cohen's *A Deal Undone: The Making and Breaking of the Meech Lake Accord* (Vancouver: Douglas and McIntyre, 1990). Lucien Bouchard's autobiography *On the Record* (Don Mills: Stoddart, 1994) was translated by Dominique Clift. Susan Delacourt's *United We Fall: In Search of a New Canada* (Toronto: Penguin, 1994) is a compulsively readable and authoritative work on the Charlottetown Accord. Delacourt has written well about McKenna's role on the national unity stage, recounting his movement away from Trudeau Liberalism, and this chapter relies on her work on that point.

Chapter Seven
THE HUSTLER
Throughout the 1990s, several national magazines published in-depth profiles of McKenna, his politics and role as an economic development hustler. Among the best are Merle MacIsaac's "Faith, Hope and Hold the Charity," *Canadian Business*, December 1992; John Lownsbrough's "The Win Win World of Frank McKenna," *Report on Business*, March, 1993; and John Demont's "Fast Frank," *Maclean's*, April 11, 1994. All three of these articles were valuable sources for this chapter. Donald Savoie's *Pulling Against Gravity* was also an essential source. William J. Milne's study *The McKenna Miracle: Myth or Reality* (Toronto: University of Toronto Press, 1996) explores the missing echo generation in New Brunswick.

Chapter Eight
PREMIER FRANK
The scene of Frank McKenna clashing with union protesters was filmed by CBC Television cameraman George Andrews, who endured all manner of indignities to stay with the Premier during his long march through the crowd. The tape in the CBC archives is marked "Never Erase; Keep Forever." Gordon Gregory provided his extensive files on his case against the government of Frank McKenna. Gregory's documents and observations in interviews were helpful in this chapter and elsewhere in the book. Don Richardson's description of Fern Landry after the negotiations with CUPE was published in the Fredericton *Daily Gleaner* on August 7, 2001. Catherine Dunphy's *Morgentaler: A Difficult Hero* (Toronto: Random

House, 1996) offers a comprehensive account of Frank McKenna's battle with Henry Morgentaler.

Chapter Nine
TRIUMVIRATE

Again, Susan Delacourt was an indispensable source on the Charlottetown Accord. Donald Savoie provided a copy of the paper he co-authored with McKenna and added his insights to this chapter. Robert Pichette and Université de Moncton professor Roger Ouellette helped put McKenna's stand on Meech Lake and minority language rights in the context of the politics and aspirations of the people of Acadie.

Chapter Ten
JULIE

Richard Hatfield's comments on political families appeared in a feature by Joan Sutton that was published in the *Toronto Star* in 1980 and re-printed by Michel Cormier and Achille Michaud.

Chapter Eleven
HEALING GAME

The description of the golf game in this chapter is a small part of Donald Savoie's important and remarkable work, *Governing from the Centre: The Concentration of Power in Canadian Politics* (Toronto: University of Toronto Press, 1999). Jeffrey Simpson's column appeared in the *Globe and Mail* on September 4, 1997. Simpson offered the best national commentary on McKenna's work throughout his years in the premier's office. Dalton Camp's column on McKenna's career, "The Barefoot Boy From Apohaqui," was published in the *Telegraph-Journal* on October 8, 1997.

PHOTO CREDITS

INDEX